Instructional Leadership Handbook

James W. Keefe
John M. Jenkins
Editors

National Association of Secondary School Principals
1904 Association Drive
Reston, Virginia 22091

About the editors:
- James W. Keefe is NASSP director of research and a former principal and professor.
- John M. Jenkins is principal of the P.K. Yonge Laboratory School, University of Florida, Gainesville.

Published by the National Association of Secondary School Principals
- Executive Director: Scott D. Thomson
- Editorial Director: Thomas F. Koerner
- Assistant Editorial Director: Carol Bruce
- Assistant Editor: Patricia Lucas George
- Proofreader: Eugenia C. Potter

Copyright 1984, NASSP
All Rights Reserved
ISBN 0-88210-161-7

Contents

FOREWORD

INTRODUCTION

FORMATIVE ELEMENTS

Trends in Content Fields

1. English/Language Arts
2. Reading Programs
3. The Arts
4. Foreign Languages
5. Mathematics
6. Physical and Health Education
7. Science
8. Social Studies
9. Vocational and Technical Education
10. Interdisciplinary Approaches

Trends in Organization and Staffing

11. Building Design/Modification
12. Graded/Nongraded Organization
13. School-Within-a-School Organization
14. Middle Level Education
15. School Guidance Programs
16. Cocurricular Programs
17. Administrative Teams
18. Instructional Teams
19. Master Teachers
20. Paraprofessional Personnel
21. Adult Volunteer Program
22. Collective Bargaining

Trends in Media and Methods

23. Library/Media Center
24. Textbook Selection
25. Computer-Based Education
26. Computer Software
27. New Technologies
28. Teacher-Developed Materials
29. Personalized Education
30. Direct Instruction
31. Mastery Learning
32. Cooperative Small-Group Learning
33. Contract Teaching
34. Study Skills
35. Thinking Skills
36. Talented and Gifted Programs
37. Advanced Placement Programs
38. Special Education
39. Experiential Education

PLANNING ELEMENTS

40. Conducting Needs Assessment
41. Critical Analysis of the School Program
42. Goals for the School
43. Goal Indicators
44. Subject Area Goals
45. Student Competencies
46. Performance Standards
47. School Improvement Plans
48. Staff, District, and Community Support
49. Budgeting for Instructional Improvement

IMPLEMENTATION ELEMENTS

Organizing the Program

50. Selecting Staff
51. Scheduling the School
52. Staff Development/Inservice
53. School Learning Climate
54. Change Facilitator Style

Supervising Classroom Management

55. School Attendance
56. Student Discipline
57. Classroom Management
58. Instructional Planning
59. Development of Curriculum Guides

Supervising the Diagnostic Process

60. Developmental Traits
61. Learning Style
62. Learning History

Supervising Prescription and Placement

63. Advisement
64. Educational Plans
65. Student Placement

Supervising Instruction

66. Teaching Styles
67. Supervision Models
68. Class Size
69. Grouping Practices
70. Use of Time
71. Use of Space

72. Instructional Media/Materials
73. Instructional Strategy
74. Homework

EVALUATION ELEMENTS

75. Assessing and Reporting Student Progress
76. Teacher Performance Appraisal
77. Program Evaluation
78. Community Feedback
79. Program Modification and Revision
80. Communicating the Program

Foreword

A few years ago, J. G. March characterized educational administration as "a bus schedule with footnotes by Kierkegaard." March described school administration essentially as making the organization work. Instructional leadership must surely have been one of the functions March had in mind. Making it work is the problem.

A growing body of evidence on effective schooling, school learning climate, learning styles, and personalized education emphasizes the critical role of the principal in school improvement. More and more research on the principalship affirms that certain skills are necessary for the principal to be effective. No more complex or dynamic set of skills exist than those of instructional leadership. And none more necessary.

Familiarity with instructional knowledge and skills diminishes after a teacher leaves the classroom. The same is true of a principal who neglects the skills of instructional leadership. As personal teaching skills diminish and college training becomes dated, school administrators often find themselves increasingly uncomfortable as instructional leaders. All too frequently, principals seek consolation in the less demanding tasks of day-to-day building supervision.

Principals should be encouraged by the renewal of national interest in improving instruction. A new body of knowledge on effective instructional practice clarifies the principal's role and cries for implementation. State-of-the-art information is available on subject, organizational, and methodological trends. Principals intent on becoming real instructional leaders must find the time to become involved in the academic life of the school. NASSP's *Instructional Leadership Handbook* is intended to be a basic reference for this task.

Many persons contributed to this *Handbook*. The need was identified by NASSP's Communications Committee, and enthusiastically endorsed by the Curriculum Committee. Special recognition is extended to the many writers who contributed much time and effort in preparing the pieces that make up this *Handbook*. The editors accept responsibility, of course, for its final form.

The *Handbook* is a comprehensive but succinct resource for the instructional leader not heretofore available. As such, it is both a beginning and a promise of things to come. We trust that periodic updates will make subsequent editions even more helpful.

NASSP extends to principals the right to photocopy *Handbook* entries for staff inservice activities without need for further authorization.

James W. Keefe
NASSP Director of Research

Introduction

The original model for the American principalship was the European headmaster, the best teacher in the school. But what began as an adjective to describe the chief teacher was transformed in time into "principal," a noun with a variety of meanings, most of them dealing with school management.

More recently, national studies of secondary education have emphasized the importance of the principal to the academic excellence of the school. It may be that schools today are returning to an old and basic premise: that the principal should be an instructional leader. This trend in no way diminishes the principal's responsibility for managing school resources. Rather, it extends the management function beyond the commonplace daily operations of the school.

If current educational issues reflect social change, as many observers contend, the focus of the schools and the role of the principal require a new look.

Instructional Leadership

Instructional leadership is the principal's role in providing *direction, resources,* and *support* to teachers and students for the improvement of teaching and learning in the school. This *Handbook* will review that role in four broad domains: formative, planning, implementation, and evaluation.

FORMATIVE: The principal must operate from a firm and secure knowledge base. If teachers cannot teach what they do not know, principals cannot lead where they have not been. Knowledge forms the base on which the principal builds integrity and respect. Personal reading, workshops, observation, formal classes, and annual conventions all offer ways for the principal to gain information about what is happening in learning and instruction. An effective instructional leader knows the trends in school curriculum, the new approaches to organizing schools, and the state of the art in instructional media and methodology.

The astute principal devotes a portion of the day to self-education. Budgeting time on the job to read and to develop new skills is a long-term investment insuring against professional obsolescence.

PLANNING: Understanding educational trends gives the principal an appropriate knowledge base for the planning dimension of instructional leadership. Instructional planning involves helping teachers organize for instruction:

- Assessing current student and program needs
- Establishing goals for the school
- Helping teachers see the relationship of goals to the instructional program
- Developing goals for the various areas of instruction
- Translating instructional goals into operational objectives
- Formulating a plan for school improvement
- Securing appropriate resources to support the program.

Excellent schools need principals who plan carefully and completely. Excellence is attainable only when goals are defined clearly and without ambiguity. Goals and objectives are the framework, in turn, for organizational, programmatic, and budgetary decisions.

IMPLEMENTATION: The planning process leads naturally to activities for enhancing the quality of teaching and learning. The process begins with the selection and employment of first-rate teachers. It goes forward with proper deployment of resources, setting high expectations for teachers and students, and instructional supervision. The principal needs to know the attributes of quality instruction to validate effective practices and to help teachers find better ways when what they are doing is not working. Most teachers have special gifts to bring to the overall program. The principal establishes an environment in which individual teachers can give their best to the entire school.

Research into school effectiveness shows that academic emphasis, the quality of student-teacher interactions, and the type of incentives and rewards all make a difference in student outcomes. The school's climate for learning is the product of the collective efforts of the principal, the teachers, the parents, and the students. Successful principals know how to orchestrate the talents and abilities of these groups to produce conditions of quality. Effective schools, like effective classrooms, can be places for learning, places for sharing, and places for joy. Discipline problems are minimized. People work hard, enjoy what they do, and feel good about their accomplishments.

EVALUATION: If the school really helps students to learn and grow, it will be evident from a number of vital signs:

- Average daily attendance
- Library and media usage

- Number of students participating in cocurricular activities
- Number of incidents of vandalism caused by students
- Number of students referred for discipline
- Percentage of students receiving passing and failing marks
- Percentage of students from all socioeconomic backgrounds electing advanced courses
- Success of the graduates.

Program evaluation should monitor student test scores. Schools can be compared against state and national norms. Teachers and classrooms can be assessed against criterion-referenced tests to determine the percentage of students who achieve course objectives.

Surveys of community opinion are helpful. Informal contacts with community leaders and parent groups can provide valuable feedback on the impact of the school program.

Evidence collected systematically can serve as the basis for program improvement and community support. It is not uncommon today for the public to ask tough questions of educators. The effective principal responds with evidence that supports instructional policy. Basing educational decision making on carefully gathered information establishes a professional posture that wins public respect and support.

Effective Leadership

The most consistent finding of the research on successful schools is the positive effect of leadership on student achievement.

Researchers echo similar views of the need for strong leadership by the principal. Four key traits associated with successful principals emerge in this literature.

1. Principals hold high expectations for teachers and students.
2. They spend a major portion of their day working with teachers on improving the educational program.
3. They work at identifying and diagnosing instructional problems.
4. They become deeply involved in the schools "culture" (climate) to influence it in positive ways.

Leading a school to excellence in its academic programs is a complex and challenging process. The complexity may at times seem beyond the capacity of one person. Principals must develop professional support systems including a strong supervisory-management team, effective instructional planning, and collaborative supervisory practices.

The purpose of this handbook is to provide the knowledge base for instructional leadership. Principals who understand the formative, planning, implementation, and evaluation dimensions of instructional leadership are well on the way to affecting the educational quality of the school. No more important role exists in education.

J.M.J.
J.W.K.

■ FORMATIVE ELEMENTS

Trends in Content Fields

English/Language Arts

Stephen Tchudi

The broadest, most comprehensive trend in English/language arts instruction this century has been a shift from the "particle" approach to language instruction to the "holistic" teaching method. Research indicates that language skills are *learned by doing*, by actual use in communication situations rather than by isolated instruction and drill. Despite recent demands from the public to return to "basics"—often interpreted as instruction in formal grammar—most knowledgeable English teachers continue to use skill-based instruction in reading, writing, listening, and speaking.

The Teaching of Writing

Writing instruction focuses on the *process of composing:* pre-writing (or idea gathering), drafting, editing, and copy editing. Instead of instructing students about the formal outline or the nature of the comparison/contrast essay, teachers show students a variety of ways to plan compositions and to structure their writing to achieve their own purposes. Traditional skills in spelling, grammar, usage, and mechanics are incorporated in the editing and copy editing phases as students learn to work their manuscripts into forms acceptable to their readers.

In an effort to enlarge the range of discourse that students can use comfortably, English teachers are providing opportunities for students to write nonfiction, fiction, drama, and even poetry in addition to the usual essays. Teachers are also exploring *peer editing*, in which novice writers sharpen their skills by responding to one another's writing and by teaching each other proofreading and editing skills.

The Teaching of Reading and Literature

The holistic approach to reading and literature instruction very simply is getting the right book into the hands of the right student at the right time. Many English/language arts teachers have had considerable success with "free" or "guided individualized" reading programs in which students choose from a variety of reading materials proposed by the teacher.

Stephen Tchudi is president, National Council of Teachers of English, Urbana, Ill.

In-class paperback and magazine libraries greatly energize such programs. Teachers still present selected "classic" works, but they are integrated into thematic or topical units rather than presented in a chronological parade. Students then expand their reading from the core selections of traditional literature and come to appreciate the connection between schoolroom reading and reading as a potential lifelong pursuit.

More and more students visit reading centers and laboratories for assistance with regular classroom reading. These centers no longer just offer isolated skill development or the conventional diagnostic/prescriptive approaches to reading; students learn to read by reading, with help as needed from the English and reading specialists. Many of these centers now provide similar help in writing as well.

The Teaching of Listening and Speaking

Oral language skills have traditionally received short shrift in English/language arts classes. Educators, however, are recognizing that reading and writing must be firmly based on a foundation of oral skills. In the 1970s, many English teachers moved beyond the once-a-year impromptu speech to a variety of oral language activities: panels and debates, small-group discussions, formal talks and presentations, interviews, public readings, and peer evaluation.

Interest is growing in classroom drama, both as a means of evaluating literary study and as a way of allowing students to experience a variety of identities and roles. Indeed, the oral/dramatic element in the classroom can provide a showcase for student writing and considerable motivation for pursuing the more demanding forms of written composition.

The Curriculum

The English/language arts curriculum is changing. The elective curricula of a decade ago are gone, probably to the relief of most administrators who were faced with scheduling nightmares. Unfortunately, the loss of electives has also provoked many English teachers to return to conventional teaching-by-textbook methods rather than to design reading and writing programs to meet the specific needs of individual students.

An encouraging development in some secondary schools is the movement to synthesize electives and

English/Language Arts

traditional grade-level English programs into *developmental, thematic* curricula. In these programs, courses center on the emerging psychological and linguistic needs of students.

Instruction at the junior high/middle school level focuses on the *personal uses of language* (keeping daily writing journals, reading literature for young adults, writing about the concerns of adolescents); at the senior high level on *language and human concerns* (writing for broader audiences, reading about increasingly abstract and world-centered topics). These new curricula are threatened, however, by public pressure for students to use conventional textbooks and to complete the kinds of English homework assignments that lost pedagogical respectability 30 years ago.

Curriculum and Program Evaluation

Perhaps the greatest problem for administrators and teachers today is that public pressures restrict evaluation efforts to the rather narrow focus of standardized test scores. The Scholastic Aptitude Test, which even its makers acknowledge is an inaccurate measure of secondary school education, stands in the public mind as an acceptable assessment of competence in language. State and local testing programs are proliferating at what English teaching professionals regard as an alarming rate.

Other measures of excellence and accountability are available. The single best example is the *experience portfolio*, in which language arts students keep copies of their most representative writing, lists of books read in and out of school, and records of parent/teacher/student conferences. Since holistic, learn-by-doing English programs emphasize actual "on the job" performance, these portfolios provide clear and direct evidence of the quality of the local program. Principals in particular can support significant improvements in English/language arts by supporting these performance-based approaches to evaluation and program revision.

Reading Programs

John N. Mangieri and Deborah H. Mangieri

Reading at the secondary school level has changed dramatically during the last two decades. In the past, reading instruction at the secondary level was often equated with *remedial reading*—instruction geared to individuals who are reading approximately two or more years below the expected norm at their grade level.

Remedial reading programs still exist in most secondary schools, but recently two other types of reading instruction have come of age. Students involved in *developmental/enrichment reading* are *not* remedial readers, but capable readers whose programs are based on the expectation that their competence will be further enhanced. Developmental instruction includes critical reading, vocabulary growth, study skills, and reading rate and efficiency training.

The second dimension of reading instruction that has gained popularity at the secondary school level is *reading in the content areas,* promoted largely by the work of Harold Herber (1980). Content reading focuses on helping students master the unique vocabulary and concepts of a particular subject content. The major difference between content, remedial, and developmental/enrichment reading is that in the former, the content teacher—as opposed to the reading teacher—is responsible for instruction. The social studies teacher, for example, instructs students in the techniques and strategies that enable them to read and better understand social studies textbooks and other related resources.

State-of-the-art reading programs, then, are comprehensive; they feature *all* three dimensions of reading (remedial, developmental/enrichment, and content), and are responsive to *all* students' reading needs.

An Action Plan

A middle level or senior high school principal interested in comprehensive reading instruction in the school has two options. First, at those sites without a comprehensive reading program, the principal should ask the following five questions (Mangieri and Olsen, 1974):

1. Do we need a reading program?
2. How great is the need?
3. What type(s) of reading program(s) does the school need?
4. Do we have the necessary staff, space, and materials to implement the new program?
5. Is the necessary funding available and/or obtainable to finance the program?

If a reading program already exists in the school, principals should consider evaluating its efficacy. The December 1981 issue of the *NASSP Bulletin* (Mangieri and Corboy, 1981), provides a questionnaire to facilitate this kind of evaluation. The following seven questions provide an excellent basis for most program evaluations.

1. Is your school reading program comprehensive in nature?
2. Is the reading program organized in a manner to promote continual and optimal achievement in reading?
3. Does the program offer instruction that is learner-oriented in philosophy and practice?
4. Are adequate resources available to the students, teachers, and administrators involved in the program?
5. Does the program produce students who have the *will* to read as well as the *skill* to read?
6. Do parents and community members understand and support the program?
7. Is the program regularly evaluated, both informally and formally, by school and district personnel and "outside" persons?

Concluding Comments

A comprehensive reading program is not a luxury for a middle level or senior high school. It should be as integral to the curriculum as the school's science or mathematics offerings. Such a program cannot be developed in a day, nor will it necessarily experience immediate success.

The planning and evaluating questions above are not ends in themselves. The evaluation data must be used judiciously. The principal should be actively involved in the collection, discussion, and dissemination

---

John N. Mangieri is dean, School of Education, and Deborah H. Mangieri is a graduate student in educational administration, both at Texas Christian University, Fort Worth.

of findings. Only with strong administrative leadership can a school hope to maintain a strong and responsive program.

References

Herber, Harold L. *Teaching Reading in Content Areas.* Englewood Cliffs, N.J.: Prentice-Hall, Inc., 1978.

Mangieri, John N., and Olsen, Henry D. "Planning Secondary School Reading Programs." *NASSP Bulletin,* October 1974, pp. 66–70.

Mangieri, John, and Corboy, Margaret. "Quality Reading. Programs—What Are Their Ingredients?" *NASSP Bulletin,* December 1981, pp. 62–66.

The Arts

Charles M. Dorn

The arts is among the six academic subjects listed in the College Board's *Academic Preparation for College* that can assist students in preparing for college. The others are English, mathematics, science, social studies, and foreign language.

The College Board suggests various concepts and skills in the arts that students should study in the secondary school. The Board statement goes beyond prescribing years of study to describe what students actually need to learn to get full value from their college education:

> The arts—visual arts, theater, music, and dance—challenge and extend human experience. They provide means of expression that go beyond ordinary speaking and writing. They can express intimate thoughts and feelings. They are a unique record of diverse cultures and how these cultures have developed over time. They provide distinctive ways of understanding human beings and nature. The arts are creative modes by which all people can enrich their lives both by self-expression and response to the expressions of others. . . . Preparation in the arts will be valuable to college entrants whatever their intended field of study. The actual practice of the arts can engage the imagination, foster flexible ways of thinking, develop disciplined effort, and build self-confidence. Appreciation of the arts is integral to the understanding of other cultures sought in the study of history, foreign language, and social sciences. Preparation in the arts will also enable college students to engage in and profit from advanced study, performance, and studio work in the arts. For many others, it will permanently enhance the quality of their lives, whether they continue artistic activity as an avocation or appreciation of the arts as observers and members of audiences.

The College Board statement lists five competencies that are achieved through study of the arts:

- The ability to understand and appreciate the unique qualities of each of the arts.
- The ability to appreciate how people of various cultures have used the arts to express themselves.
- The ability to understand and appreciate different artistic styles and works from representative historical periods and cultures.
- Some knowledge of the social and intellectual influences affecting artistic form.
- The ability to use the skills, media, tools, and processes required to express themselves in one or more of the arts.

The Current Situation

Support for the arts has increased perceptibly since the National Endowment for the Arts was established more than a decade ago. Not only has commitment been strengthened at the federal and state levels, but there has been phenomenal growth in arts programs in schools and communities. A wide range of organizations and agencies now work with schools that are interested in increasing access and participation in all forms of the arts. Many small and interesting curriculum projects have emerged, but as yet, no substantive agreement has been reached on standards for a comprehensive arts curriculum. Arthur Steller, in the November 1979 *NASSP Bulletin,* said:

> American education is presently in a state of depression. Declining student enrollments which result in teacher layoffs and school closings, pressures for reducing school taxes, and lower test scores, contribute to the problem. American education is in need of a catalyst to generate a resurgence of enthusiasm.
>
> The arts just might fill that need. . . .
>
> The concept of the arts leading American education to a new level of optimism and respectability is not as far-fetched as it may seem. The enthusiastic support for a good high school music program is an indication of what we could possibly achieve for all of education through healthy thriving arts programs. The fine arts possess a natural regenerative power.

Several national organizations in addition to the College Board have proposed programs that recognize arts education as basic for all students and essential for the nation's future artists and performers. Various state departments of education and local school dis-

---

Charles M. Dorn is professor of art and design, Department of Creative Arts, Purdue University, West Lafayette, Ind.

The Arts

tricts support efforts to mainstream the arts into the academic curriculum. These efforts include such programs as the following:

- *Idaho Comprehensive Arts in Education Program:* Strategies and methods to help schools enliven their total curriculum with the arts, expand and strengthen existing arts programs, and utilize new and varied resources for teaching the arts.
- *Rosemore School District, Whitehall, Ohio:* An exemplary comprehensive art curriculum developed for the district that includes units of study on making art, understanding how artists work, and appreciating how society expresses values and beliefs in art forms.
- *Pine Bluff Humanities Program, Pine Bluff, Ark.:* Pine Bluff High School offers a humanities program to eleventh and twelfth graders organized around nine-week units such as tribal man, Renaissance man, man and self, man and society, and man and the future. The courses integrate visual arts, music, drama, literature, philosophy, and religion in historical and critical frameworks.

Certainly the most extensive efforts in the arts have been organized to meet the needs of the gifted and talented and the handicapped. Dozens of specialized art schools established at the state and local levels include magnet schools in the visual and performing arts, school-within-a-school organizations, outreach or bus-in programs for partial-day instruction, and programs for the deaf and blind.

For more detailed information on the great variety of new arts curricula and programs, see the March 1983 NASSP *Curriculum Report,* "The Arts: A New View from the Tower."

Foreign Languages

C. Edward Scebold

"In an increasingly interdependent world, foreign language study must be a vital part of the core of common learning. We recommend that all students become familiar with the language of another culture. Such studies should ideally begin in elementary school, and at least two years of foreign language study should be required of all high school students," writes Ernest Boyer in *High School: A Report on Secondary Education in America* (1983).

The recommendations to increase accessibility and to lengthen the sequences of second language study are echoed in the recent College Board report, *Academic Preparation for College: What Students Need to Know and Be Able to Do* (New York: The College Board, 1983). Focusing on the students' ability to function effectively in college and university study, the report recommends that course completion be shifted from time requirements and Carnegie units to performance-based indicators.

The Boyer report and the number of other studies of American education that have been issued in recent months do not propose any new recommendations. Each has been voiced at another time, in another context; however, the force of this focused debate may be greater now than at any point in recent history. Never before has the pressure on the principal to stay informed and to respond to the questions, concerns, and needs of students, parents, and faculty been greater, nor the scope of the information to be grasped broader.

Proficiency Guidelines

Since 1981, the American Council on the Teaching of Foreign Languages (ACTFL) and the Educational Testing Service (ETS) have engaged in numerous projects to provide clear statements of student performance as the basis for measuring the proficiency gained through second language study. These statements, outlined in the ACTFL Provisional Proficiency Guidelines, describe progressive stages of functional language use. The guidelines (although not intended as a curriculum guide) provide a framework, or organizing principle, to help educators design a second language curriculum and assess the overall skills attained by students in speaking, listening, reading, and writing. Tentative guidelines also are available for culture (cultural assimilation and learning) but they are in need of significant further refinement.

The effort to provide a usable framework for defining proficiency in a second language must be coupled with an assessment of oral skills. This assessment provides a realistic picture of a learner's ability to function in unpredictable, real-life situations. (See Figure 1 for an illustration of such a process adapted from the original oral interview developed by the Foreign Service Institute and subsequently modified by the Interagency Language Roundtable.)

Trends in Instruction

Foreign language instruction today focuses more and more on communication skills. Phillips (1982) describes the trend in this way:

The dominant trend in foreign language teaching is toward greater concentration on developing communication skills. It may seem surprising to the lay person that this has not been a primary emphasis all along. One need only recall, however, the many people who acknowledge an exposure to two years of studying a language even as they testify to the fact "I can't speak a word of it." Several forces have contributed to this communicative orientation, but it was the report of the President's Commission (*Strength Through Wisdom*, 1979) that brought the issue to the attention of the government and the public.

The commission reported that the United States suffers from a lack of foreign language "proficiency," meaning communicative ability, on all fronts. . . . In the final analysis, the commission recommended that all possible support be given to increase foreign language enrollment, but it is in the classroom that the goal of communicative ability must be fostered. Research and curriculum must henceforth provide the language learner with a real world context, that is, linguistic content in its full cultural environment.

Much of the current research suggests that a second language is most readily learned in an intensive setting or through extensive reading and listening practice. Intensive instruction immerses the learner in the study of other academic subjects *through* the second language. Emphasis on appropriate practice may lead to reinstatement of updated language laboratories that offer current magazines and tapes for "real life" input rather than boring and repetitious drill. Indeed new

---

C. Edward Scebold is executive director, American Council on the Teaching of Foreign Languages, Hastings-on-Hudson, N.Y.

Foreign Languages

Figure 1. *Oral Proficiency Rating Scales*

Government (FSI) Scale	Academic (ACTFL/ETS) Scale	Definition
5	Native	Able to speak like an educated native speaker
4+ / 4	Superior	Able to speak the language with sufficient structural accuracy and vocabulary to participate effectively in most formal and informal conversations
3+ / 3		
2+	Advanced Plus	Able to satisfy most work requirements and show some ability to communicate on concrete topics
2	Advanced	Able to satisfy routine social demands and limited work requirements
1+	Intermediate-High	Able to satisfy most survival needs and limited social demands
1	Intermediate-Middle	Able to satisfy some survival needs and some limited social demands
	Intermediate-Low	Able to satisfy basic survival needs and minimum courtesy requirements
0+	Novice-High	Able to satisfy immediate needs with learned utterances
0	Novice-Middle	Able to operate in only a very limited capacity
	Novice-Low	Unable to function in the spoken language
	0	No ability whatsoever in the language

Source: Judith E. Liskin-Gasparro. *ETS Oral Proficiency Testing Manual.* Princeton, N.J.: Educational Testing Service, 1982.

technology may open the way to new levels of proficiency by automating *formal* language instruction, freeing the teacher for dialog and tutoring.

The current national effort to develop a consensus on realistic expectations for second language study in the schools is the result of nearly three decades of ferment. Time, study, and experimentation have shown that the issue is not one of classroom methodology; any number of instructional approaches may achieve the desired outcomes. The focus today, then, is less on how an individual teacher may choose or organize instruction, and more on the expected outcomes of instruction and how these outcomes can be accurately measured.

This performance focus is especially important to the school administrator as a basis for addressing the issues of expectations versus outcomes. Mechanisms for designing curricula that identify realistic, achievable outcomes do exist in second language education, and the tests to measure these outcomes exist or are being developed.

The current reports on education repeatedly emphasize two crucial needs: redesigned teacher education and increased inservice education to provide teachers with required skills. Experienced teachers in particular need the time and resources to update their knowledge, the chance to use the language or languages they teach, and the opportunity to work with colleagues. The needs in second language education are even greater at this juncture because of the tremendous work involved in revising curricula to address performance-based criteria.

Second language education as a discipline continues to mature. School administrators hold the key to retraining opportunities, and through hiring practices, can improve preservice training programs.

References

Boyer, Ernest L. *High School: A Report on Secondary Education in America.* New York: Harper and Row, 1983.

Phillips, June K. "Foreign Language Education." In *Encyclopedia of Educational Research,* edited by Harold E. Mitzel. 5th ed. New York: The Free Press, 1982.

Strength Through Wisdom: A Critique of U.S. Capability. Report to the President from the President's Commission on Foreign Language and International Studies. Washington, D.C.: U.S. Government Printing Office, 1979.

Mathematics

Catherine D. Tobin and Mark Driscoll

National awareness about students' need for mathematics as a prerequisite for additional education opportunities and future employment is increasing. Students are finding that their job and career choices are limited when they lack mathematics skills. The case is graphically illustrated in the chart below from the National Council of Supervisors of Mathematics.

Curriculum Trends

Today, mathematics is experiencing several important trends.

- Results of the Third National Assessment of Educational Progress have shown that computational skills in mathematics have remained stable but problem solving skills are in need of a concerted effort for improvement.
- "The Agenda for Action" published by the National Council of Teachers of Mathematics (April 1, 1980) recommended that "problem solving should be the focus of school mathematics in the 1980s."
- Much greater emphasis is evident today on problem solving skills at all levels of education. Good supplementary materials are available to help students and teachers with problem solving, and problem solving materials are being incorporated into the new textbooks.
- A concern for higher level thinking skills is apparent in all curriculum areas. In particular, schools are giving much more attention to the computer-related problem solving skills of organizing and interpreting data.
- Acceptance of the calculator as a mathematical tool is more noticeable at the secondary than at the elementary level. Calculators give students more time for the important thinking and problem solving processes.

Mathematics Requirements

State legislatures, state boards of education, and local school boards are mandating more mathematics and computer literacy requirements for high school students. In some instances, students not only enroll in a specific number of credits in mathematics, but must also pass the courses. In general, if students were required to take two mathematics courses in the past, they must now take three courses. This regulation affects not only students in the academic track, but all students. These expanded course requirements may cause problems in some high schools if meaningful coursework is not available for students who would ordinarily take as little mathematics as possible.

Scope of Skill Development	Expected Outcomes
EXPANDED SKILLS	**POTENTIAL LEADERS**
Mathematical skills beyond those described here plus a desire to learn more.	Employment and educational opportunities will continue to increase as mathematical skills continue to grow.
BASIC SKILLS	**EMPLOYMENT VERY LIKELY**
Problem Solving; Applying Mathematics to Everyday Situations; Alertness to Reasonableness of Results; Estimation and Approximation; Appropriate Computational Skills; Geometry; Measurement; Reading, Interpreting, and Constructing Tables, Charts, and Graphs; Using Mathematics to Predict; Computer Literacy.	Employment opportunities are predictable. Doors to further education opportunities are open.
MINIMAL SKILLS	**LIMITED OPPORTUNITIES**
Limited skills, primarily computation. Little exposure to the other skill areas described here.	Unemployment likely. Potential generally limited to low-level jobs.

Catherine D. Tobin is program director, hm Study Skills/NASSP, Newton, Mass., and Mark Driscoll is with Northeast Regional Exchange, Chelmsford, Mass.

Mathematics

Mathematics Teachers

The shortage of mathematics teachers is not decreasing; if anything, it is escalating. Not enough mathematics teachers are training in our colleges and universities, and good teachers are still leaving the profession. Many persons teaching mathematics are not certified to do so, and a substantial number of teachers are teaching mathematics by rote, an approach indicative of a low level of mathematical skill. Retraining programs are insufficient to guarantee that all students will have certified and competent mathematics teachers.

Whether mathematics departments should be responsible for school computer courses is debatable, but in reality, math teachers are usually called on to direct these programs. The offshoot is that good mathematics teachers are lost to computer instruction and subsequently leave the schools for jobs in industry.

Implications for Action

The current trends in mathematics strongly suggest the need for some specific curriculum and personnel initiatives:

- Career counseling for students on the importance of mathematics beginning in the junior high or middle school, with information on coursework needed for further mathematics study, specific careers, and future employment
- Development of a meaningful curriculum for those students who usually do not take two or three years of mathematics
- A flexible math program that allows movement between courses and a greater number of options
- Attention to problem solving strategies within each strand and topic of the curriculum
- Use of technology in the higher level courses that have small enrollments
- Computer literacy courses that emphasize the computer as a tool for learning, problem solving, and time saving
- Pairing of qualified, experienced math teachers with new teachers, for guidance and training
- Inservice courses for ongoing teacher training and the updating of skills
- Math programs that are straightforward enough to aid working teachers who themselves need more training in mathematics.

Physical and Health Education

Betsy Zimmer

People generally are more aware today of the importance of quality physical and health education to our total educational effort. They realize that programs of physical and health education provide knowledge and understanding essential for developing quality lifestyles.

The value people place on physical activity increases as people have more leisure time. This increasing emphasis on fitness challenges traditional physical education programs.

Americans today enjoy a healthier and longer life than ever before, largely because of new medicines, better health care, and health education programs. Unfortunately, even with recent medical advances, many students are not living at optimal levels of health.

Physical Education Programs

The quality physical education program provides a wide range of physical activities:

- The curriculum teaches students both the basic skills as well as an understanding of the importance of physical activity in adult life.
- A reasonable balance between cooperative and competitive activities helps students achieve success and builds confidence for a lifetime.
- Individualized programs accommodate students' unique needs, interests, and incapacities.

With the introduction of coeducational activities in recent years, more program options are available for students and teachers. Some of the most effective current programs are interdisciplinary. Personal physical fitness programs, for example, use microcomputers for analysis and/or record keeping. They strongly emphasize lifetime sports which the student can enjoy in adult years, a positive attitude toward exercise, and recognition and management of stress.

Health Education Programs

According to Ernest Boyer, "no knowledge is more crucial than knowledge about health." Many schools launch enthusiastic attacks on the health problems of teenagers through "crash" education programs, but the most effective health education comes from a coordinated curriculum that is compatible with schoolwide goals and comprehensive in nature, reaching students at every grade level.

Trends in health education include instruction about nutrition, drug use and abuse, family life and sexuality, fitness, and personal safety. Traditional health education subjects such as anatomy and physiology are now a part of the biology curriculum. The developing health curriculum emphasizes disease prevention rather than disease treatment, "wellness" rather than sickness, and positive decision making about personal health rather than memorization of cognitive information. The study of healthy lifestyles is now considered an essential part of any health curriculum.

Health services (i.e., nursing care, screening tests, emergency procedures, etc.) and school environmental health (i.e., the attitudes of students and staff, the safety of facilities, etc.) round out the unified health program of the school.

School health education thrives on support from school personnel, parents, and community agencies. A health education advisory committee is one way to marshal such support. This committee can draw on the expertise of health professionals and materials from community agencies to encourage good working relationships and to provide essential backup in times of controversy.

Functional Health and Fitness

Recent research findings highlight the effects of exercise on health. The American Alliance for Health, Physical Education, Recreation, and Dance (AAHPERD) makes available to schools a Health Related Physical Fitness Test. The test targets functional health rather than athletic or motor performance. The test battery measures cardiorespiratory function (distance run), body composition (skin fold measure), and musculo-skeletal function (sit-up and sit and reach measure). National norms on the four-item test are available for ages 5 through 17.

Another useful aid in the assessment and promotion of physical fitness is the Fitnessgram. A computerized fitness report card, the Fitnessgram provides students (and their parents) with a fitness profile and an "exer-

Betsy Zimmer is director of the office of public information and special projects for the American Alliance for Health, Physical Education, Recreation, and Dance, Reston, Va.

Physical and Health Education

cise prescription." The Fitnessgram also enables teachers and administrators to assess the fitness level of each class and the entire school.

For more information on the Fitnessgram and the other curricular resources below, contact AAHPERD at 1900 Association Drive, Reston, Va. 22091.

- *Basic Stuff Series I* (body of knowledge supporting physical education)
- *Basic Stuff Series II—Adolescence* (ages 13-18 instructional activities)
- *Guidelines for Middle School Physical Education*
- *Guidelines for Secondary School Physical Education*
- *Health Education Teaching Ideas: Secondary*
- *Ideas II: A Sharing of Teaching Practices by Secondary School Physical Education Practitioners*
- *Physical Education and Sport for Secondary School Students*
- *Implementation of Aerobic Exercise Programs*

Science

Milada Benca

"Across the United States, there is escalating awareness that our educational systems are facing inordinate difficulties in trying to meet the needs of the nation in our changing and increasingly technological society. We appear to be raising a generation of Americans, many of whom lack the understanding and the skills necessary to participate fully in the technological world in which they live and work."

This call to upgrade science education, an excerpt from the 1982 Report of the National Science Board Commission (National Science Foundation), epitomizes the challenge facing secondary school principals. They must consider several important questions on the issue.

What Is the Study of Science About?

The public tends to view science as a method rather than as a process. The study of science requires a questioning and critical attitude in addition to a knowledge of fundamental principles and facts. To observe and interpret aspects of science requires curiosity, objectivity, and honesty. The ability to distinguish between scientific evidence and opinion implies three basic skills:

- How to use observation and experimentation to develop scientific ideas
- How to use a library and perform simple experiments
- How to organize material and communicate the results.

What Mathematical Skills Are Necessary?

Mathematical skills are required to communicate most scientific results. The single most important means of upgrading science education in a school is to provide students with a strong mathematical background. The following mathematical skills are recommended for college bound students who take science courses (see the College Board study *Academic Preparation for College*):

- Ability to interpret data from graphs or tables
- Ability to draw conclusions from data

Milada Benca is associate professor, Physical Science Department, Kennedy-King College, Chicago, Ill.

- Ability to select and apply mathematical relationships to scientific problems
- Ability to explain mathematical relationships in nonmathematical language.

In reality, these skills are needed by *all* secondary school students.

What Course Content Is Included in Science?

Societal issues such as environmental pollution and threat of nuclear war are often discussed in nonscience courses. To intelligently discuss these issues requires an understanding of concepts in the fields of biology, chemistry, and physics. The most helpful science course content stresses unifying concepts such as geological evolution, cell theory, and chemical bonding. In recent years, secondary schools also have added such useful courses as geology and interdisciplinary science to the traditional curriculum.

Advanced Placement courses in the high school science curriculum are advantageous both as college level offerings for students of high ability and motivation, and as a resource for all classes in that discipline. Community science resources (industry, colleges, retired professionals) also are useful to reinforce and to expand the scope of the school program.

How Can Administrators Promote Better Science Education?

Principals must provide adequate time for science instructional tasks such as setting up demonstrations and laboratory equipment, preparing solutions, and programming computers. Allotting additional preparation time to lab teachers and hiring laboratory aides can promote the effective use of faculty and keep morale high.

Science teachers should be encouraged to exchange ideas and plan together. Some of the best ideas for program improvement can come from within the school or district.

What About New Directions?

In the October 1983 NASSP *Curriculum Report*, Robert Yager suggests that "school science programs must come closer to considering the essence of real science. Science is an exploration of the universe in

Science

which each person exists—explaining the objects and events encountered and testing such explorations for accuracy. These three ingredients—i.e., exploring, explaining, and testing—must be central to every science course."

Yager goes on to recommend several features that should characterize exemplary science programs of the 1980s.

- A science/technology curriculum built around major societal issues unique at a given time and/or to a given community
- Basic science knowledge derived from direct applications
- An environment where students can explore, offer explanations, and test such explanations
- Presentation in a social context that emphasizes what people do, what the consequences of these actions are, their ethics and values.

Social Studies

John P. Lunstrum

Citizenship education for more than a century has been viewed as the central goal of social studies. Unfortunately, the meaning of citizenship varies. Some educators see it simply as the indoctrination of traditional patriotic and free enterprise virtues. Others argue for a broader meaning consistent with the changing character of American democracy and call for critical thinking and political participation skills.

In the 1960s and '70s, the goal of education for citizenship was eclipsed by prestigious, federally-funded national curriculum projects that attempted to bridge the gap between teaching and research in the social science disciplines. The "back to the discipline movement" mustered the help of prominent scholars to create special programs for secondary schools in sociology, anthropology, behavioral and political science, and analytical history.

Despite the efforts of the reformers, little remains of the "new social studies." A plausible explanation for the demise is that scholars did not understand the realities of the classroom and therefore did not involve administrators and teachers in the critical decisions about content and teaching methods.

Curriculum Patterns

The prevailing pattern today is the framework established by the 1916 NEA Commission Report. After more than 60 years, the following courses still predominate:

- Grade 7: World History/Cultures/Geography
- Grade 8: U.S. History
- Grade 9: Civics/Government or World Cultures/History
- Grade 10: World Cultures/History
- Grade 11: U.S. History
- Grade 12: American Government and Sociology/Psychology.

The remarkable persistence of this basic pattern does not tell the whole story. More social, economic, and cultural content is included in many U.S. history courses, and some states and districts have turned the junior year course into American studies, stressing themes and topics as opposed to chronology.

Another interesting development runs counter to the uniformity of the basic pattern. An analysis of local and state curriculum guides points up the great variety of topics taught under the rubric of the social studies. This enthusiasm for including timely new topics is both a blessing and a curse. It is a positive influence insofar as it infuses vital new content and meaningful issues in the curriculum. Unfortunately, it also encourages a kind of curricular evangelism or "mindlessness" (Morrissett and Haas, 1982) that ignores the relationship between purpose, content, and organization.

Concerns of Teachers

To understand the challenges facing the social studies, principals must understand how teachers perceive their problems and needs. In recent studies, junior high teachers report three major problems: limited student reading ability, lack of individualized learning materials, and lack of student interest. Problems perceived by senior high social studies teachers were quite similar. Heading the list were "inadequate student reading abilities," "lack of student interest in the subject," and "lack of materials for individualizing instruction." Virtually two-thirds of the senior high teachers saw "inadequate articulation across grade levels" as a serious problem.

These problems are not insurmountable. The principal can do much to help teachers cope with such concerns as inadequate reading abilities. Carefully planned workshops in basic skill development may be a starting point. An informed and concerned teacher can do much to make textbooks more comprehensible and more interesting. It might be feasible to set some time aside during the summer to enable teachers (with expert guidance and direction) to develop individualized materials. Basic skill development (reading, writing, and study skills) can be integrated with the teaching of content (Lunstrum and Irvin, 1981). The role of the microcomputer is worth exploring for individualizing instruction and facilitating skill development, but much of the available courseware is inadequate, appearing most often in the form of electronic workbooks.

John P. Lunstrum is professor of social studies, education, and reading, College of Education, The Florida State University, Tallahassee.

Social Studies

Instructional Practices

Despite recommendations from several generations of social studies reformers, teachers still cling to traditional instructional practices. The most widely used methodology is the lecture (Goodlad's expression "teacher talk and demonstration" is probably more accurate). Rivaling teacher talk in popularity is discussion/recitation. Discussion here may mean an exchange of ideas or simply a rapid-fire question and answer process. Student individual assignments ("seatwork") are also widely used. Students spend much time completing assignments—usually writing answers to questions following a teacher lecture or teacher-led discussion.

Newer instructional practices tested and advocated in the social studies projects of the 1960s have not found many converts, despite the continued need to motivate students. Inquiry/discovery learning, for example, is used regularly by only about 20 percent of senior high school teachers in the analysis of social problems. Values analysis and clarification—a major reform thrust of the 1960s and '70s—has few adherents, probably because of the negative reaction from the community.

Despite much concern expressed in professional journals, controversial issues are not perceived as a serious problem. Decisions in federal courts in the last few years have buttressed the concept of academic freedom in schools, providing more latitude to deal with the difficult issues.

Community/experienced-based education, which opens many possibilities for senior high social studies, is not widely practiced. Little interest remains in modules/LAP packages and programmed instruction, probably because teachers perceive them as counterproductive to the interaction essential in a social studies classroom. Proponents of continuous progress materials respond by pointing out the ways teachers have misused these materials.

Instructional Materials

The textbook is still the most widely used type of instructional material. State and local curriculum guides do not appear to exercise much influence over what is taught. Teachers seem content with their textbooks, and publishers anticipate that texts will continue to be the foundation of social studies content.

Challenges for the 1980s

The consultants and staff of Project SPAN, a recent extensive national study of social studies priorities, practices, and needs, identified six critical problems for the 1980s. Four of the problem areas appear to be directly related to the issues and decisions facing principals.

1. *Improving student learning in social studies*
Many students leave school without knowledge, skills, and attitudes that are important and desirable outcomes of social studies programs. In addition, many students do not like or value social studies as much as other subjects.

2. *Changing the culture of the school*
The culture and organization of schools, especially at the secondary level, focus much of the teachers' and administrators' energy on management and control rather than on the teaching and learning of social studies—particularly on the teaching and learning of higher level thinking skills, participation skills, and democratic values.

3. *Improving teacher practices*
Instruction in the social studies is generally characterized by limited kinds of learning experiences and by inattention to the implications of educational research.

4. *Strengthening the curriculum*
The social studies curriculum—courses, materials, and content—is focused primarily on specific facts and broad conclusions from history and other social science disciplines rather than on critical-thinking skills, social science concepts, values and attitudes, and social participation. The curriculum, moreover, is not based on student developmental needs and does not emphasize important societal issues and effective participation in the social world.

References

Lunstrum, John P., and Irvin, Judith L. "Integrating Basic Skills into Social Studies Content." *Social Education,* March 1981.

Morrissett, Irving, ed. *Social Studies for the 1980s.* Alexandria, Va.: Association for Supervision and Curriculum Development, 1982.

Morrissett, Irving, and Haas, John D. "Rationales, Goals and Objectives in the Social Studies." In *The Current State of the Social Studies: A Report on Project SPAN.* Boulder, Colo.: Social Science Education Consortium, 1982.

Vocational and Technical Education

Michael J. Dyrenfurth and L. Alan Phelps

The shifting purposes and missions of the high school will continue to affect administrators, school boards, and the public during the 1980s. Several trends in vocational, technical, and practical arts curricula are worthy of serious consideration in the light of this changing environment.

1. High schools are being asked to expand their role in developing technological literacy. Clearly, young adults must be functionally literate in the technology that affects their future roles as workers, parents, and life-long learners in an information-based society.
2. Vocational and technical education is beginning to look at ways to improve *both* the academic and basic skills of students. Vocational subjects can and must be systematically linked with mathematics, science, and English curricula to more clearly illustrate the relevance of academic learning to the world outside the school.
3. High schools serve an increasingly broader range of students (Orientals, Hispanics, the limited English proficient, the handicapped, dropouts, and potential dropouts). Vocational education programs are serving a vital role in keeping many of these students in school, enabling them to learn basic and interpersonal skills, and assuring that they develop useful job skills.
4. Considerable attention is also being given to the major, long-term goals of vocational education. All students need exposure to comprehensive and sequential career awareness, to exploration, orientation, and preparation programs. This vocational continuum enables students either to enter the world of work or to pursue further education with greater purpose and insight into their career interests.

Curriculum Issues and Trends

Several changes are developing in the design and implementation of high school vocational education curricula. Some of the more critical and substantive curriculum issues are discussed below:

Michael J. Dyrenfurth is professor of industrial education, Department of Practical Arts and Vocational Technical Education, University of Missouri-Columbia, and L. Alan Phelps is professor of vocational education, Office of Career Development for Special Populations, University of Illinois at Urbana-Champaign.

- National studies (Sherman, 1983; National Institute of Education, 1981; Task Force on Education for Economic Growth, 1983) have called for a closer relationship between vocational education and business, industry, and labor. Private sector personnel should be put to better use for curriculum development and program evaluation. Collaborative participation by corporate personnel directors, executives, skilled journeymen and women, and others representing the range of corporate employment opportunity is essential if vocational education is to be optimally effective.

- The demands for accountability continue to motivate the development of competency-based vocational curricula. Numerous regional, state, and local curriculum projects have produced extensive lists of job tasks, competencies, performance objectives, and performance standards for many career clusters and specific occupations. Regrettably, most of the competency-based activity to date has focused on the psychomotor and lower-level cognitive skills required for entry into specific occupations. Only minimal attention has been given to affective and other highly transferable skills.

- As schools assume a greater role in technology-related education, practical arts programs such as industrial arts and general business will become increasingly important. Recently added high school graduation requirements in mathematics, science, and language may jeopardize students' ability to take orientation-level and particularly preparation-level vocational education courses.

- Rapid changes in the workplace necessitate that high schools launch major efforts to upgrade/update their vocational education equipment and facilities. Much of the equipment used in the schools was purchased 10-30 years ago. Given the rate of change, continued use of such obsolete equipment is ludicrous!

- The articulation of high school curricula with community colleges, elementary, and middle level programs has been an important focus in recent years. Curriculum coordination with community colleges and other agencies continues to occur in many communities (e.g., those sponsored by the Jobs Training Partnership Act). These efforts attempt to avoid duplication of training programs in specialized areas such as welding or electronics.

Vocational and Technical Education

Efforts are underway to assure that elementary and middle school students are developing the important basic skills and competencies necessary for career development. In many states, area vocational high schools still have strong advanced vocational programs. Recently, however, these centers have encountered financial difficulties because of declining enrollments, tight budgets, and greater attention paid to traditional academic subjects. Comprehensive high schools in many communities are attempting to structure sequential curricula in high technology fields to ensure that the electronics and drafting courses taken in high school, for example, articulate with the electronics, mathematics, and technical drawing courses offered in postsecondary institutions.

Instructional Trends

Like most other subjects, vocational/technical education has plunged headlong into the use of microcomputers. Students use micros as an instructional tool and they study them as an *object* of instruction. Individualized and/or self-paced instruction is delivered by interactive microcomputers. Micros help instructors manage the ever more complex inventory, record-keeping, and performance charting requirements of competency-based vocational laboratories. And vocational education is beginning to explore the potential of interactive video instruction.

Other continuing instructional trends include cooperative education, i.e., school-supervised work experience in real work settings, and student vocational groups organized in every vocational subject area *including* industrial arts and home economics.

Trends in Student Services

The large numbers of students served by vocational education have placed greater demands on guidance and counseling and other specialized personnel. More mentors/role models from the private sector are needed to clarify the job and attitudinal demands of the real world.

Complex technology and its preparatory programs demand systematic exploration in the schools. The industrial arts and career education programs, for example, should expose students to a significant variety of technological areas and careers. Mere wood shop and sewing courses are not enough.

Placement and follow-up services are becoming more important because they also provide the most widely accepted standard for judging program success. In these tight financial times, continued funding is usually based on good performance.

Evaluation Trends

Advisory councils and other business/industry/labor participation are regularly called for by policymakers. Placement and follow-up data are the ranking criteria for evaluating vocational program success. Other criteria are emerging, however, particularly those related to the new basics: i.e., skill in work-related communication, calculation, and comprehension. Technological literacy (a much more important concept than computer literacy) is receiving considerable attention (see *High School* by Ernest Boyer).

Action Recommendations for Principals

Vocational educators often feel that their administrators "just don't understand them." Sometimes this impression is correct. The field is a broad and complex one with significant links to *many* of the central purposes of education. Principals can lend their support by showing an interest in vocational and technical education and undertaking the following initiatives:

- Attending vocational advisory council meetings (state or local) with their vocational staff
- Enhancing the extent/effectiveness of the schools' linkage with the business/industry/labor sector
- Analyzing the equipment and facility needs of the vocational education programs—particularly for technologically appropriate learning
- Assessing the effectiveness and extent of articulation among the vocational program's various components.

References

Contemporary Challenges for Vocational Education, American Association Yearbook, 1982.

Centergram and other publications of the National Center for Research in Vocational Education. *VocEd* and other publications of the American Vocational Association.

Interdisciplinary Approaches

Nancy Tondre Jones

A major challenge of instructional leadership is how to allocate resources—time, money, and personnel—to ensure not only that the most important instructional goals are accomplished, but also that students are provided opportunities to pursue areas of individual interest. Although the goals of any content field can be argued convincingly by proponents, overriding educational goals transcend the scope of any particular field of knowledge. Interdisciplinary approaches attempt to deal with these broad domains.

Compartmentalization in content fields is understandable, due to both traditional teacher training and the increasing complexity and specialization of teaching today. Teachers cling to subject barriers; change is difficult. But there is so much to teach, and students need a broad educational background.

Interdisciplinary approaches to content help students make connections between subjects and apply their knowledge to real problems. Interdisciplinary alternatives also offer the advantage of greater educational impact with available resources.

Interdisciplinary approaches take many forms. In the past, an interdisciplinary approach meant team teaching or combining two or more related topics into one course. Current interdisciplinary efforts include a number of approaches, from simple correlation of content to significant restructuring of the school day.

The following is a framework for establishing an interdisciplinary curriculum.

- *Philosophy.* District and school philosophy are the starting points for any investigation of interdisciplinary focus. After goals have been agreed upon and priorities have been established, the opportunities for interdisciplinary work within the curriculum can be identified.
- *Skills.* Most district/school philosophies and goals identify basic skills for all students, with communication at the top of the list. Too often, however, the responsibility for teaching communication skills rests with the English/language arts department. Research suggests that students learn to communicate better if teaching and application occur in a variety of contexts. When math, science, social studies, and arts teachers share an area of responsibility—like reading improvement or teaching problem solving—a natural bridge to other collaboration forms.
- *Natural Linkages.* Some subjects or courses are more naturally linked than others because of similar content. Algebra II and chemistry, mathematics and physical science, American literature and United States history, geography and earth science are typical examples. Teaching these subjects to present key ideas that make sense to students can be coordinated without extensive curriculum or staff development.
- *Common Topics.* Common topics exist in several curricular areas. Technology, nutrition, health, and careers are commonly taught and retaught through various courses. More meaning and depth can be developed in the same amount of available time with an interdisciplinary approach.
- *Themes.* Topics that are of high interest or recognized importance to students offer significant opportunity for interdisciplinary development and the possibility of making schooling more relevant to the community at large. Political issues, environmental concerns, futures, and global understanding are themes that can tie various courses together. These themes change over time and with student interests. Emphasizing these kinds of topics in two or more courses/subjects helps students to see beyond disciplinary lines.
- *New Subjects.* Some fields have or are developing crossover disciplines that integrate related subjects. After a thorough grounding in the separate subjects, interdisciplinary courses provide the linkage. Ecology and marine science, for example, are crossover courses that require a background in biology, chemistry, and earth science. Communications and visual language are other crossover subjects.

  The computer can provide opportunities to bring subject areas together. Interest in new technology is intense and there are fewer preconceived notions. One such collaboration among graphic arts, business education, journalism, and English composition has resulted in an interdisciplinary approach to writing.

- *General Education.* The history of education records divisions among subjects and a search for core learnings. Recent secondary school studies have

---

Nancy Tondre Jones is staff assistant in the Office of Curriculum Assessment and Development, Virginia Beach City Public Schools, Virginia Beach, Va.

Interdisciplinary Approaches

made strong recommendations about general education. Several of these studies recommend interdisciplinary courses in a seminar setting that would enable students to apply knowledge to the real problems of contemporary life. Gordon Cawelti, Theodore Sizer, Mortimer Adler, and others have stressed the importance of the interdisciplinary seminar in developing student capability to use knowledge.

Barriers to interdisciplinary thinking are strong. Single discipline thinking and alliances are both traditional and convenient. Lack of understanding of common educational goals is probably the greatest obstacle to progress.

Reorganization of departments is one way to overcome disciplinary thinking and to encourage thinking in broader fields. Possibilities include: communications, aesthetics, technology, career and vocational studies, societal studies, and physical education and health.

Important Steps To Take

- Involve staff, students, and community in determining philosophy and core goals.
- Identify specific areas where interdisciplinary approaches are feasible and needed
- Provide time to plan
- Allow understanding to grow; subject area specialists speak different languages.

Remember that even a few linkages can change the atmosphere from territoriality to collaboration. A few well-planned interdisciplinary approaches that work can open up many other valuable and informal collaborative opportunities.

Trends in Organization and Staffing

Building Design/Modification

William S. DeJong

The design of the school building has a definite impact on curriculum and instruction. Whether the physical structure creates the program or vice versa, however, is open to question.

The similarity in high school buildings and programs across the country is hardly arguable. Most secondary buildings include standard classrooms, special laboratories, and general purpose spaces built or renovated to accommodate a curriculum of the 1960s and 1970s. Space is often allocated according to required course offerings and student elective requests. Both have changed dramatically during the past decade.

The Impact of Program Change

State legislatures and local school boards responding to public pressures in many areas of the country have increased graduation requirements, emphasizing the academic subjects and downgrading elective subjects and prevocational programs. Translating these actions to the building level requires more science laboratories, more classroom space, fewer home economics and industrial arts facilities, and even a microcomputer lab or two.

The educational specifications of the past that created many of the school buildings are, in some respects, out of step with the needs of the present. Facilities once important are no longer needed or are needed to a lesser degree. New facilities are required. Some existing facilities are either moderately useful or in need of major redesign and modification.

When building changes are necessary, at least two imperatives should be given priority:

- When converting space, strive for flexibility so as to be able to convert again as needed.
- Opt for modular equipment and furniture insofar as possible.

The Impact of Enrollment Fluctuations

A second force affecting the use of school buildings is fluctuation in student enrollment. It is not uncommon today for schools that were once bulging at the seams to be half filled with students.

William S. DeJong is assistant executive director, Council of Educational Facility Planners International, Columbus, Ohio.

When enrollment decreases occur, principals and their staffs are left with spaces no longer needed for academic programs. Frequently what could be an opportunity for increased flexibility in building use and program results only in a larger faculty lounge or expanded administrative offices. Sometimes rooms are used one or two hours a day to house tutoring programs or itinerant speech therapists.

This unplanned use can result in space-use patterns that are difficult to reverse if enrollment increases, consolidation occurs, or if alterations are needed to respond to program innovations. Some rules of thumb are helpful to principals of schools with declining enrollments:

1. Monitor the actual use of space closely, just as you would if the school enrollment did not change.
2. Assign space for a specific function and for specific blocks of time. Do not assign space to persons or programs.
3. Make space allocations based on need, not simply on availability.

Matching the Facility with the Instructional Program

The traditional school building assumed instructional programs that did not readily acknowledge differences among students. The 750 to 900-square-foot classroom might have been an appropriate space for teacher presentation and general discussion, but it was not very good for cooperative teaching or variable grouping. As instructional programs shift to focus on needs of individual students, the form of the facilities should follow the functions that are required.

What can be done to convert inflexible buildings into the kind of space needed to implement the requirements of personalized and adaptive educational programs?

To begin with, know what you want to do. The school's goals and objectives should be written and understood so that they can be used to ensure appropriate building modifications. If larger spaces are needed, walls can be removed. If smaller spaces are required, classrooms can be divided for discussion areas or teacher offices. Auditoriums and cafeterias, when properly equipped and scheduled, can be used for large-group instruction. In light of the research data that show the positive impact of cooperative teacher planning on student academic learning, perhaps planning areas will be a priority.

Building Design/Modification

Support for these kinds of changes is given more readily when they are grounded in thoughtful planning. School boards and central office staffs are more receptive to proposals that link building changes with improved program options for students. Buttressing requests with research findings that show the relationship of new approaches to increased student performance can be particularly convincing.

Current research suggests, for example, that students benefit when teachers rearrange classroom space to accommodate diagnosed student learning style differences. (See Article 61.) Space redesign can account for differences in such preferences as formal or informal setting; independent, paired, or group experiences; teacher-directed or peer-oriented learning. A growing body of research supports the decision to change classroom space to permit more adaptive instructional programs.

A Final Perspective

Our information society is changing at such a rapid rate that predictions for the future are risky. Yet, planning is necessary if school buildings and programs are to keep in step. The wise principal keeps abreast of curricular changes and their implications for schooling by reading, attending conferences and workshops, and interacting with informed persons in the community. When educational specifications are developed for building additions or modifications, it is good to get a second professional opinion. And ask community members to review them and give their honest reactions. The lessons of the open space era underline our startling proclivity of trading one inflexibility for another.

Principals can see themselves trapped by the shape of the school building, but choices and options are always available. A new direction can set in motion thought waves that cause principal and staff to look more imaginatively at utilization of existing space.

Education is changing continuously. New information about learning and about the needs of society create new contingencies to which schools must be ready to adjust. The design and use of our buildings is a public statement of our willingness to accommodate change.

Graded/Nongraded Organization

Roger B. Worner

School administrators continue to debate the practical and philosophical merits of graded vs. nongraded patterns in school organization.

From a practical point of view, graded organizational patterns are efficient, easily understood by the observing public, and less controversial. In the main they have worked fairly well. Nongraded patterns, however, better address the proven diversity that exists in a randomly selected group of students. This is a fact parents intuitively understand.

Given a like-aged group of students, their learning rates, learning styles, ability to handle concepts of differing levels of abstraction, and ability to acquire and retain information vary greatly. At the same time, the practical issue remains: Can school districts, principals, and teachers effectively organize and implement nongraded organizational patterns?

Research conducted from 1968 to 1973 (primarily at the elementary level) shows conclusively the benefits of nongraded organization. Student achievement scores and student attitudes toward school were higher for students in nongraded schools. Student retentions were low in nongraded schools and these schools were especially beneficial for minority students, males, and underachievers (Heddens, 1982).

Nongraded Organizational Options

Fortunately for those who agree that a school district or school should address known student differences in the classroom, several nongraded options exist. The level of sophistication is up to the building principal and staff who are largely dependent upon the degree to which differences will be acknowledged and personnel committed.

- *Nongrading Within the Self-Contained Classroom.* Teachers, independently of one another, organize and deliver instruction differently for students whose placement spans two or three grade levels within a single classroom.
- *Nongraded Grouping Within the Same Grade Level.* Two or more teachers at the same grade level collaboratively organize materials and teach students whose placement spans two or more grade levels. Students are grouped and regrouped, as appropriate, to maximize the number of potential instructional groups.
- *Multi-Grade Level, Cross-Grade Grouping.* Two or more teachers with different grade level assignments organize materials and teach students whose placement spans two or more grade levels. Students again are grouped for instruction and exchanged to maximize groupings and take advantage of the subject matter expertise of the teachers.
- *Schoolwide Nongraded Organization.* All staff members participate in a multi-grade level, cross-grade grouping structure.

One feature of nongraded organization is that the school administrator and staff can begin the implementation process as conservatively as personal attitudes and curricular materials dictate; and, as confidence and sophistication build, they can develop more complex and refined forms of nongraded instruction. The advantages of this increasing sophistication are more appropriate placement and instruction delivery for students. The major disadvantage is the difficulty of managing the system. Students must be moved from group to group as they show progress or decline.

Workability of Nongraded Patterns

Some educators would have us believe that nongraded organizational patterns have been tried and have failed. In reality, nongraded organizational patterns have failed only when the responsible personnel were ill-prepared to administer the system or, more often, when the delivery system was so ill-conceived that failure was predictable.

Well-conceived, soundly-designed, effectively-implemented nongraded organizational patterns do not fail. Regardless of the form of past nongraded structures, the majority that failed did so because of inappropriate delivery systems. Weakest of the system components have been the diagnostic tests, curricular materials, and accounting system/organization. In many instances, school districts operated programs with committed personnel but with an archaic set of tools. Staff members tried but eventually succumbed to the "wear and tear" of a poorly organized effort. A quality nongraded delivery system is characterized by several elements.

1. Reliable and accurate skill/content-based (criterion-referenced) tests are critical to assess student programmatic weaknesses and to match students

---

Roger B. Worner is superintendent of schools, Mason City, Iowa.

with materials and instruction that will enhance their learning.
2. The delivery system requires a multiple option, multi-grade level curriculum that allows for speedy placement, prescription, and, as necessary, remediation. Classroom teachers working with a variety of groups cannot be expected to develop all the necessary materials in the evening after a taxing day's work. Instructional materials must be readily available and keyed to the diagnostic tests.
3. Successful nongraded programs are characterized by systems for diagnosis, placement, prescription, grouping, regrouping, correction of homework/seatwork, grading, progress recording, attendance, and student monitoring that are philosophically consistent, organizationally articulated, understandable, and efficient. Clearly, microcomputers provide a base for conquering the management problems of nongraded structures. We have no reason to relive the unpleasant experiences of the open schools and open classrooms of a decade ago. With careful planning and use of the technology now available, accounting and organizational problems can be managed quite reasonably.
4. The nongraded organizational pattern requires individual commitment to make the process work. Unquestionably, school districts and schools have staff members qualified to implement organizational patterns that are soundly designed, professionally rewarding, and that hold reasonably high probability of success. Securing personnel commitment will be less difficult if principals understand why "once-burned" staff members may show reticence about jumping on a nongraded bandwagon again, unless design deficiencies are carefully resolved *before* implementing this important organizational pattern.

The Dilemma

Research and considerable experience affirm that the nongraded organizational pattern is philosophically stronger than its comparatively trouble-free cousin, the graded organizational pattern. The nongraded approach—if well conceived and implemented—deals with the differences that characterize students of the same age. Graded approaches, on the other hand, poorly address diversity in student learning styles, and capabilities for distraction, acquisition, and retention. But, nongraded approaches are more demanding.

A myriad of technological advancements make the implementation of nongraded organizational patterns more practical today than at any previous time in the history of American education. For creative administrators and dedicated teachers, the nongraded structure represents one of the most promising links in the framework of personalized education.

References

Brown, B. Frank. *The Nongraded High School.* Englewood Cliffs, N.J.: Prentice-Hall, 1963.

Buffie, Edward G., and Jenkins, John M. *Curriculum Development in Nongraded Schools.* Bloomington, Ind.: Indiana University Press, 1971.

Heddens, J. W. "Elementary Education." In *Encyclopedia of Educational Research,* vol. 2, edited by H. E. Mitzel. New York: The Free Press, 1982.

School-Within-a-School Organization

Gilbert R. Weldy

During the baby-boom years of the 1950s and 1960s, school district consolidation as well as the urbanization and suburbanization of our population produced larger and larger schools, particularly at the secondary level. Schools of 2,000-5,000 students were thought to be superior in their capability to provide broad programs and more specialized services.

Unfortunately, individual students tend to get lost in large schools. They are swallowed up in the anonymity of large impersonal structures. Some, after being assigned a number, are never heard from again unless their computer cards are folded, spindled, or mutilated.

High schools of 5,000 are more often the exception than the rule today, but the idea that "bigger is better" still persists in some circles. The personalization of learning, characteristic of small schools where all students are likely to be well-known, is sacrificed for more course offerings and more diverse facilities.

One of the organizational plans that can break down this bigness and make the larger school more suitable for the individual student is the school-within-a-school plan. This plan simply divides all the students and staff into smaller units, identifying them with a smaller subschool, and perhaps assigning them to a certain area of the building for their home base. Schools use two to four such units, depending on the student enrollment, the building, and the staff. The units are variously referred to as "houses," "units," "halls," "divisions," "small schools," or "subschools."

Characteristics of the Plan

Some school buildings are designed and constructed with several identical halls or wings to accommodate this organization. In this "ideal" design, the structure of each small school usually contains all of the following:

- An administrator (called a "house" or "unit" principal, director, or subprincipal)
- Guidance counselors
- Homerooms
- Some office staff
- Separate classroom facilities

Gilbert R. Weldy is assistant superintendent, Niles Township High Schools, Skokie, Ill.

- Teachers of "basic" subjects (English, math, social studies, science, and possibly foreign language).

The small school is as self-contained as possible, with students spending as much as one-half to three-fourths of their school time there. The school-within-the-school is their home base. Their counselor and basic or core classes are located there. Attendance and discipline are administered by the principal or director of the small school.

The faculty assigned to each subschool is multidisciplinary, making it possible to organize teaching teams and interdisciplinary programs, particularly at the middle level. Except in the very largest schools, students share common areas such as cafeterias, libraries, gyms, and auditoriums.

Students remain with the same subschool throughout all their years in the school. Subschools are labeled in a great variety of ways: "A, B, C, D" (at Niles North High School, Skokie, Ill.); "Michael, Boltwood, Bacon, and Beardsley" (at Evanston Township High School, Evanston, Ill.); "Oracle, Olympian, and Omega" (at Old Orchard Junior High School, Skokie, Ill.).

Students are randomly assigned so that each subschool is as nearly like the others as possible, with equal numbers of boys, girls, honor students, and special-need students. Colors and mascots are adopted to give students pride and identity in their subunits. Intramural competition among small schools is encouraged, but athletic teams for interscholastic competition are selected from the entire school.

School-within-a-school organizations like those described here have often been very successful, but they do have certain shortcomings. Subschools can never be totally self-contained, since a large part of the school program demands specially trained staff and special facilities. Only required courses, with multiple sections schoolwide, can be scheduled without conflict in each small school. If students cannot be scheduled for a course in their own unit, they must be assigned one elsewhere. A student's program of choice has priority over the assignment of classes in subschools. Consequently, students in honors programs or specialized courses may have few if any classes in their own small school.

A different kind of drawback is that most school buildings were not designed for this plan, making it difficult to decentralize many of the functions.

Students entering a large, impersonal high school are encouraged and reassured by their small school

School-Within-a-School Organization

assignment—knowing who their homeroom teacher, counselor, and subprincipal will be, where their school office is located, where their locker will be, and which of their friends are assigned with them. As school enrollments decline, however, school-within-a-school plans must be modified. In some situations, four small schools are reduced to three, or even two. In other instances, functions that can no longer be effectively separated are combined or centralized. In some cases, the plan may be abandoned altogether because the school is too small.

Some Alternatives

Aside from the standard school-within-a-school organization, some additional variations have begun to emerge. The objective is the same (personalization), but the organizational focus is more specialized. Alternative education and special education use subschool plans. These "schools-within-schools" are part of the larger school organization, but are not based on random student assignment.

- The *alternative school* offers personalized schooling to students who have not done well in the larger school setting. Generally, these "continuation" students have low grades, frequent disciplinary referrals, and high rates of absence. The school-within-a-school offers them a home base where the student-teacher ratio is small enough to furnish individual attention and support. As in more general models, alternative education students use the resources of the larger school when appropriate.
- *Special education* programs often operate as schools-within-the-school. Special and mainstreamed classes are characteristic of these programs. Riverdale High School in Fort Myers, Fla., for example, organizes its special education program as a departmentalized team. Students complete their basic academic requirements with special education teachers who have a subject specialty. Students take elective courses in the school at large. This approach allows special students to complete state-mandated graduation requirements without having to compete with students in the regular program.
- Some schools have organized *small units, centers, or grade level subunits* within the total school to accommodate the special needs of students. This approach is dictated by the educational needs of students, not by the desire to reduce bigness or anonymity. Where numbers are sufficient, for example, it may be useful to remove students from the mainstream for programs that require special facilities, staff training, or other services. Schools can assist groups of students whose educational interests and learning styles suggest an accommodation apart from the mainstream. Typical of these programs are action learning, the arts, vocational training, and interdisciplinary studies such as global or international studies.

The school-within-a-school model has been used successfully in large schools to subdivide by grade level—most often for ninth graders in four-year high schools. This approach has many advantages for orienting new students and providing a highly supportive curriculum. The school-within-a-school organization makes good educational sense, particularly when it is focused on the developmental needs of students.

Middle Level Education

Conrad F. Toepfer, Jr.

Middle level education encompasses grades 5 through 9, with programs for youngsters between the ages of 9 and 14. Variously described as young adolescents, early adolescents, emerging adolescents, even "transescents," these youngsters approach or realize puberty during their middle level school years. They are at a unique stage of growth and development and require educational experiences different from those that elementary and high schools emphasize. Teachers in these schools must have or develop appropriate pedagogical skills and an understanding of the human and educational needs of young adolescents.

Developing Middle Level Staff and Program

Middle level education today has a researched data base at least the equal of elementary and high school education. The middle level principal can utilize material from medical, neuroscientific, and educational findings to upgrade and improve the knowledge of staff members.

The knowledge explosion in middle level psychology and pedagogy requires periodic inservice and staff development for all middle level professionals. The successful teacher at either the elementary or high school level cannot automatically expect success at the middle level with the same instructional techniques. An effective eleventh grade chemistry teacher, for example, can become an effective middle level science teacher by developing instructional strategies grounded in the learning characteristics of middle level youngsters. Middle level teachers learn that students at this level are not miniatures of the later adolescents they taught in high school.

The middle level principal must show the way for teachers to understand the characteristics of middle level learners in such important respects as physical stability, emotional maturity, cognitive level, and attention span. Teachers gaining this perspective find greater satisfaction in their work and achieve greater success in diagnosing learner readiness and capability.

Developing a middle level perspective among building staff is perhaps the major task of middle level principals. The vast majority of teachers are still trained for the elementary or high school levels, with various supplemental experiences required for individual state certification at the middle level. Gruhn long ago identified the need for middle level schools to be transitional from elementary to high school learning. (See *Schools in the Middle: A Report on Trends, Practices.* NASSP, June 1983). Teachers with both child-centered and subject-based preparation are important for transitional middle level programs.

The principal should bring together both elementary and secondary-prepared teachers to discuss buildingwide middle level programs. Groups should be organized around the content and developmental issues of the school's program. Assigning one or two elementary teachers, for example, to work with secondary language arts teachers on an English/reading sequence allows both perspectives to be incorporated. One or two secondary science teachers might work in a similar way with elementary teachers on a fifth or sixth grade science program.

Middle Level Staffing Trends

Cooperative Planning. Principals more and more recognize the need to maximize cooperative planning on the staff. The diverse and dynamic needs of middle level youngsters are best served when teachers working with the same groups can meet regularly for planning. The principal should try to schedule teachers with the same classes in a common planning period. These teachers can meet regularly, share information, and discuss mutual problems. Counselors can meet with planning groups as necessary. Cooperative planning results in a more responsive program and greater staff awareness of student instructional needs.

Teacher Scheduling. Experienced school administrators know that a three-grade middle level school offers students better stability and learning experience than a two-grade school, regardless of the particular grades involved.

Students take a year to adjust to a new physical setting, student population, and new program. Today, many two-grade schools exist (usually cut-back junior highs). In these schools, students have only one year before moving to high school. A promising trend is to schedule teachers with the same groups of students for both years. The advantage of the approach is that it allows teachers to plan and teach a two-year sequence

---

Conrad F. Toepfer, Jr., is associate professor, Department of Curriculum Development and Instructional Media, State University of New York-Buffalo, Amherst, N.Y.

Middle Level Education

of content. Proponents believe that it gives teachers greater control during the two years for which they are responsible. Some two-year schools enhance the approach with an adviser-advisee program. (See Article 63.)

Even three-year middle level schools are adopting a variation on the plan. Usually the final two years are structured as a unit. Proponents argue that the approach improves the articulation of the entire middle level experience.

House Plan. The house plan or school-within-a-school approach continues to be popular for personalizing the environment of the large middle level school. (See Article 13.) No conclusive research establishes the optimal size of middle level schools, but practice shows that when a school exceeds 800 pupils, students are less known as individuals. The transitional nature of middle level education (from elementary to high school) is well served by house plans. These mini-schools allow teachers to know students better and to build carefully on the instructional environment of the elementary school.

The houses provide the general education experience. Students from all houses are combined for exploratory programs, physical education, and cafeteria. Students expand their relationships with the total student body and staff members from the secure and personalized base of the school-within-a-school.

Organization/Staffing Patterns

For better or worse, no optimal pattern exists for organizing and staffing middle level schools, but the size of the school definitely has an impact on the available choices. The smaller the staff and student body, the more limited the organization and staffing choices will be. The degree to which the staff is made up of teachers with elementary, secondary, and middle level preparation has an important bearing on decision making in the school.

Self-contained, departmentalized, team teaching, core curriculum, and other instructional approaches permit a matching of student needs with staff instructional skills. A middle level school can offer combinations of these approaches. A school with three different grades and a student population in excess of 300 can include departmentalized, team teaching, and self-contained classes. The larger the numbers of students and staff in the school, the wider the range of organization/staffing possibilities.

Several guidelines may be helpful as principals seek to improve organization and staffing in their schools.

1. Consider organizational/staffing issues in terms of instructional needs. While economic and other concerns cannot be overlooked, decisions to change organization or staffing patterns should be grounded as firmly as possible in real instructional considerations.
2. Consider the strengths and weaknesses of the present organizational/staffing arrangements. Explore areas in which specific changes might offer program improvement and carefully identify the inservice needs and staff development needs which those changes would require.
3. Do not consider any organizational/staffing changes unless they are found to be necessary.

A final caveat: Principals should weigh all organizational/staffing patterns in terms of their appropriateness for middle level education. Articulation with elementary and high school programs is central to a successful middle level program. Real effectiveness depends on principals understanding the uniqueness of the middle level and organizing instruction accordingly.

School Guidance Programs

Frank Burtnett

Redesigning school guidance programs to meet student needs and to support the instructional process is a major challenge to school administrators.

Mitchell and Gysberg (1978) have listed the characteristics of a comprehensive guidance program:

1. The program is student-centered, based on student needs and desired outcomes
2. All students are beneficiaries of the program
3. The program is consistently implemented across student populations
4. The program is articulated for the student's entire career in the school/district
5. The program is developmental
6. The emphasis is on enabling students to participate in their own development
7. Interventions are growth and development-oriented rather than problem-oriented
8. The counselor is accountable for program implementation and outcomes.

In reality, school guidance programs often fall short of supporting the instructional and human development mission of the school. They have evolved with a crisis or problem-solving orientation and many are chiefly responsive to the needs of subpopulations. Others fail to take advantage of the unique competencies and skills of professional counselors. These and other deficiencies can be remedied by: (1) comprehensive analysis of student needs; (2) an audit of the existing guidance program, its program components, organizational structure, and staff competencies; and (3) the redesign, implementation, and continual evaluation of a quality program.

The Helping Process

Assisting students in the secondary and middle level schools calls for an awareness of the developmental needs of early and later adolescents. The skills and knowledge of the counselor are most effective in alerting principals and teachers to those aspects of personal development most associated with life success.

A comprehensive secondary school guidance program will include the following student services:

Frank Burtnett is assistant executive director for association and professional relations, American Association for Counseling and Development, Alexandria, Va.

(1) individual and group counseling; (2) occupational, educational, and financial aid information; (3) testing and appraisal; (4) school orientation; and (5) program placement.

These services are available to all students as a part of their general educational experience and tailored, whenever appropriate and possible, for students with special needs (e.g., handicapped, gifted, etc.).

Program Development and Management

To what extent is the guidance program structured and operated on sound development and management principles? The following elements deserve consideration:

Planning concerns
- Overall program goals are clearly stated
- Desired student outcomes are identified
- Existing program is assessed for content and relevance
- Program priorities are established.

Design concerns
- Specific objectives are developed
- Program strategies are identified
- Staff competencies are analyzed
- Program responsibilities are assigned
- Staff development is provided
- Resources and tools are identified and acquired
- Adequate physical facilities are provided.

Implementation and evaluation concerns
- Program is installed as planned
- Evaluation strategies are carried out
- Planning and design receive ongoing attention
- Program is modified and maintained according to the above process.

Principals should think of this process as cyclical and ongoing.

Guidance Program Development

To what extent do all members of the school community participate in the development of the guidance program? Certainly, professional counselors and guidance staff members have a major stake in the program, but to what extent do other staff members participate? What provisions are made for student,

School Guidance Programs

parent, and community participation?

Two-way communication and participation in guidance program development ensure that everyone's expectations are clearly defined. Many schools have institutionalized participation through a guidance advisory committee in which student, parent, and staff representatives join the counseling staff to determine program priorities and objectives.

Principals have a direct responsibility to ensure that guidance services do not become an "island" within the school. Professional counselors should serve a consultative and collaborative function and work with teachers and other staff members. They also can serve as links between the school and the home.

Some schools have instituted teacher adviser programs in order to be more responsive to the needs of students. (See Article 63.) Acknowledging that the typical 300-400 counselor-student ratio is a serious impediment to individual counseling, schools have reorganized their guidance programs to utilize teachers as advisers. Adviser loads range from 15 to 30 students, allowing time for more one-to-one contact.

In schools where teacher adviser programs exist, professional counselors work closely with the teaching staff, accepting student referrals and providing inservice education. Freeing counselors from simple advisement gives them more time to work intensely with students in career, college, and personal counseling.

Staffing Roles and Responsibilities

What type of staffing model is useful for a secondary school guidance program? Unfortunately, the roles and responsibilities of guidance personnel are not clearly defined in many schools. Principals and counselors must share the responsibility for this confusion and communicate realistic expectations to students, staff, and community. Adequate human resources must be available to carry out the program. The following concerns are worthy of special consideration:

1. Professionally trained and certified counselors should be the core of the guidance program staff.
2. Guidance program specialists, both professional and paraprofessional, should be employed to complement the work of the counseling staff.
3. Guidance programs require managerial attention.
4. Professional and support personnel have general and specific inservice education needs.
5. The identification and selection of professional counseling personnel demand continued attention.
6. Teachers have sufficient background in academic decision making to be of assistance to students.

Herr (1979) has written that "the rise of school counseling has been accompanied by shifts and debates about where and by whom leadership and management of guidance and counseling should be located." Active leadership and direction by the secondary school principal is vital to the success of the school guidance program.

This We Believe (1975), a statement of the National Association of Secondary School Principals, sums up the issue well: "The Association is convinced that the delivery of guidance services can be improved significantly. Expectations for counselors and other school personnel must be clarified and the organization of guidance services must be recast and strengthened.... Improvement in the area of service to youth is central to a quality secondary school program and requires careful attention."

References

American School Counselor Association. *The Practice of Guidance and Counseling by School Counselors: A Position Statement of the American School Counselor Association.* Alexandria, Va.: ASCA, 1981.

Herr, Edwin L. *Guidance and Counseling in the Schools: Perspectives on the Past, Present and Future.* Alexandria, Va.: American Association for Counseling and Development, 1979.

Mitchell, A., and Gysberg, N. C. "Comprehensive School Guidance and Counseling Programs: Planning, Design, Implementation and Evaluation." In *Status of Guidance and Counseling in the Nation's Schools.* Alexandria, Va.: American Association for Counseling and Development, 1978.

National Association of Secondary School Principals. *This We Believe.* Reston, Va.: NASSP, 1975.

Cocurricular Programs

Terry Giroux

The cocurricular program in middle level and senior high schools is a vital educational experience. Among the benefits are improved school spirit, lessons in leadership, applications of classroom learning, and skills preparatory for adult life. Student organizations offer participants a creative outlet that enhances personal growth and fulfillment.

A basic philosophy helps set the direction for a student activity program: A program should promote continued educational development, student involvement, and citizenship, and it should link closely with the formal instructional program. Student organizations that grow out of the instructional program can provide unique opportunities for students to test newly acquired knowledge or to compete for honors. Assembly programs can complement career education or motivate students to move in-depth academic learning.

Staffing and Managing the Program

Appointing a qualified and dedicated faculty member as an activities adviser is the first and most important undertaking. Look for faculty members who previously have participated in student activities. Invite nominations from administrative staff and department chairpersons. Ask student leaders for suggestions. Students already involved in a particular organization are motivated to find committed and enthusiastic advisers to lead the way.

The newly nominated adviser needs a comprehensive review of rights and duties before beginning the assignment. Establishing a chain of command in the cocurricular program is essential. Questions such as, Who approves activity projects? When can they be held? and, Who unlocks the school building for an evening activity? come up repeatedly. Activity advisers need guidelines for the limits of their responsibility and to whom they should go for program scheduling, building use, and project approvals.

Consider holding monthly or quarterly meetings with the student activities director and/or activity advisers. Keep communication channels open. Give all interested parties ample opportunity to raise concerns, review annual objectives, and promote student cooperation. One of the most helpful organizational tools is the master calendar. Creating and reviewing the calendar is a key function; careful scheduling avoids needless conflicts and provides control over scheduled events.

In schools where a sizable portion of the student body is bused, special activity periods allow student organizations to meet during the regular school day. Some schools combine the activity period with homeroom and schedule student activities several times each week to permit students to participate in more than one organization.

Funding and Fund Raising

The cocurricular program is currently in transition. Budget cuts typically affect cocurricular programs, and some districts simply terminate funding as the easiest solution to the money crunch. Eliminating a student organization should be the last resort. In any reduction process, consider several factors:

1. How closely do the student organization's goals and objectives correspond to the cocurricular program philosophy?
2. How many students participate in the organization?
3. What is the cost per pupil?
4. What is the revenue per pupil?

Fund raising is essential for the survival of the cocurricular program. Many businesses, community organizations, and parent groups are interested in supporting specific and worthwhile causes. L. D. Bell High School in Hurst, Texas, has developed "10 W's of Project Planning" that may be used as a broad framework for development activities.

- What are you planning to do?
- Why do you want to do this project?
- When and where will the activities or events take place?
- Who will benefit from the project?
- Who needs to approve the project?
- When will the basic planning be done (time line)?
- What funds are needed? When will the money be needed and who will get it?
- What kind of publicity is needed? When is it needed?
- What committees are necessary? (List committees, task, chairperson, and deadlines.)

Terry Giroux is director of student activities, NASSP, Reston, Va.

Cocurricular Programs

- Was the project worthwhile? How do you know? What changes are needed?

Evaluation

The student activities program, like any other program offered by the school, needs periodic evaluation. Ideally, the program should be evaluated yearly. Minimally, however, the general program and each of its constituent parts should receive a thorough evaluation every two or three years. The school administrator (or the student activities director) should involve advisers and student leaders in the evaluation process. Outside consultants can be helpful. Methods of evaluation vary, but student questionnaires, interviews, observation, and analysis of participation data can be used.

The following questions are useful for evaluating the student activities program:

A. Are the general program and each specific activity meeting objectives for student knowledge, skills, attitudes, and/or values? What is the evidence that objectives are being met?
B. What is the extent of student participation in the total program and in each activity? Are a majority of students participating in the program? What is the evidence of degree of student participation?
C. What types of students are participating in the program, and what is the nature of their participation? Do the non-college-bound participate to the same degree as the college-bound? If not, why? Do girls participate to the same extent as boys? If not, why? Do some students spend too much time in the student activities program?
D. Is the student activities program well-balanced and comprehensive, or do some activities dominate the program? Are student interests and needs adequately met by the program?
E. Is the total program and each of the activities well organized?
F. Are all aspects of the program adequately supported in terms of facilities, funds, school time, personnel, and recognition? Are some activities disproportionately supported?

In the final analysis, the success of the student activities program will depend to a large extent on the vision and commitment of the people who provide its leadership.

Administrative Teams

William Georgiades

Secondary school principals have one of the most complex jobs in American education. They are expected to provide leadership for an institution that has become all things to all people. They must be instructional supervisors, money managers, mediators of diverse points of view, counselors to teachers and parents, and "Rotarian" citizens.

Of all these responsibilities, the role of instructional leader bears most heavily today.

Principals play a significant role in bringing about instructional improvement. Leadership at the building level is a key factor. In most respects, a school is but a reflection of its principal and its community. Unfortunately, some administrators lack the skills to help their teachers improve instruction. Preparation programs for principals emphasize school law, building management, school finance, and other noninstructional responsibilities, often to the neglect of curriculum.

If instruction is to improve in American secondary schools, principals must be willing to work directly with teachers toward that end. The principal can delegate many routine matters in order to preserve energy and talent for instructional leadership. The findings of the Ford Foundation in *A Foundation Goes to School,* were echoed by the National Association of Secondary School Principals' Model Schools Project. The most significant person in the change process is the principal. District offices may assist, but instructional improvement is basically undertaken by a school faculty, its management team, and supporting community.

The Supervisory-Management Team

With demands on their time increasing, most principals are unlikely to spend a majority of time working directly on instructional improvement. One workable solution to the time problem—the supervisory-management team—was developed during NASSP's Model Schools Project. The supervisory-management team is a differentiated staffing approach that acknowledges the importance of school management, but affirms that the principal cannot do it alone. The composition of the team varies with the size of the school and the variety of school programs. In some schools, the team consists of the *principal,* who serves as instructional leader and supervises instruction; the *assistant principal,* who builds the master schedule and assists the principal; the *director of student activities/community relations,* who schedules school events and coordinates community activities; the *student services director,* who coordinates guidance and school discipline; the *building manager,* who administers the buildings and oversees the financial programs; and *professional counselors.*

The success of this organizational alternative is tied to several assumptions:

1. The responsibility for making different kinds of decisions can be successfully delegated.
2. The principal should work with teachers (and students) toward instructional improvement without letting other matters interfere.
3. Various styles of instructional leadership are possible and allowances should be made for individuality.
4. Regularly scheduled meetings are important to discuss problems and successes, and to coordinate activities.
5. Effectiveness should be measured in terms of the instructional goals of the school.

Instructional Improvement

The school leadership team should adopt a systematic process for instructional improvement. The following model may be helpful:

- *Awareness.* The school staff must be aware that instructional improvement is needed. Schools which emphasize that they are doing a good job and that there is no reason to change, obviously are not interested in looking ahead. Schools, like other social institutions, tend to live on past reputations. Outside consultants can help at this stage.
- *Information.* Once an awareness of the need for instructional improvement has developed, teachers and administrators should investigate the available alternatives. Where can teachers learn more about instructional improvement? How can they avoid purchasing gadgetry that looks modern, but produces few real results? How do they avoid the "instant conversion" syndrome, the myth that programs "buy" instructional improvement? Other successful schools can provide a starting point.

William Georgiades is dean, College of Education, University of Houston, Texas.

Administrative Teams

- *Assessment.* How does a school determine what will be most effective in its setting? The experiences in NASSP's Model Schools Project demonstrated that instructional improvement demands total involvement of community, students, teachers, and the school management team. Develop a systematic plan for change.
- *Modification.* After a school has proceeded through the stages of awareness, information, and assessment, specific steps must be agreed on to meet the instructional needs of a particular school. The change plan needs to be fleshed out with concrete strategies. The next step is to pilot the basic ideas for one or two years. In the initial phase of piloting, involve only interested, committed persons.
- *Monitoring.* After the program has been adequately implemented, it should be systematically evaluated. Evaluation should be formative in the early stages to facilitate mid-course corrections. Data can be gathered with standardized tests, criterion-referenced tests, attitudinal instruments, by observation, and the like.
- *Institutionalization.* The last step is schoolwide implementation after the pilot program and the monitoring process have indicated that the program is ready for use.

Changing educational practice is intrinsically disruptive. Change threatens people, upsets established routines, takes extra energy and time, and challenges the status quo. Improving instruction often demands different instructional methods and/or new materials. The principal and his or her team must recognize that improvement is necessary and create a shared concern by involving teachers and others to accomplish the task. A functioning supervisory management team extends the influence of the principal and makes the difficult goal of instructional leadership more feasible, more attainable.

Instructional Teams

John Daresh

Instructional teams in schools are not new. Beginning in the 1950s with the Franklin School (Lexington, Mass.), teaming in several forms has been used to increase the opportunities for teachers to work together. Team teaching was truly one of the most visible, innovative practices in the 1950s and 1960s. During the 1970s, however, it began to lose some of its glamour. Too many team teaching experiences had become "turn teaching" with the same teachers working successively with larger groups.

Team planning, however, is another matter. Most personalized education programs have emphasized the value of teachers (and administrators) working collaboratively to improve instruction. Of particular relevance are Little's findings (1981) that, in unusually effective schools, a high degree of interaction occurs among teachers. Specific kinds of interactions are teacher talk about the practice of teaching; observation of teaching; working together to plan, design, research, and prepare materials; and teaching each other. All of these activities are characteristic of cooperative teaching.

Types of Teams

Teachers can be brought together for instructional collaboration in a number of ways. Vern Cunningham of Ohio State University noted four distinct kinds of instructional teams:

- *Team leader type:* One member of the team has high status and more responsibility than the other team members. The team may be organized according to a single subject, or on an interdisciplinary basis.
- *Associate type:* No individual teacher is designated as a leader. Design is expected to emerge from the mutual preferences of the team members. Again, the team may be single-subject or interdisciplinary.
- *Master teacher-beginning teacher type:* Teaming is used primarily as a way of helping new teachers enter the profession and tends to be a short-term arrangement.
- *Coordinate team:* A team of this type is not responsible for the same group of students over a long period of time. Teams consist of teachers who teach the same subject, but different students. Emphasis is placed on planning and resource development rather than instructional collaboration.

Some of the questions that principals can ask to determine the advantages and disadvantages of alternative teaming arrangements are:

1. What impact would each type of team have in assisting students in a particular school?
2. Which type(s) appear to promote increased staff planning time?
3. Which type is most efficient in terms of time required of staff?

Advantages of Teaming

Instructional teams, regardless of type, require more work, but the results seem to justify the effort. Teaming increases opportunities for teachers to work together cooperatively to plan, carry out, and evaluate instruction. Teachers no longer need to remain isolated from their peers. Students benefit because identifiable groups of teachers are available for support whenever needed.

Several instructional factors support teaming. First, teaming enables teachers to draw on strengths and expertise of other teachers in the school. Second, teaming arrangements encourage ongoing, formative peer review. Busy schedules prevent principals from observing teachers frequently. When teachers work in teams, they give each other constructive feedback on a regular basis. Third, teaming can help build continuity in a school program. The departure of one key staff member is not so likely to destroy a program when teachers share instructional planning and review.

A few words of caution are also in order. Some teachers lack the collaborative interpersonal skills that are essential for effective group membership. Group decision making also requires more time and is not always appropriate. The coordinate team approach emphasizing collaborative planning rather than instruction may well be the most applicable model in light of the current research.

Getting Started

Most schools already have some instructional teams. Many high schools are organized into subject departments (coordinate teams) with chairpersons desig-

---

John Daresh is assistant professor of educational administration, University of Cincinnati, Ohio.

Instructional Teams

nated as leaders. Middle level schools often operate in interdisciplinary teams. Modification of what exists may not be useful; the real issue might be how to increase the ability of teachers to function more effectively in existing teams. People are always less resistant if what they are asked to do is structurally familiar and related to existing practices.

Reference

Little, J. W. *School Success and Staff Development: The Role of Staff Development in Urban Desegregated Schools.* Boulder, Colo.: Center for Action Research, Inc., 1981.

Master Teachers

Jon Schaffarzick

Effective teachers can help their principals be instructional leaders. Principals can assign to a cadre of master teachers instructional improvement responsibilities beyond their regular teaching duties.

This strategy can magnify the principal's efforts and make available to less experienced teachers, as well as others requiring assistance, the skill and wisdom accumulated by the school's most effective teachers. It may also give the best teachers added motivation to remain in teaching by giving them recognition, a measure of prestige, and a needed change of pace.

Responsibilities of Master Teachers

In support of instructional improvement, master teachers may be asked to:

- Observe and assist other teachers: Serve as mentors to beginning teachers, teachers who are experiencing difficulty, or student teachers.
- Train other teachers: Teach demonstration lessons so others can observe and learn and critique others' teaching in the manner of an academic coach.
- Direct instructional development projects: Take a leadership role in developing and/or implementing new instructional programs.
- Evaluate other teachers' performance: Assist the principal in the process of teacher evaluation in a specific department, much as department chairpersons now do in some school districts.

Master teachers may be released from some of their regular instructional duties to perform these special tasks. Most administrators are fearful of taking the best teachers out of the classroom, however, and disrupting instructional continuity through increased use of substitutes. Accordingly, master teachers are often paid for the extra hours required to carry out their additional responsibilities.

Some schools/districts deal with the time problem by assigning master teachers as team leaders on a differentiated teaching team. A larger number of students are scheduled with the master teacher who in turn is assisted by regular teachers, beginning teachers, student teachers, and aides. Several benefits result from this organization. The master teacher:

- Teaches the major portion of the day
- Has direct influence over more students
- Serves as a model for other teachers
- Works directly with beginning teachers and student teachers
- Interacts daily with other teachers on the practice of teaching.

Career Ladders

Career ladders have been the subject of considerable recent interest in response to a growing concern about attracting highly qualified persons to teaching and retaining superior teachers.

Career ladders typically have three or four levels, with some combination of entry, continuing, senior, and master teacher categories. All new teachers must begin at the entry level while they are on probation. Minimum and maximum number of years at the entry level may be specified (with dismissal possible if a teacher fails to qualify for the next level by the end of the period). Teachers with previous teaching experience entering a district normally are placed in the entry level category for a shorter period than first year teachers.

Advancement to higher levels in the career ladder is predicated on a specified number of years at the current level, and on some combination of performance, years of experience, and level of educational attainment. As teachers advance to higher levels, they are given new titles (which carry with them some prestige), higher pay (e.g., $1,000-$3,000 per level), and more responsibility. Master teachers are at the top level.

Dangers

Master teacher and career ladder arrangements pose some potential dangers. The best teachers may be out of the classroom too much of the time. The continuity of instruction may be disrupted by too many scheduling changes and too heavy a reliance on substitutes. Master teachers may be asked to spend time on tasks that are less important than teaching itself. The danger also exists of creating a new mid-level bureaucracy with responsibilities like those of existing administrators (i.e., supervisors and subject specialists).

Jon Schaffarzick is managing consultant with Cresap, McCormick and Paget, Washington, D.C.

Master Teachers

Advantages

Master teacher and career ladder schemes have several significant advantages:

- Enhancing the principal's instructional leadership efforts by expanded participation
- Building commitment to the school's goals
- Helping institutionalize innovative programs that improve instruction
- Encouraging good teachers to stay in teaching by providing advancement within the profession
- Counteracting teacher stagnation by providing new responsibilities and activities every few years
- Linking merit, higher pay, and increased responsibility
- Upgrading the school's teaching and learning environment
- Rewarding superior teachers with increased recognition and prestige as well as financial remuneration.

Paraprofessional Personnel

Carl A. Grant

Recent reports and empirical studies suggest that teacher aides provide valuable support and have a positive impact on student achievement (Grant, 1983). Because of financial cutbacks, however, fewer aides are hired today. Many principals are successfully dealing with this quandary by using parents and other community volunteers as teacher aides to:

- Contribute to improved student achievement, especially in basic skills, language arts, and mathematics
- Relieve teachers from clerical and other nonprofessional duties
- Permit teachers to give students more personalized and individualized attention
- Enable individual students and small groups of students to be tutored
- Improve community relations and participation in the school.

Duties of Aides

A *teacher aide* is an employee or volunteer who assists with the educational programs of the school. According to Brighton (1972) a *volunteer aide* is "a person engaged by the school system, who voluntarily devotes time to the performance of various duties, either within or without the classroom, as agreed upon by legally responsible, educational supervising personnel." A *paid teacher aide* is "any person within a school system who is legally and specifically employed to assist certified teachers in the discharging of their teaching and ancillary duties and is paid for (his or her) services." A recent report by the Educational Research Service (1983) documents that paid instructional aides work an average of 30 hours per week, 37 weeks per year, for $5.28 an hour. The same report indicates that noninstructional teacher aides work an average of 28 hours per week, 37 weeks per year, for an average of $5.01 an hour.

Aides are paraprofessional in the sense that their primary responsibility is not to innovate or initiate education (DaSilva and Lucas, 1974). They are assistants who take direction from a teacher, principal, or supervisor. Aides may perform both instructional and noninstructional duties:

Carl A. Grant is professor, Department of Curriculum and Instruction, University of Wisconsin-Madison.

- Prepare instructional materials
- Serve as school-community liaison
- Assist non-English speakers to learn English
- Help in guidance and counseling
- Facilitate independent study
- Perform clerical and housekeeping chores
- Monitor halls, the cafeteria, or bus loading zone
- Work in the instructional materials center, subject area resource centers, or media centers.

Although some teachers still are hesitant about working with aides, more and more teachers in recent years have come to welcome and value their support. Teachers have discovered that another adult in their classroom does not threaten their authority. They find that staff relationships are not strained by personality clashes and differences in philosophy or background. They come to realize that aides can effectively participate in the instruction of students.

Guidelines

Paraprofessional guidelines are important to a school. Determine first whether the district office has a specific policy statement about the use of paraprofessionals. In establishing guidelines, give attention to the following areas:

1. *Selection.* Criteria for selection should be developed and consistently used in the employment of aides.
2. *Orientation and Inservice.* An orientation program should be developed that includes an introduction to the whole school as well as to the area of assignment.
3. *Assignment.* Job assignment must take into account teacher needs and requests, and aide availability, experience, and skills. Persons with one or two years of college can be assigned as instructional aides while those with clerical skills can prepare instructional materials.
4. *Evaluation.* Aides should be evaluated regularly by their direct supervisors in terms of their specific job descriptions and assignments. Some type of self-assessment might also be included.

Teachers and the principal can help aides become valuable members of the school team by:

- Exercising patience and showing them respect
- Making certain they are welcome and accepted in the staff room

Paraprofessional Personnel

- Providing them with a personal place to work; e.g., a desk in the classroom
- Giving them personalized responsibilities and duties
- Setting performance goals for them
- Helping them develop professional growth plans
- Assisting them in self-evaluation.

Some Important Decisions

The principal, the administrative team, and at least some teachers should develop a paraprofessional plan with purpose, duties, responsibilities, and assignments spelled out. The plan should be available in writing for aides to read and initial.

Conflict is inevitable if aides are seen as cheap labor, a way to avoid hiring certified teachers. This problem rarely occurs if the use of aides is consistent with the school's instructional plan and teachers have been involved in the decision to employ them.

Ask teachers whether they want aides to attend staff meetings. Collect teacher opinion and know your own mind. Establish a policy. The decision, of course, will be influenced by the role and duties of aides in the school.

The positive effects of paraprofessional personnel on the total school program have been well documented. Classroom instruction and student achievement can be improved and the classroom teacher and the school obtain an important ally. Using paraprofessionals is one sure way of decreasing student-adult ratios in the school and providing a more personalized environment for students.

References

Brighton, H. *Handbook for Teacher Aides.* Midland, Mich.: Pendell Publishing Co., 1972.

DaSilva, B., and Lucas, R. D. *Practical School Volunteer and Teacher-Aide Programs.* New York: Parker, 1974.

Educational Research Service. *Spectrum* 1(1983):27.

Grant, C. A.."Teacher Aides." *Encyclopedia of Educational Research.* 5th ed., vol. 3, 1983.

Adult Volunteer Programs

William Clay Parrish

Thousands of volunteers are performing essential duties in schools across the country. Working with curricular and cocurricular programs, volunteers perform services that would otherwise represent sizable expenditures. The principal plays a key role in recruiting and organizing these volunteers.

Organizing the School Volunteer Program

The volunteer coordinator is central to the success of any school volunteer program. Many large secondary schools hire a full or part-time staff person for this role. In smaller schools, a teacher's class load can be reduced to provide time for him or her to coordinate the volunteer program.

Many school districts have established formal policies governing volunteer service in schools. In the absence of a specific school board policy, the principal and faculty should determine what duties are appropriate for volunteers.

Recruiting the Volunteers

School volunteer programs work best when all faculty members are involved in planning. Staff needs should be assessed early in the school year. Aides can perform a variety of services, primarily by relieving teachers of noninstructional responsibilities.

Volunteers perform these duties in many schools:

- Tutoring
- Calling the homes of absent students
- Working in the library
- Staffing the student job placement office
- Giving instructional support
- Helping in the school clinic
- Preparing school newsletters
- Filing, typing, other clerical duties
- Assisting in the college and career guidance center
- Reading/grading English papers.

Most educators agree that students profit particularly from the presence of parents and senior citizens in the school, although volunteers may be recruited from a variety of sources.

William Clay Parrish is assistant director of research, NASSP, Reston, Va.

Ways of advertising the volunteer program include:

- Announcements in school publications and the local press
- A "town meeting" to launch a volunteer project
- Notices in local church and synagogue bulletins
- Contacts with civic organizations
- Radio and television public service announcements
- Sign-up tables at school programs attended by parents
- Community bulletin boards
- Fliers and brochures placed in community business and professional offices.

Staff and Volunteer Orientation

Both staff members and volunteers must clearly understand the volunteer's role in curricular and cocurricular programs. Faculty involvement in planning minimizes the need for formal staff orientation, but be very sure that everyone understands volunteer job assignments. Following state and local board policies, the principal, school volunteer coordinator, and staff should develop guidelines in several areas:

- *Administrative procedures:* Simple and convenient procedures should be developed for handling the typical problems that arise. In particular, these procedures should deal with the kinds of situations that can have a negative impact on the total program (e.g., aides exceeding their authority or scope of responsibility).
- *Supervision of volunteers:* Individual staff members are responsible for supervising the volunteers assigned to them, but the school should have guidelines for the process. These guidelines should outline the responsibilities of the school coordinator as well as other members of the administrative staff.
- *Evaluation of the program:* Procedures for evaluation may range from informal to highly structured. Oral and written comments from supervisors and volunteers provide a valuable basis for program improvement.
- *Recognition of volunteers:* Parents and other citizens who volunteer their services do so willingly and enthusiastically. Maintaining a high level of volunteer participation, however, demands some attention from the staff. Appropriate methods of showing appreciation are important, as public recognition of

Adult Volunteer Programs

volunteers is an indispensable component of a viable program.

The formal orientation is one of the most important aspects of a successful volunteer program. Usually the volunteer coordinator conducts the orientation, but the principal, administrative staff, and faculty should be highly visible. The goals and purposes of the school volunteer program, state laws, local board policies, and school procedures must be covered thoroughly. In addition, ample time should be allowed for discussion and questions.

A group orientation session should be held before the opening of school or early in the year, and individual and group follow-up sessions should be scheduled as needed throughout the year. A tour of the building and a "get acquainted" social are also valuable welcoming strategies.

A handbook should be issued to each volunteer. The handbook should cover all aspects of the volunteer program. (Much of it can be extracted from the student and faculty handbooks.) Important topics are:

- Insurance and liability
- Parking
- Health examination requirements
- Volunteer code of ethics
- Confidentiality
- Student and faculty relations
- Scheduling of assignments
- Cafeteria
- Lounge and locker facilities
- Emergencies.

Summary and References

A strong school volunteer program is dependent on systematic and supportive leadership. Administrators and teachers should look to the resources in their own communities, but the following references will also be beneficial:

Educational Volunteerism, A New Look, by Susanne E. Taranto and Simon O. Johnson. Springfield, Ill.: Charles C. Thomas, 1984.

National School Volunteer Program (NSVP), 300 North Washington St., Alexandria, Va. 22314, (703) 836-4880.

Retired Senior Volunteer Program (RSVP), a federally-funded program with regional offices in 10 states. For information, call toll free (800) 424-8580.

Collective Bargaining

Larry Janes

The collective bargaining process and the bargained contract have intruded into the classroom. As a result, today's principals may see their instructional leadership role either strengthened or eroded by arrangements that govern their ability to structure and manage staff programs.

To exercise some control over instruction in their schools, principals must be knowledgeable about three areas of collective bargaining:

- The language of contracts and the impact of specific language
- The hidden content of the negotiation process
- Methods for maintaining and/or strengthening their instructional leadership role through contract administration.

Contract Language and the Principal

Although most principals do not single-handedly organize staffs or make programmatic decisions, most are influential in the decision-making process. Collective bargaining can place serious constraints on that influence. Consider these contract language examples:

- *Preparation Time*—Many boards have negotiated preparation periods without regard for the need for student supervision during those times.
- *Class Size*—Class size limitations have great emotional appeal, and provide union security against reduction in force. In some cases, contract language has made employment of additional staff necessary without regard to available classroom space, scheduling of services, and instructional resources.
- *Assignment Limitations*—Some contracts forbid the assignment of teachers to other than their major field of study or transfer to other assignments without the staff member's (and in some cases the union's) approval.
- *Annual Performance Evaluation*—Evaluation clauses in a contract can severely restrict a principal's use of supervisory data to make program and staffing decisions. Contract language often places the complete burden for instructional improvement upon the principal and the staff member. Some principals have the responsibility to make resources available and to provide options for instructional growth.
- *Seniority Provisions*—Language that allows assignment of staff based on competency alone is seldom acceptable to teachers' unions. Reduction-in-force (RIF) language can force principals to place senior staff into subject positions they have never taught or have not studied since college. Quasi-administrative positions such as department or area heads and committee chairs may be mandated under contract language for senior but less qualified staff.
- *Program Reduction*—Several boards have agreed to language that guarantees current course offerings in the curriculum. This kind of language prevents principals from canceling classes with limited enrollments or otherwise modifying the class schedule.

Hidden Impact

Not all that is collectively bargained will be in the final copy of the negotiated agreement. During the course of bargaining sessions and prior to the signing of a contract, both districts and unions have the opportunity to deliver a number of intended and unintended messages that can greatly alter the principal's scope of leadership.

Scenarios could be drawn in which the principal's ability to staff and organize the instructional program is eroded, either by the bargaining language or the content of the process. Policy modifications, new chains of command, additional paperwork, even potential negative relationships with other members of the management team, are distinct possibilities for principals not represented on the district negotiating team.

Minimizing the Impact

Three main mechanisms can lessen the erosion and ensure the principal's involvement in staffing and organizational bargaining decisions.

1. *Contract Items Analysis.* A formal monitoring process such as the Contract Items Analysis (CIA) model developed by Janes and Lovell can be implemented as a management practice. CIA involves three steps: The principal:

- Identifies specific items that should be modified in the current contract or in the union's current proposals

---

Larry Janes is an associate of the Illinois Association of School Boards and professor, Eastern Illinois University, Charleston.

Collective Bargaining

- Specifies how current language will affect building operations in such areas as personnel, curriculum, finance, and general administration
- Provides acceptable compromise language, actions, or counterproposals.

A sample CIA item is illustrated in the figure.

2. *Negotiating Team Membership.* Many seasoned bargainers believe the only way to protect building level authority is to place a principal on the management team. This approach offers a number of distinct advantages:

- Team membership can lead to improved managerial communication
- The principal brings a unique perspective to evaluating contract impact on the operation of the school
- A principal's presence in the caucus room and/or at the table allows building positions to be defended firsthand and factually.

If the district size permits, a rotation system can be used to give different principals experience and provide a sense of ownership.

3. *Central Management.* The greatest loss of a principal's rights probably occurs in poor contract management. Certain practices are basic to good contract management at the building level:

- All administrators need inservice on the total contract. Any substantive or procedural changes in the contract should be given major attention. Agreement about the meaning of language is essential.
- Periodic meetings should be held between principals and central office personnel to review policy and concerns and to discuss contract provisions, grievances, and strategies.
- A procedure for handling grievances at the building level should be established and understood by all administrators.
- Uniformity and consistency should be districtwide goals in contract administration and in the resolution of grievances.

The principal must provide unbiased administration of contractual procedures. Should a grievance occur, the principal must be able to defend a teacher when the facts support such an action. No principal has ever prospered by allowing the grievance process to become a battleground for indefensible positions.

Contract Item Analysis
Example of Staff Assignment Item

ITEM: Assignment of Staff	Building: Central H.S.	Respondent: Principal
(1) Proposed or Existing Language	(2) Implications	(3) Alternative Language/ Counters Actions
Employees shall be assigned to unstaffed classes by order of seniority with all teachers holding the proper certificate given the right of first refusal according to seniority.	A. *General Administration:* Completely denies me the right to place the most appropriate person into a vacant class. The use of *classes* as opposed to a total assignment could lead to making a collage out of the staff. B. *Finance:* Would have to develop and have a legal staff review a massive seniority bump list. Potential exists for grievances and arbitration and litigation due to challenges. C. *Personnel:* Could start a domino effect. Inexperienced but certificated staff could claim positions desired by more recently trained or experienced personnel. D. *Curriculum:* The possibility of poor instruction is greatly increased. E. *Other:* No time bars as to when they must possess the certificate. Could be gained over summer. Define: proper certificate.	A. *Alternative Language/Counter:* The administration shall fill vacant classroom assignments after considering experience in the vacant position, certification for the assignment, and availability of the personnel for the specific assignment. B. *Compromise:* None. C. *Action Recommended:* Reject as not in the best interest of the students and staff.

Trends in Media and Methods

Library/Media Center

Edward John Kazlauskas

Probably the most important current development in the library/media center is the use of the microcomputer to support instruction and to assist in center management.

The library/media staff in many schools is responsible for managing and maintaining microcomputers and for providing related instructional support to classroom teachers. The library/media center is an ideal location for microcomputers since the micro is basically one more tool in the total array of media alternatives. A systematic plan is needed for the selection and use of microcomputer hardware/software, with the library/media specialist as a key member of the planning team.

Microcomputers now allow smaller library/media centers to automate functions, including ordering, subscription maintenance, catalog production, "booking," and circulation control. Automatic processing was used in the past only by large college or public libraries. A considerable amount of "off-the-shelf" software is available for this automation. Typically, it is more cost-effective to select and use "canned" programs than to develop custom management software locally. Even traditional library/media suppliers now carry a line of computer software, hardware, and related equipment and supplies.

Media Resources

Visual media, particularly films, play an increasingly important role in the library/media center. For some time centers have utilized 16mm film, but the same subjects are now available on videocassette. Although cost is a major consideration, centers are now able to catalog one or both of these formats, acquire multiple copies of a film, or purchase the rights to copy the videocassette. Copying may become the most cost effective approach as more topics are made available in the video format.

Other media being introduced to the library/media center include cable, videodisc technology, and off-site data bases. Off-site services such as *The Source* or *Dialog* can be accessed through a terminal or microcomputer hook-up. These data bases give library/media centers access to a wide range of information not previously available. Computer-based bibliographic utilities (such as the OCLC inter-library cataloging system) now play an important role in catalog copy production, interlibrary loan, and resource sharing.

Physical Site

Concern for the design of the physical site is a strong library/media center issue. Flexibility is the major consideration, with specific emphasis on:

- Adequate space for hardware and software, and storage for collections of materials;
- Browsing space for all materials;
- Shelving that accommodates a wide variety of media types;
- Adequate electrical and electronics outlets;
- Appropriate environmental controls such as lighting and sound;
- Necessary space for offices and processing work; and
- Adaptable areas to allow space for individual and group work.

Personal computers in the home may have an impact on designs yet to come. Learners working at home with a personal computer can access a wide variety of instructional resources and informational data bases. Less space may be needed in the library/media center if home learners actually use the resources available to their computers in a consistent and systematic way.

Personnel Training

Education and training continue to be important to the operation of the library/media center. Staff members need experience in center management, resource use, bibliographic methodology, and the new technologies, particularly the microcomputer. Staff training must increasingly focus on the expanding roles. Indeed, the library/media professional is becoming a key instructional specialist, helping students develop information skills and positive attitudes toward life-long, independent learning.

Edward John Kazlauskas is associate professor, School of Library and Information Management, University of Southern California, Los Angeles.

Textbook Selection

J. Patrick Mahon

Saying that the textbook largely determines what students will be taught is not an understatement. Because of this, the selection of textbooks and supplementary materials must be a thoughtful, well-planned process.

The principal's responsibility for selecting textbooks and other instructional materials varies from one school system to another. In smaller systems, the principal and teachers usually have major input into the process; in larger systems, a representative committee generally makes the decisions. In some cases, statewide adoptions curtail the choices of the principal and building staff, particularly when state funds can be used only for state-approved textbooks.

Recently, textbooks and curriculum materials have come under scrutiny by various pressure groups. Some materials have been labeled sexist, some racist, others too "humanistic." The administrator must balance these competing claims at the building level.

Some criticisms of textbooks are justifiable; others are largely a matter of opinion. School officials must somehow balance the desirability of exposing students to a variety of ideas with community's interest in promoting its own ethical and cultural standards. The ever present danger is that a vocal minority will succeed in giving the impression that it represents the thinking of the entire community.

The Legal Issues

State or local boards have the right to specify textbooks, and courts are reluctant to substitute their judgments for those of school boards unless it can be shown that the educational agency abused its discretion. Teachers also have some latitude on making reasonable decisions about content and methodology. In the absence of specific board or school policy, teachers may choose among textbooks and other materials, provided they bear a reasonable relationship to the curriculum. Teacher discretion is not unlimited, however, since in many places, a prescribed curriculum must be followed and materials used must relate to that curriculum. The principal is often called on to adjudicate issues in the gray zone between teacher and community wishes.

Since the decision of the U.S. Supreme Court in *Tinker v. Des Moines* (1969), schools have moved to protect student constitutional rights that may not be abridged. Although the Court's most recent decision in *Pico v. Island Trees* (1982) left some issues unresolved, the following principles can be used as general guidelines to administrative action:

1. Boards and administrators have more latitude in selecting curriculum materials than they have in removing library books.
2. Students have the right to be exposed to a variety of viewpoints.
3. Boards and administrators have the authority to see that "traditional" values are inculcated through the curriculum, but they do not have the authority to select textbooks solely on the basis of their own personal views.
4. Boards and administrators should not select textbooks simply because they represent viewpoints that are religiously, scientifically, politically, and philosophically orthodox.
5. If textbooks are challenged, boards and administrators must show objective reasons for their decisions. The general criteria for judging textbooks and other instructional materials are:
   - Is the material relevant to the curriculum?
   - Is the material suitable for the grade level and the age of the students?
   - Is the material accurate and up-to-date?
   - If religious, political, scientific, and philosophical viewpoints are expressed, does the material expose the students to a variety of such viewpoints?
   - Is the material obscene?
6. The special criteria for determining obscenity are:
   - Does the material appeal to prurient interests? (Note that offensive language is not necessarily obscene.)
   - Does the material, as a whole, lack serious artistic, literary, or scientific value?
7. Boards and administrators must establish and follow formal procedures for selecting textbooks and supplementary materials.

J. Patrick Mahon is principal, Central Gwinnett High School, Lawrenceville, Ga.

Textbook Selection

Recommendations

The principal is the link between the district and the building staff, and must ensure that all curriculur policies are observed. The following principles may prove helpful in doing so:

- Guidelines for the selection of books and materials should reflect input from both professionals and citizens (especially on community standards from the latter).
- Board procedures should permit citizens to challenge books and materials. These procedures should cover controversial materials and methods and should advise teachers of their prerogatives within the confines of the classroom. A citizens' complaint form should be available.
- School districts/schools should develop curriculum guidelines which clearly specify goals, objectives, content, and materials. Teachers, administrators, and lay persons should have a voice in their development. Care should be taken to exclude materials and methods that would not withstand serious challenge. At the same time, the right of teachers to individualize or personalize learning should be meticulously protected.
- Principals should be fully informed on legal requirements governing textbook selection and applicable board policies and procedures.
- Principals should not take sides when controversy arises, but should maintain professional neutrality so that district or school guidelines are carefully followed.
- Principals should require that teachers observe mandated curriculum guidelines and choose materials and methods wisely.
- Teachers should maintain academic neutrality when they teach controversial topics. These topics emphasize the value in a democracy of considering and discussing a variety of viewpoints.

Figure 1. *REQUEST FOR RECONSIDERATION OF INSTRUCTIONAL MATERIAL*

Media consists of all types of print and nonprint materials; i.e., books, films (16 mm and 8 mm), filmstrips, tapes, records, study prints, pictures, transparencies, and all other printed or published items.

Name of Item _____ Type of Material _____
Publisher or Producer _____ Date of Publication _____
Name of person, organization (group) or community seeking reconsideration
Address _____
    Street   City   State   Zip
Occupation _____ Telephone _____

1. Did you read, view, or listen to the complete item? Yes ___ No ___
2. How was the item acquired? (Assignment, free selection, from a friend, etc.)
3. Is item part of a set or series? Yes ___ No ___
   If yes, did you read, view, or listen to all of the set or series? Yes ___ No ___
4. What is objectionable regarding the item and why? (Be specific)
5. How did you react to the objectionable part of the item? _____
6. Were there good sections in the item? Yes ___ No ___
   If yes, please list them _____
7. Did you locate reviews of the item? Yes ___ No ___
   If yes, please cite them _____
   If no, why not _____
8. Did the review(s) substantiate your feelings? _____
9. Is there any educational merit to the item? Yes ___ No ___
   If yes, indicate such and provide approximate grade level(s) _____
10. How do you see the item being utilized in an educational program? _____
11. List the person(s) with whom you have discussed this item.
    Name   Title-Occupation   Address
12. What were their reactions and/or opinions? _____
13. What do you suggest be provided to replace the item in question? _____
14. What do you suggest be done with the item in question?
    ___ Do not assign to my child
    ___ Withdraw it from all students as well as my child
    ___ Send back to Curriculum Adoption Committee for reevaluation
    ___ Other

Date   Signature of Complainant

Citizens' complaint form, Board of Education of Carroll County, Westminster, Maryland (based on the model form of the American Library Association and the National Council of Teachers of English).

Computer-Based Education

Keith A. Hall and J. Mark Tisone

A great deal of enthusiasm and excitement has greeted the use of computers in education. One significant difference from the enthusiasm surrounding past educational innovations, however, is that parents and school board members have frequently been the driving force behind the computer movement. This role reversal reduces the educator's task of soliciting financial resources for the program, but sharply increases public attention and demand for effective curricular planning and implementation.

Some Simple Definitions

- **Hardware:** All of the electrical and mechanical devices and attachments used with computers, including *disk drives* for storing and transferring programs to other computers; *monitors* (sometimes referred to as *display screens* or *terminals*) for displaying text and graphics; *keyboards, game paddles, joysticks,* or a *mouse* for entering information into the computer; and *printers* for making copies of material.
- **Software:** The computer programs that enable computer hardware to perform desired tasks, such as *word processors* for writing, editing, and printing textual material; *data base systems* for storing and retrieving data on request; and *electronic spreadsheets* used (in schools) for budget planning or grading.
- **Computer-Based Education (CBE) Courseware:** A special kind of software that provides personalized instruction to students in any subject area without them knowing much about computers. Courseware may provide *computer-managed instruction* that relies on the record-keeping and summarizing power of the computer to assess, diagnose, prescribe, and monitor each learner's progress; *interactive instruction* (tutorial and drill-and-practice) that presents instructional material to the learner, accepts and judges responses, provides feedback, and alters the flow of subsequent instruction depending on the learner's responses; and *instructional simulations* that allow learners to analyze, integrate, and synthesize their knowledge by solving "real life" problems.

Keith A. Hall is a professor and J. Mark Tisone a graduate student in instructional design and technology, Department of Educational Theory and Practice, The Ohio State University, Columbus.

Levels of Computer Use

Not all computer users need the same levels of expertise. The various levels of computer skills can be compared to differing levels of musical skill: Music traditionally has been considered valuable to all persons, but at varying levels of skill. Students and teachers can be found at all levels regardless of grade in school or area of teaching. This same diversity across ages and grades poses perhaps the most difficult problem for computer-based education in the schools. (See Figure 1)

Getting Started

Program Support. Community and teacher support are critical, and can best be achieved through a computer advisory committee composed of community representatives who have knowledge and experience in the computer field and teacher representatives from a broad range of school departments. (If only math and science teachers participate, the myth will be perpetuated that computers are most useful in these fields.)

Initial Expenditures. Approximately one-third of the initial budget should be allotted for purchase of hardware, one-third for software and courseware, and one-third for teacher education.

Policy Development. Model computer implementation policies are available from school districts throughout the United States. Implementation policies should be developed and written by a curriculum council appointed by the principal for approval by the board of education.

Computer Program Policies

Evaluation and Selection of Software/Courseware. Software should be reviewed before selecting any hardware. *General purpose* software (data base systems, electronic spreadsheets, word processors) is a relatively safe investment because many persons can use these programs in a broad range of applications. Each user can adapt the software to specific applications through a selection of options. Programs of this nature are the wave of the future.

Courseware selection, on the other hand, is full of potential hazards:
- Courseware design is a relatively new discipline and available courseware is not always of high quality

Computer-Based Education

Figure 1. *Hypothetical Levels of Musical and Computer Skills*

Levels of Skill	% of Population	Musical Skills	Computer Skills
Basic	100	Group singing, enjoyment of existing music	Using existing hardware and software to run limited purpose programs (e.g., CBE lessons)
Intermediate	10	Learning to play an instrument in groups or to sing in a chorus	Using a variety of software to meet various needs, writing simple programs for personal use
Advanced	1–5	Solo-quality skills for amateur performance	Write complex programs, modify existing software, add non-standard hardware for personal use
Professional	less than 1	Professional performance and composing	Designing and developing software for others

- Many teachers lack experience with computer applications and should develop sensitivity to good and poor features before attempting to select courseware
- Courseware is generally designed for specific objectives at certain grade levels. If a program does not meet the needs of the intended students, it probably cannot be used elsewhere in the school system.

Only courseware that comes with a 30-day money-back guarantee should be purchased. A useful reference for selecting courseware is *T-E-S-S: The Educational Software Selector* (New York: EPIE and Teachers College Press, 1984), a comprehensive catalog of courseware evaluations for a broad range of microcomputer systems.

Evaluation and Selection of Hardware. Hardware choices should be based on the intended uses and software/courseware availability. Decisionmakers should address the following issues:
- How many computers are needed?
- How will cost of repairs be handled? Most school districts allocate about 5 percent of their total computer budget for maintenance. Maintenance contracts generally are more costly than paying for repairs as needed.
- Who will take equipment for repair?
- How long will equipment be retained (replacement policy)?

Implementation Policies. Several important issues should be addressed before initiating any computer program:
- Where will the computers be placed in the school (e.g., media center, computer classroom, or moved from room to room as needed)?
- In what courses will computer use be needed (e.g., word processing in English for writing themes, stock market data base in economics to assess trends, or computer simulation in civics to study presidential elections)?
- What specific computer courses will be developed (e.g., a computer concepts and skills course, programming in BASIC or Pascal)?
- Will students have equal access to computers? Care must be taken that use not be limited to the gifted, to more affluent schools, etc.
- What safeguards will be installed to prevent violation of copyright laws?

Education of Faculty, Administration, and Staff. Principals play a vital role in the development of faculty computer skills. The principal's interest in computer-based education is a major factor in teachers' acceptance and acquisition of computer knowledge and skill. Staff development ideas can include the following:
- Provide released time and/or expenses for teachers interested in computer-based education. If teachers are unable to attend classes in the evening, urge them to consider weekend or summer session courses.
- Schedule weekly clinical sessions for teachers to review new courseware, to discuss computing problems, and to develop new strategies for implementing courseware in the curriculum.
- Invite vendors to your school to display the latest hardware/software/courseware products.
- Develop explanatory slide-tape presentations and micro "loaner" programs, or sponsor a micro user group to facilitate teacher interest in computer-based education.
- When hiring new teachers, give preference to candidates who have successfully completed CBE courses in their teaching areas.

Computer Software

James P. Pollard and Donald C. Holznagel

Educators today are demanding software that makes the microcomputer an effective tool for the daily work of the student, the teacher, and the administrator. This trend embraces software in virtually every subject and every type of management application.

The use of computers is not new to the nation's secondary schools. Computer science, mathematics, and computer literacy classes have long used these machines as "number crunchers." As the microcomputer has moved to other parts of the school building, however, its role has changed to that of tutor, teacher's aide, and even entertainer. Teachers are increasingly asking that the microcomputer be allowed to act like a computer.

Assessing the Trend

In assessing this trend, it is helpful to look at the success of *Bank Street Writer,* a word processing program developed at the Bank Street College of Education in New York City. The program is used in English classes, in social science classes, even in natural science classes. The appeal of this software is not so much that it instructs in word processing (which it does), but that it makes the student's life easier in the same way that word processors make other lives easier. By simplifying the task of getting words on paper, *Bank Street Writer* enables teachers to concentrate on improving the content and arrangement of those words.

As a content free program, *Bank Street Writer* is versatile and as appropriate for reporting the results of a chemistry experiment as for teaching composition or writing a speech. The unifying factor is that the computer is being used as a tool to help the user accomplish various tasks.

Word processing, of course, is not the only "real world" use of a computer as a computer. In the science laboratory, courseware for instructing students about chemical reactions is being replaced by programs that help students analyze reactions they have actually observed. The student enters data from the experiment into the computer, manipulates the data, and perhaps constructs a graph or a table. In short, the student uses the computer in the same way that a chemist would use it.

Computer software is available for virtually every subject area in secondary education (although the programs have generally been written for uses outside the schools). Teachers interested in determining whether a computer program might be helpful in a particular class must analyze whether the classroom tasks would be performed by a computer in the "real world" of work.

Software can be incorporated into a curriculum through data base programs, spreadsheets, accounting systems, time management aids, graphics packages, music synthesizers—almost every general-purpose program used outside the classroom. Most school programs, however, will be shorter, with fewer user options than the commercial packages. These changes will not only simplify the programs but will also lower prices.

Teachers selecting software for class use will also need to be cognizant of the trends in the home market. Students who use the *Bank Street Writer* at home to prepare written assignments will find a different word processing program at school difficult to manage.

This compatibility problem has no easy answer. Compatibility between home and school is currently a desirable goal rather than an imperative. For the present, administrators and teachers can use trends in personal computer "best sellers" as a barometer of what students might be using at home.

In the near future, faster and more powerful hardware will surely be available to schools. As hardware prices go down, software that needs large chunks of computer memory (such as integrated business packages) will become more practical for schools. More "user friendliness" in both hardware and software should also help make functional computer literacy an attainable goal for both students and teachers.

James P. Pollard is a program associate and Donald C. Holznagel is program manager in the computer technology program, Northwest Regional Educational Laboratory, Portland, Oreg.

New Technologies

Lawrence P. Grayson

Videodiscs, microcomputers, computer graphics, "intelligent" electronic terminals, fiber optics, lasers, communications satellites that broadcast through low-cost terminals, and a whole array of devices that communicate through telephone lines are making possible new approaches to learning that were technically or economically unfeasible in the recent past.

The telephone, for example, is usually thought of as a device for transmitting conversations. Yet, the telephone can be used to send data and a variety of pictorial information from freehand drawings, photographs, and still pictures to paper facsimiles and computer-generated graphics. Visuals can accompany audio instruction or any dialog that takes place. Full-motion video telecommunication offers even greater promise, as it becomes economically feasible to transmit television lectures or conduct "face-to-face" seminars across great distances.

Teachers and administrators are confronted with so many technological options today that they must weigh very carefully the reasons for implementing any technology, examine the way it will be used, and determine its implications for funding, staffing, and classroom organization. Almost all technologies have been used successfully in education, but when these same technologies serve unclear purposes or are implemented ineffectively, they contribute nothing to learning improvement.

Most people think of technology in terms of its hardware. This perspective should not limit the school administrator or teacher, however, from taking a broader view of technology in the total learning environment.

The new technology for education can be categorized in several ways. Figure 1 presents one schema based on hardware *capability* (audio or audiographic, computer, or video) and *accessibility* (used locally or over a distance).

Any analysis of the role of technology in schools should treat various aspects of teaching, learning, and information delivery. The following are important questions that planners are confronting:

- What educational goals should the technology address? Is a technological approach the best way to achieve those goals?
- What kinds of experiences should students have? Should they interact or just observe, listen, and take notes? Should they manipulate physical equipment or objects, or simply use print or visual information? Should they concentrate on problem solving, recall, or drill-and-practice activities?
- What role should/will teachers play? Will they dispense the content as instructors, or serve as facilitators, helping students find and interact with information?
- How large will classes be? Is there enough equipment for all students to use it effectively? Will each student have enough time on the equipment?
- Will the equipment be used in a traditional classroom setting, an open classroom, or in a media facility or resource room?
- Who will supervise the students—a teacher, a special resource person, or both?
- How will courseware and other software be obtained? Will it be produced locally, borrowed from a media center, or purchased from a commercial source? Will enough copies be available for all students to have access?
- Who will evaluate the software before use? What criteria will be used? How will student learning be evaluated?
- Will teachers need training in the use of the technology? Who will offer the training? Will follow-up experiences be available to teachers after they have some experience using the technology? Will training be available to new teachers?
- Is the budget satisfactory not only to purchase equipment, but to train teachers, to maintain and expand the program (if successful), and to purchase materials on a continuing basis?

The decision to utilize technology in a school is a significant one. Technology can bring great benefits to the educational process, but it also can fail without proper planning and implementation. Administrators should carefully consider purpose and use before moving into technological innovation.

Lawrence P. Grayson is institute adviser for mathematics, science, and technology, National Institute of Education, United States Department of Education, Washington, D.C.

New Technologies

Figure 1. *Classification of Various Technologies Used in Education*

| CAPABILITY | ACCESSIBILITY ||||
| | Used locally || Used over distance ||
	Hardware	Typical applications	Hardware	Typical applications
Audio and audiographic	Audiotape Audiodisc	Stored lectures and discussions Instructions	Radio Telephone Dial access Electronic blackboard Slow-scan television (SSTV) Facsimile	Preproduced and edited programs Lectures, seminars, and discussions Retrieval of audio information Transmission of documents, still images, and handwritten information Audio conferencing
Computer	Minicomputers Personal computers	Computer-assisted instruction (CAI) Computer-managed instruction (CMI) Computer-aided testing Problem solving	Central computers Remote terminals Time-shared computing	Information retrieval Computer-assisted instruction (CAI) Computer-managed instruction (CMI) Computer-aided testing Problem solving Electronic message delivery Computer conferencing
Video	Videotape Videodisc	Stored lectures and presentations Interactive instructional programs	Instructional Television Fixed Service (ITFS) Cable Satellites Broadcast television	Preproduced and edited programs Lectures, seminars, and discussions Video conferencing

Teacher-Developed Materials

Rita Dunn

Increased academic achievement, improved attitudes toward school, and reduced numbers of discipline problems are the results when students' learning styles are matched with complementary instructional approaches, according to researchers at major universities.

The most effective way to introduce new and difficult objectives, particularly with large classes and inadequately prepared teachers, is through materials that teach the way individual students learn.

A successful program of instruction requires a systematic blend of commercial media, computer-based instruction, and locally prepared materials. Schools that strive for a workable blend of these elements tend to achieve effective programs sooner than those that rely on a single approach. Teacher-developed materials are essential to this process, but are time consuming to prepare and revise—usually from three to five years. Adapting commercial programs for local use is an efficient way of beginning the developmental process.

Various types of teacher-developed materials have proven useful in individualized instruction, from traditional handouts and checklists to the complex learning packages of the 1960s. Three examples of these materials that illustrate the range of possibilities are discussed below.

Contract Activity Packages

Academically gifted and talented students learn more, learn more easily, and tend to retain information better when assisted by contract activity packages (CAPs) rather than by whole-class instruction.

CAPs are subject matter outlines that list clearly-stated objectives for students who need structure, and provide options for those who thrive with choices.

CAPs contain various resource alternatives: *auditory* (tapes, records, cassettes); *visual* (books, magazines, journals, transparencies, graphs, pictures); *tactual* (learning circles, task cards); *kinesthetic* (games, trips, interviews, and realistic experiences); and *multimedia* (videotapes, computer cassettes, televised sequences).

Students use the materials of their choice to complete the objectives. They are encouraged to study new information through their strongest perceptual channel, reinforce it through a secondary one, and if they are having trouble remembering, reinforce again through a tertiary channel.

After being exposed to new and/or difficult information, students are required to *apply* what they have learned by completing at least one activity and reporting experience for each objective. Figure 1 shows one example.

CAPs also include team learning to introduce new and/or difficult material, "circle of knowledge" to reinforce what has been learned, brainstorming for problem solving, and either case studies or group analyses to build higher level thinking skills. Pretests and posttests assess the quality of the student's knowledge.

Programmed Learning Sequences

Programmed learning sequences (PLS) are highly structured, visual materials that teach a specific topic, skill, or value. PLSs are designed for learners who have a strong need for structure and who extract meaning by seeing either the written word, representative pictures or drawings, graphs, and/or tables. Because visually-oriented students tend to profit from initial visual exposure followed by tactual and then auditory reinforcement, PLSs often include a tactual game, task cards, or tapes (the latter for those whose reading level is not quite up to the text).

PLS objectives (the same as those of a CAP) indicate what must be learned. Then, like a book, the material actually *teaches* the subject matter, but in very small doses. (See Figure 2) The back of each frame (page) gives the answers to the questions on the front. Pre and posttests again evaluate the quality and quantity of what the student has learned.

Multisensory Instructional Packages

The learning styles of underachievers differ drastically from those of the gifted. Youngsters who perform below grade level more often learn with their hands (tactually) and/or through direct involvement (kinesthetically) than by listening to someone or by reading. Indeed, learning disabled students and underachievers who are taught reading and mathematics tactually achieve significantly better than when they are taught through lecture/discussion or printed ma-

Rita Dunn is professor, School of Education and Human Services, and director of the Center for the Study of Learning and Teaching Styles, St. John's University, Jamaica, N.Y.

Teacher-Developed Materials

Figure 1. *Contract Activity Package Applications on the Topic of Understanding Brain vs. Mind*

Activity Alternatives	Reporting Alternatives
1. Write or tape record a conversation between your mind and brain, showing how they differ.	1. Ask at least two other students to read or listen to your conversation and evaluate whether you have demonstrated the differences clearly. Have each person write a one-sentence overview of your analysis.
2. Write an article for a magazine in which you explain the differences between your mind and your brain.	2. Send your article to the editor(s) of your school magazine or newspaper. Request that it be published.
3. Draw a picture which illustrates the brain, the mind, and their functions.	3. Display your picture and give a two-minute description of the differences.
4. Develop a three-dimensional sculpture of the mind and the brain. Explain their differences with labels.	4. Display the sculpture in class and ask at least three classmates to critique it.

terials. Underachievers appear to learn best in an active environment where they can concentrate on small amounts of information at a time, be around friends, and take occasional breaks. Multisensory Instructional Packages (MIPs) literally teach objectives through four different senses—auditory, visual, tactual, and kinesthetic. A cassette tape guides students through the contents. Students actually make their own MIPs in some schools.

Figure 2. *Programmed Learning Sequence Frame Illustrating How the PLS Teaches Subject Matter in Small, Sequential Steps.*

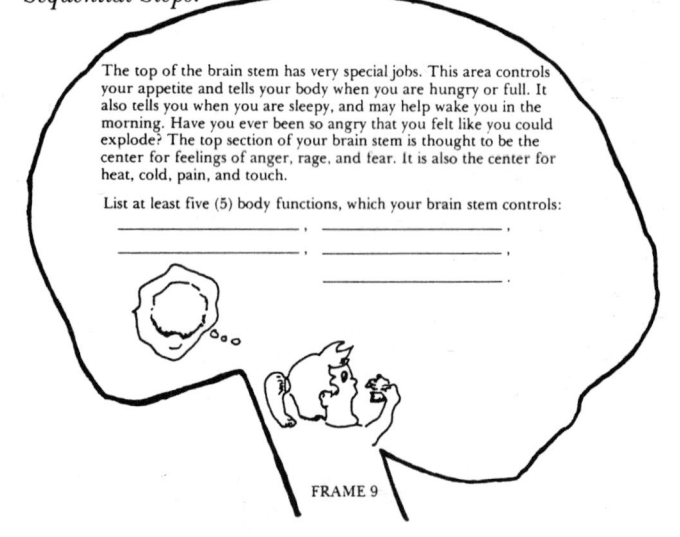

> The top of the brain stem has very special jobs. This area controls your appetite and tells your body when you are hungry or full. It also tells you when you are sleepy, and may help wake you in the morning. Have you ever been so angry that you felt like you could explode? The top section of your brain stem is thought to be the center for feelings of anger, rage, and fear. It is also the center for heat, cold, pain, and touch.
>
> List at least five (5) body functions, which your brain stem controls:
> _____ ; _____ ;
> _____ ; _____ ;
> _____ .

FRAME 9

Developing Teacher-Made Materials

Teacher-developed materials are critical to adaptive instruction. Underachievers, for example, do not learn well by lectures, but need multisensory materials. The gifted can function without special materials, but they can become bored with conventional group-paced instruction. They flourish at their own pace. Visual students needing structure perform much better with programmed learning sequences.

Principals who are instructional leaders will urge teachers to develop their own materials and provide time to develop them. Once teachers perceive the advantages of resources matched to students' learning styles, they will urge students to make the materials; encourage parental or volunteer assistance, and gradually build an arsenal of such materials for use in their classes.*

---

*Practical, easy-to-follow directions for developing CAPs, PLSs, MIPs, and tactual/kinesthetic materials at the secondary level may be found in Dunn, R., and Dunn, K., *Teaching Students Through Their Individual Learning Styles: A Practical Approach*, Englewood Cliffs, N.J.: Prentice Hall, Inc., 1978.

Personalized Education

James W. Keefe

Personalized education means neither individualized instruction nor open classrooms. While it does reach back to these and other forerunners, it is more flexible and at the same time more structured than any of them. It is a practical, eclectic approach to effective teaching and learning.

No educational program can be successful without attention to the personal learning needs of individual students. A single approach to instruction, whether traditional or innovative, simply does not do the job.

Contemporary research on learner and teacher traits is building a conceptual base for change in conventional instructional practice. This research gives support to the concepts of personalized education and adaptive instruction—more precisely, to a teaching/learning cycle of diagnosis, prescription, instruction, and evaluation (DPIE).

Some Definitions

Personalized education is a systematic effort to take into account individual student characteristics and effective instructional practices in organizing the learning environment. Carroll (1975) calls it "an attempt to achieve a balance between the characteristics of the learner and the learning environment. It is the match of the learning environment with the learner's information, processing strategies, concepts, learning sets, motivational systems achieved, and skills acquired. It is a continual process...."

Ideally, personalization tailors teaching to the individual. In practice, it may take many forms, depending on the available human and instructional resources. No one way of personalizing education is best.

The forerunners of personalized education are nongraded education, continuous progress education, and individualized instruction.

- Nongraded education is primarily a *grouping practice*. Students of different ages are grouped in classes based on skill levels or academic achievement. Cross-age grouping does not necessarily demand substantial changes in instructional organization and can operate in a conventional setting. Research establishes its effectiveness.
- Continuous progress education is a *scheduling strategy* or management system, a way of organizing the school program to facilitate individual student progress. Each course is organized as a learning sequence allowing students to progress at their own pace and according to their own needs. Continuous progress has been difficult to implement in many schools, but it can be very effective.
- Individualized instruction is a *teaching methodology* encompassing instructional objectives, content sequences, multiple learning resources, flexible scheduling, systematic management procedures, and (often) differential staffing arrangements. Individualized instruction exhibits strong effects in college-level applications (e.g., Keller's Personalized System of Instruction), but meager results in general applications at the middle and senior high school levels (Bangert, Kulik, and Kulik, 1983). Some individualized strategies, however, do greatly enhance achievement (Slavin and Karweit, 1984).

A Model of Personalized Education

Personalized education begins with learner needs and adaptive instructional strategies to build the learning environment. From a teaching-learning perspective, the process can be conceptualized as a cycle of diagnosis, prescription, instruction, and evaluation. Unlike nongraded education, personalized education can function under various grouping arrangements. Unlike traditional classrooms, continuous progress education, and individualized instruction, it neither assumes nor demands a specific instructional strategy.

Diagnosis is concerned with student traits. It encompasses student developmental characteristics, learning history, and learning style. (See Figure 1)

1. Developmental characteristics are those specific stages in individual maturation when certain capacities for learned behavior appear (e.g., visual perception, language pronunciation, cognitive thinking skills). These characteristics tell us *when* a student is developmentally ready to learn something; they indicate individual physiological readiness for learning.

2. Learning styles are characteristic cognitive, affective (motivational), and physiological behaviors that serve as relatively stable indicators of how students perceive, interact with, and respond to the learning environment. They can be measured by a variety of assessment techniques. Learning styles tell us *how* a student learns best.

3. Learning history reveals *what* a student knows at a given point in his or her learning career—the knowledge and skills possessed before the learner begins a new learning experience. These achievement levels may be measured by curriculum-referenced (local) or normative (standardized) tests.

James W. Keefe is director of research, NASSP, Reston, Va.

Personalized Education

Figure 1. *Model of Personalized Education*

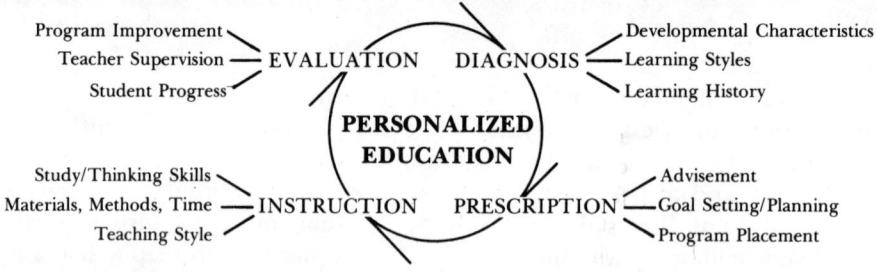

Program Improvement, Teacher Supervision, Student Progress → EVALUATION
DIAGNOSIS ← Developmental Characteristics, Learning Styles, Learning History
Study/Thinking Skills, Materials, Methods, Time, Teaching Style → INSTRUCTION
PRESCRIPTION ← Advisement, Goal Setting/Planning, Program Placement

PERSONALIZED EDUCATION

Prescription is concerned with advisement, goal setting, program planning, and placement. Teachers determine appropriate instructional objectives and activities, suggest grouping and scheduling arrangements, and advise small groups of students.

4. Advisement brings the student into continuous contact with persons, places, and activities that facilitate development of his or her talents and interests. The teacher adviser is the key person in this process.

5. Goal setting begins with a diagnostic profile developed for each student from the diagnostic data available to professional counselors and teacher advisers.

6. Program planning builds on the student's diagnostic profile and personal/career goals. Both one-year and four-year plans are useful. The four-year plan outlines long-range educational goals based on mutual agreement among parents, teachers, and the student. The one-year plan focuses on the student's program of study for the current year.

7. Program placement involves scheduling the student in courses, with appropriate learning activities, materials and methods for individual development, skill needs, and learning style. The school schedule provides both the structure and the flexibility for this purpose.

Adaptive instruction embraces teacher styles, teaching methodologies, time use, and thinking skills. Teachers structure the learning environment, train students in thinking skills and time use, communicate information, etc.

8. Teaching styles are characteristic instructional behaviors reflective of teacher personality and educational philosophy. Different teaching styles create different learning environments.

9. Various materials and methods are appropriate for differing student styles, needs, and interests. Personalized methodologies can include computer-based instruction, individualized instruction, cooperative group activities, experiential learning, tutorial work, mastery learning, direct instruction, lecture-recitation, etc. Instruction is monitored and students are given feedback on the quality of their time use, study habits, and academic work.

10. Thinking skills are learned capabilities that enable the individual to manipulate knowledge and experience. Formal thinking skills training is important for all students, with practice and reinforcement in the content areas.

Evaluation looks at learners, teachers, and programs.

11. Student achievement is assessed and reported in terms of (absolute) performance or skill standards rather than relative criteria. Grades do not indicate class standing, but rather what a student has or has not learned.

12. Teacher evaluation assesses instructional competence and mutually agreed upon goals. A process of performance appraisal or clinical supervision is employed.

13. Administrator growth profiles help school principals and vice principals to identify personal strengths and weaknesses and to work toward constructive goals.

14. The total school curriculum is evaluated in terms of district/school philosophy, goals, and objectives.

15. Feedback using data from student assessment, teacher appraisal, and program evaluation is the basis for: a) continuation, modification, or termination of a given program; b) continuing diagnosis of student needs; and c) repetition of the entire DPIE cycle.

References

Bangert, R. L.; Kulik, J. A.; and Kulik, C-L. C. "Individualized Systems of Instruction in Secondary Schools." *Review of Educational Research* 53 (1983): 143–158.

Carroll, A. W. *Personalizing Education in the Classroom.* Denver, Colo.: Love Publishing Co., 1975.

Georgiades, W. D.; et al. *Take Five: A Methodology for the Humane School.* Los Angeles, Calif.: Parker Publishing, 1979.

Slavin, R. E., and Karweit, N. L. "Mathematical Achievement Effects of Three Levels of Individualization: Whole Class, Ability Grouped, and Individualized Instruction." Baltimore, Md.: Center for Social Organization of Schools, Johns Hopkins University, Report No. 349, January 1984.

Direct Instruction

Barak Rosenshine

Direct instruction is a summary term for recent findings on effective teaching. It refers to a systematic method of effective teaching that emphasizes proceeding in small steps, checking for student understanding, and achieving active and successful participation by all students. The term is interchangeable with other terms such as active teaching, systematic instruction, explicit teaching, interactive teaching, and effective teaching for achievement gain.

The conclusions about effective teaching have been primarily based on reading and mathematics research conducted in urban elementary and junior high schools, but the procedures are relevant to any instruction designed to teach skilled performance or mastery of knowledge. Specifically, these procedures are applicable to reading, math, foreign language, English grammar, science, and parts of social studies and language arts. They are less applicable for teaching students to develop higher level thinking skills, to construct their own creative responses, or to learn to appreciate the aesthetic elements of the world.

The research has found that teachers effective in direct instruction procedures use most of the following techniques:

- Begin a lesson with a short statement of goals
- Begin with a short review of previous, prerequisite learning
- Present new material in small steps, with student practice after each step
- Give clear and detailed instructions and explanations
- Provide frequent active practice for all students
- Ask numerous questions, check for student understanding, and obtain responses from all students
- Guide students during initial practice
- Provide systematic feedback and corrections
- Obtain a student success rate of 80 percent or higher during initial practice
- Provide explicit instruction for seatwork exercises, and where necessary, monitor students during seatwork.

Direct instruction emphasizes teaching in small steps with student practice after each step, guiding students during initial practice, and providing all students with a high level of successful practice. All teachers utilize some of these behaviors some of the time, but the most effective teachers use most of them almost all of the time.

The Steps in Direct Instruction

The following six teaching functions are a useful way to summarize the research on direct instruction:

1. *Review and check previous work.* When teaching skill subjects such as reading, math, foreign language, and grammar, effective teachers begin by correcting homework and quickly reviewing previous work so that students will be firm in their knowledge and capable of applying it to the current lesson. Typical techniques include review of vocabulary or previously learned skills (as in math or foreign language), or short quizzes. These activities usually take from two to eight minutes. Effective teachers also review materials prerequisite for new learning.

2. *Presenting new material.* Effective teachers introduce new material by giving a series of short presentations with detailed instructions and many examples. They follow each presentation with active student practice. During this practice, teachers may ask more questions, call on several students, and/or ask students to agree or disagree with the answers. The purpose of these questions is to provide active practice and to check for student understanding after each step. If the students do not fully comprehend the material, the teacher goes over it again.

3. *Guided practice.* After the new material is presented, students work problems with guidance from the teacher. Students work problems at their seats, with a friend, or at the board, and the teacher provides correction and help as necessary.

4. *Provide feedback and correctives.* When students make errors during guided practice, effective teachers provide hints, break the questions down, and/or re-explain the steps to be followed. Less effective teachers simply give the answer or call on another student.

5. *Supervise independent practice.* When most of the students can work alone without error, independent practice begins. Independent work is facilitated by sufficient *guided* practice and helps students achieve confident, smooth, fluid performance. Effective teachers circulate during independent practice, or, if

---

Barak Rosenshine is professor, Department of Educational Psychology, University of Illinois at Urbana-Champaign.

Direct Instruction

they are working with a second group, show students how to get help if they need it. Frequently, independent practice is continued as homework.

6. *Weekly and monthly review.* Effective teachers schedule weekly and monthly reviews and tests. These reviews and tests provide the additional (successful) practice that students need to become smooth performers, capable of applying their skills to new areas.

Some Subject Examples

Direct instruction is most readily applicable in teaching math or foreign language, but it has been used successfully in other areas. In U.S. history, for example, a teacher might begin a lesson with a short quiz on previously presented material. Students exchange papers for grading, and the teacher reviews the correct responses to several questions. The teacher then presents new material, pauses to ask questions, and leads a discussion on a few of the points. Guided practice of the new material follows.

Most social studies teachers do not use this systematic procedure. Their classes follow a pattern of short lectures (two to four minutes), a question to the entire class, a short student answer, and then more short lectures followed by more questions and answers. This type of instruction is less effective because it neither checks for understanding, nor involves all students in active practice.

Systematic teaching can be used to teach writing. If a teacher wants students to write essays using colorful adjectives, for example, he or she begins with a review of colorful adjectives, asking students to list these adjectives and then checking their work (or having students check each other). The teacher might then present a model paragraph using colorful adjectives and ask students to write single sentences using these adjectives. When all students have demonstrated that they can form these sentences, and are checked for understanding, they begin independent practice.

In such classes, there is a delightful hum as students work confidently. A less effective teacher would likely make the assignment and then move around the room, supervising the students as they work. In these kinds of classes, students frequently complain that they do not understand the assignment.

Direct instruction is not appropriate for all teaching, but is for those times when a teacher is presenting material, demonstrating a skill, or modeling a process. Direct instruction would not be appropriate during a discussion when students are exploring new ideas or defending their views. Before discussion, however, direct instruction can ensure that students have mastered basic material on which the discussion and inquiry are based.

References

Brophy, J. "Successful Teaching Strategies." *Phi Delta Kappan* 63 (1982): 527–532.

Rosenshine, B. "Teaching Functions." *Elementary School Journal* 83 (1983): 335–351.

Mastery Learning

James H. Block

Excellence, equity, excitement, and economy are current major educational policy themes. They are addressed by a set of instructional leadership concepts known as mastery learning.

Mastery learning has enabled principals to:

- Build the school's curriculum around the types and levels of learning outcomes historically achieved only by the best students
- Tailor the school's teaching and testing techniques to ensure that virtually all students, regardless of their home background, master the curriculum
- Renew staff optimism about their capacities to teach for excellence and equality
- Generate equality and excellence by orchestrating existing rather than new human or nonhuman resources.

In short, mastery learning has helped principals to reassume their historic role as the school's chief supervisor of instruction.

What Is Mastery Learning?

Mastery learning is an optimistic theory about students' capacity to learn and teachers' capacity to teach. This theory, developed by Benjamin Bloom and his students based on the earlier work of John Carroll, asserts that any teacher can help virtually all students to learn quickly, self-confidently, and well. "Dumb" students can be helped to learn like "smart" ones; "slow" students to learn like "fast" ones; "unmotivated" students to learn like "motivated" ones.

Mastery learning is also a set of preventive instructional techniques that have helped most students to learn more effectively. Most mastery practices can be implemented without major structural changes in classroom organization. In fact, mastery learning was designed for use in the typical classroom situation:

- Where teachers must cover a required or teacher-developed curriculum in a fixed period of time
- Where students must be taught largely in groups
- Where extended amounts of instructional time cannot be spent with "problem" learners, and
- Where student learning must be graded.

James H. Block is associate professor, Department of Education, University of California, Santa Barbara.

Mastery learning techniques supplement, complement, and integrate existing management norms and structures.

How Does It Work?

Mastery learning is based on three significant teaching and learning concepts: systematic instruction, "proactive" teaching, and the management of learning.

Mastery learning is *systematic* in the sense that *what* will be taught is directly linked to *who* will be taught. Teachers learn how to base their instruction on a set of expected high-order learning outcomes and provide a variety of different teaching techniques so that each student attains these outcomes. Invariably, mastery techniques build on each staff member's customary ways of teaching.

Teaching is *proactive* in the sense that teachers ready themselves *outside-of-class* to handle their normal in-class instructional responsibilities. They clarify and explicate high-order learning expectations for classes and plan their instruction so that groups of students can be taught as if each student had his or her own tutor. Central to this planning is the development of feedback and correction systems that enable each teacher to periodically monitor the overall quality of his or her customary group teaching methods and to supplement them, as appropriate, for students who need more help and additional learning time.

School staff members manage *learning*, rather than learners, in the sense that they try to maximize both the quantity and the quality of the time students spend on classroom learning experiences. Teachers use planned mastery instruction to systematically vary how and how long each student is taught so that every individual continually experiences success. Teachers also personalize their grading techniques to reward students for competing with themselves and pre-established learning standards rather than against their classmates. Students are graded for their absolute, not their relative, learning accomplishments. (See Figure 1)

How Well Does It Work?

Mastery learning clearly promotes student intellectual and emotional development. Most students in mastery learning classes, compared to their counterparts in standard classes, learn better in terms of

Mastery Learning

Figure 1. *Mastery Learning: How Does It Work?*

CONCEPTS	TECHNIQUES
GENERAL	
A. Approach Instruction SYSTEMATICALLY: It Should Provide Bridge Between WHOM and WHAT You Teach	
1. Match Instruction to OUTCOMES	1. Base Instruction on Outcomes
2. Match Instruction to LEARNERS	2. Provide Multiple Instructional Methods
SPECIFIC: EXTRA CLASSROOM	
B. Be PROACTIVE, not Reactive	
1. Clarify OUTCOMES	1. Pre-Define Mastery and Make It Explicit
2. Provide for APPROPRIATE HELP in Learning	2. Pre-Plan Instruction for Mastery
3. Provide for APPROPRIATE LEARNING TIME	3. Pre-Plan Instruction for Mastery
SPECIFIC: INTRA CLASSROOM	
C. Manage LEARNING, not Learners	
1. Provide STUDENT ORIENTATION	1. Orient Students to Mastery Learning
2. Vary HOW and HOW LONG Each Student Is Taught as Necessary	2. Use Pre-Planned Instruction To Teach for Mastery
3. PERSONALIZE GRADING	3. Grade for Mastery

Figure 2. *Mastery Learning Flow Chart (West and Foster 1976)*

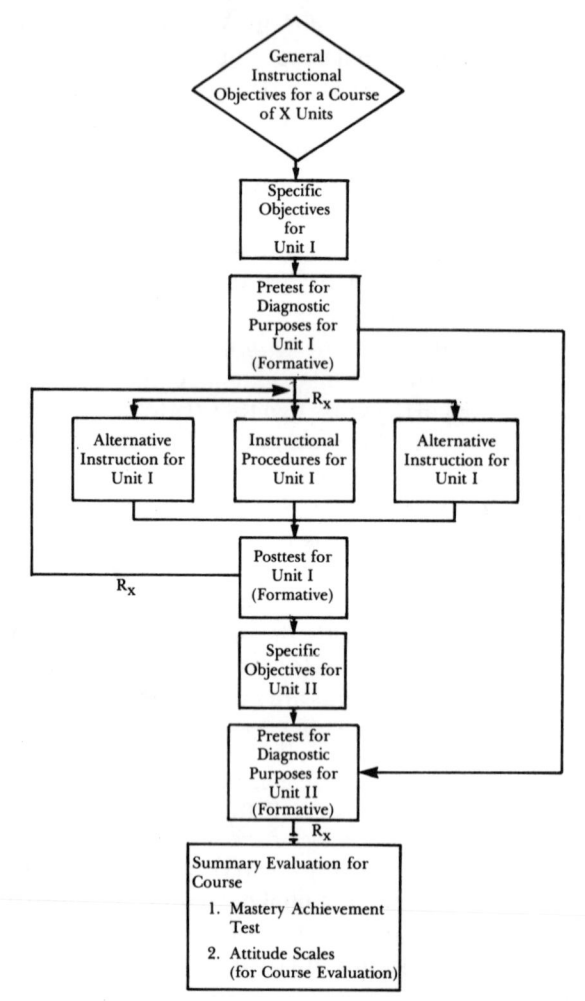

```
         ┌─────────────────┐
         │    General      │
         │ Instructional   │
         │ Objectives for  │
         │  a Course of    │
         │    X Units      │
         └────────┬────────┘
                  ▼
         ┌─────────────────┐
         │    Specific     │
         │   Objectives    │
         │      for        │
         │     Unit I      │
         └────────┬────────┘
                  ▼
         ┌─────────────────┐
         │   Pretest for   │
         │   Diagnostic    │
         │  Purposes for   │
         │     Unit I      │
         │   (Formative)   │
         └────────┬────────┘
              Rx ▼
    ┌──────────┬──────────┬──────────┐
    │Alternative│Instructional│Alternative│
    │Instruction│ Procedures  │Instruction│
    │ for Unit I│ for Unit I  │ for Unit I│
    └──────────┴──────┬──────┴──────────┘
                      ▼
              ┌───────────────┐
         Rx   │  Posttest for │
              │    Unit I     │
              │  (Formative)  │
              └───────┬───────┘
                      ▼
              ┌───────────────┐
              │   Specific    │
              │ Objectives for│
              │    Unit II    │
              └───────┬───────┘
                      ▼
              ┌───────────────┐
              │  Pretest for  │
              │  Diagnostic   │
              │ Purposes for  │
              │    Unit II    │
              │  (Formative)  │
              └───────┬───────┘
                   Rx ▼
      ┌──────────────────────────────┐
      │ Summary Evaluation for Course│
      │ 1. Mastery Achievement Test  │
      │ 2. Attitude Scales           │
      │    (for Course Evaluation)   │
      └──────────────────────────────┘
```

achievement, retention, and transfer, learn faster and learn more self-confidently in terms of subject matter interest and academic self-concept.

Most students in mastery taught classrooms learn as students do at the 85th (or better) percentile in traditional classrooms. Students in mastery classes also seem to learn *how to learn;* they take increased personal interest in and responsibility for their learning. Not only are they capable of the learning demanded of them, they also want to learn.

Where Can I Find Out More?

The National Clearinghouse of Mastery Learning. Glenn Hymel, Director, School of Education, Loyola University, New Orleans, La. 70118.

Block, J. H. "Promoting Excellence Through Mastery Learning." *Theory into Practice* 19 (1980): 66–74.

Block, J. H., and Anderson, L. *Mastery Learning in Classroom Instruction.* New York: Macmillan, 1975.

Bloom, B. S. *Human Characteristics and School Learning.* New York: McGraw-Hill, 1976.

Guskey, T. *Implementing Mastery Learning.* Belmont, Calif.: Wadsworth Publishing Co., 1984.

Klein, J. S. "Designing a Mastery Learning Program," *Educational Leadership,* November 1979.

Taylor, G. L. "Mastery Learning: A Prescription for Success." *NASSP Bulletin,* September 1983.

West, C. K., and Foster, S. F. *The Psychology of Human Learning and Instruction in Education.* Belmont, Calif.: Wadsworth Publishing Co., 1976.

Westerberg, T. "Mastery Learning for Teachers: A Competency Based Program for Improving Instruction." *NASSP Bulletin,* March 1983.

Cooperative Small-Group Learning

David W. Johnson and Roger T. Johnson

Inappropriate interpersonal competition and individualistic learning dominate instruction in American schools today. Only 7 to 20 percent of instructional time is usually spent in cooperative learning. Yet, considerable research supports the concept that cooperative learning should occupy at least 60 percent of the time in most classrooms.

Compared with competitive and individual instruction, the skillful use of cooperative learning results in:

- Higher achievement in the mastery of facts, information, and theories taught in school
- Acquisition of higher level analytical reasoning strategies
- Higher motivation to achieve by more students striving for mutual benefit and joint effort
- More positive attitudes toward subject areas (including math, science, and foreign languages) which in turn generate a continuing motivation to study, to take advanced courses, to learn more about the area, to enter related careers
- Greater competencies in working effectively with other people in career, family, and community settings
- Greater integration of caring and supportive relationships with other students, including stronger friendships, a sense of psychological support and safety, and conviction that peers support and encourage one's efforts to learn
- Greater psychological stability, health, and well-being, including positive self-esteem and a sense of autonomy.

Cooperative Learning Procedure

Cooperative learning can be structured for any age student and in any subject area. Teachers assign students to pairs or small groups and instruct them to work together so that *all* members of the group learn the assigned material to a predetermined level of excellence. Cooperation is much more than physically associating with other students, discussing material with them, helping them, or sharing knowledge with them. Each of these elements is important in cooperative learning, but four elements are basic and must be present for small-group learning to be truly cooperative.

1. *Positive Interdependence.* For a learning situation to be cooperative, students must perceive that they are positively interdependent on other members of their learning group. This relationship is achieved through mutual goals, division of labor, distribution of materials or information among group members, differing student roles, and joint rewards.

2. *Face-to-Face Interaction Among Students.* Positive interdependence is not magical in and of itself. The face-to-face interaction patterns promoted among students by positive interdependence also are critical to the educational outcomes.

3. *Individual Accountability for Mastering the Assigned Material.* The purpose of any learning activity is to maximize individual student achievement. Feedback mechanisms to determine individual student levels of mastery are necessary if learners are to provide real support and assistance to each other.

4. *Appropriate Use of Interpersonal and Small-Group Skills.* Placing socially unskilled students in a learning group and telling them to cooperate obviously will not be successful. Students must be taught the requisite collaborative skills and be motivated to use them. They must be given time and procedures for analyzing how well their learning groups are functioning and the extent to which they are using collaborative skills.

Administrators can encourage teachers to use cooperative learning by:

- Visiting classrooms where cooperative learning is practiced and reading related material to develop an understanding of what cooperative learning really means.
- Announcing support for teachers who are using cooperative learning procedures or who wish to do so.
- Organizing interested teachers into support groups that meet regularly to plan and discuss implementation procedures. Teachers should talk about the specific goals of cooperative learning, "co-plan" lessons, exchange ideas, solve problems, and observe one another teaching cooperative lessons.
- Providing the time, materials, and rewards for the teacher support groups to function effectively, and

---

David W. Johnson and Roger T. Johnson are professors, Department of Educational Psychology, University of Minnesota-Twin Cities, Minneapolis.

Cooperative Small-Group Learning

joining in their planning and observing whenever possible.
- Protecting and nurturing the implementation effort so that teachers are comfortable with the routine. This timeline may be a matter of years, not months.
- Modeling cooperative learning procedures by encouraging positive interdependence among staff members and by using the cooperative learning strategies for faculty meetings.

Real Life Skills

In the past, schools have tried to graduate as many students as possible. Today, however, emphasis is more on ensuring that students are functionally literate and employable after leaving school. Some of the most important aspects of functional adulthood and employability are: the collaborative skills to work effectively with peers, superiors, subordinates, and clients; the personal security and psychological health to maintain a stable career, family life, and community life; a basic mastery of such subject areas as math and science that form the basis for career advancement in technology, business, and industry; the ability to engage in analytical problem solving and higher level reasoning processes; and the willingness to commit oneself to organizational goals.

Classrooms where students sit in rows and learn exclusively through lecture-discussion-worksheet methods offer an unrealistic picture of the interactive realities of adult life. Business and industry are especially concerned today that the school environment become more realistic. Team work, effective communication and coordination, and division of labor to achieve mutual goals characterize most real life settings. The quality and viability of life within our society may depend on citizens developing more of a "we" and less of a "me" orientation.

Help is available for schools or districts just beginning to emphasize cooperative learning, and for principals who want to help teachers grapple with the complex processes of cooperative learning. The Cooperative Learning Center at the University of Minnesota has several publications that present lesson plans for preschool, elementary, secondary, and college level classes.

References

Johnson, D. W., and Johnson, R. T. *Learning Together and Alone.* Englewood Cliffs, N.J.: Prentice-Hall 1975.

Johnson, D. W.; Johnson, R. T.; Holubec, E. J.; and Roy, P. *Circles of Learning: Cooperation in the Classroom.* Alexandria, Va.: Association for Supervision and Curriculum Development, 1984.

Slavin, R. E. *Cooperative Learning: Student Teams.* Washington, D.C.: National Education Association, 1982.

Contract Teaching

Bonnie S. Daniel

Principals regularly exhort teachers to "do more" for their students, to motivate them, and to teach responsibility. And teachers just as regularly respond that they simply cannot add one more twist to an already convoluted instructional program. The principal who wants to offer his or her teachers a manageable strategy to achieve more personalized education and motivate students to greater responsibility should seriously consider contract teaching.

- *What will be required of the principal?* Training, guidance, and support—the things that only a principal can provide.
- *What will be required of the teacher?* Careful planning, logical organization, and periodic evaluation—the things required for any kind of effective instruction.
- *What can both principal and teacher hope to gain?* A way of meeting individual student needs that generates increased motivation and responsibility for learning—the very things that critics say present methods are failing to accomplish.

What Is Contract Teaching?

Contract teaching is an instructional method by which a teacher and a student design a learning activity—with objectives, activities, schedule, and evaluation—which the student then implements on his or her own. Contracts are not intended as a replacement for conventional methods, but provide an alternative that capitalizes on the student's need to have some control of his or her learning.

Contracts do not require additional teacher work; instead, they shift part of the workload to students, giving the teacher more flexibility. Contract teaching does require a different kind of planning and creates a subtly controlled environment in which the student can exercise responsibility.

Elements of the Contract

The format of a contract may vary, but every contract must contain certain elements to ensure adequate structure and the desired outcomes.

Bonnie S. Daniel is facilitator, Staff Development Center, Faulkner Ridge Elementary School, Columbia, Md.

1. **Directions.** A contract should contain brief instructions: how it is to be completed, who must be involved in its construction and approval, where it is to be kept.

2. **Content.** A contract should provide space for:
- *Subject:* the content to be covered
- *Objectives:* clear statements of the learning goals, stated measurably
- *Activities:* a sequential list of learning activities and conditions of learning—these activities may be independent, for pairs, small groups, etc.
- *Resources:* a list of materials the student will use
- *Time line/due dates:* a specific estimate of time to be spent on each activity, plus teacher conference dates, work due dates, and a date for sharing with peers
- *Evaluation:* a description of evaluation and grading procedures and acceptable performance levels
- *Signatures:* required from teacher, student, and parent before the contract is implemented.

A contract is usually completed in duplicate, with one copy for the teacher and the other for the student.

How Do You Start?

Successful contract teaching requires a "contract environment." Because a contract is designed to give students increasing responsibility, contract teaching requires systematic student training. The teacher must also learn to operate in a different way. The following three-step procedure is useful for gradually increasing student input and ensuring a successful teacher–student experience.

Step One. The teacher must develop alternative activities and due dates for the student to select. Selection and organization of content stays firmly under teacher control, but students begin to assume some responsibility for their own learning.

Step Two. The second step is implementation of an actual contract, as described earlier. How much of the contract is left to the student to complete will depend on the teacher's assessment of student readiness. A teacher might begin by providing objectives, activities, evaluation, and the time frame, allowing the student to choose method and style. Later the teacher might provide only objectives and content (or content alone), allowing the student more latitude in the design of the activities and evaluation.

Contract Teaching

Step Three. The final step is "free" contracting. At this stage the student assumes total responsibility for all aspects of the contract: creation of objectives; identification of content, activities, and methods of evaluation; and development of a time line and due dates.

Practical Concerns

The teacher must learn to judge student readiness and to simultaneously monitor several students on contracts. The former requires a sensitivity to student need for structure and to psychological maturity. Some students are ready for "free" contracts in a short time, while others never advance beyond the early stages of Step Two. The monitoring process requires that the teacher maintain a folder for each student, schedule a calendar of conference dates, and set aside time for those conferences.

Another consideration is the amount of course time to be allotted to contract teaching. Each teacher must weigh this variable against student readiness, individual needs, and the objectives of each course. Certainly many students can complete one or two contracts each semester.

What Are the Benefits?

- *Motivation and Personalization.* The teacher can give in-depth attention to a student's individual needs and interests.
- *Pacing.* The teacher can subtly address pacing, a problem in the typical classroom where students enter with different levels of ability and achievement and master material at different rates.
- *Responsibility.* The student can assume responsibility for some of his or her own learning, cooperating with the teacher to assess strengths and weaknesses and to establish learning objectives.
- *Creativity, Critical Thinking, and Learning Style.* Students can develop critical thinking skills and capitalize on individual learning style as they select activities and methods of evaluation.
- *Study Skills.* Students can develop planning skills as they establish time lines and due dates; they can reinforce research skills as they locate resources.

CONTRACT TEACHING IS IDEAL FOR THE . . .

- Highly able student who wants to and is capable of working ahead
- Average student who deserves recognition for working responsibly
- Slower student who needs attention to special problems
- SLD student who needs time and/or method alternatives
- ESOL student who is academically able, but slowed down by the language barrier
- Absentee who needs a way of catching up with the class.

Study Skills

David Marshak

Study skills are strategies and procedures that students have to solve their learning problems. As basic as any other skill that students learn in school, study skills are useful in every learning situation.

The College Board includes study skills in its list of basic academic competencies for the secondary school. Study skills ". . . constitute the key abilities in learning how to learn. Successful study skills are necessary for acquiring the other five competencies (reading, writing, speaking and listening, mathematics, and reasoning), as well as for achieving the desired outcomes. Students are unlikely to be efficient in any part of their work without them."

Study skills facilitate learning by teaching students to use a dictionary, take notes, develop listening and vocabulary skills, improve their memory, use time wisely, apply formulas, prepare for and take tests, ask useful questions, solve problems, etc.

Teaching Study Skills

The most effective teaching and learning of study skills is guided by several principles. Teachers must recognize:

- Which study skills are central to the accomplishment of the tasks they set for students. An assignment to read any textbook chapter, for example, will demand at least the following study skills: listening to directions; applying a systematic approach to the homework; scheduling time for the work; having a supportive study environment; reading the chapter for understanding and retention; and taking effective notes.
- That study skills instruction is most effective when integrated with the rest of the curriculum. Students learn "how to learn" as they learn the content of the course.
- That acquiring study skills causes the student to understand more about his or her own learning style. This recognition encourages students to take more risks and to exercise judgment and choice during the learning process.

- That they can systematically teach needed study skills through an organized program of instruction and help students see their use and importance in terms of their own personal values.
- That they can assist students to improve their study skills by having them practice the various skills. Teachers need to understand that study skills, like other skills, are mastered, with time, by repeated practice. They should structure their classes so students have sufficient practice in mastering new study skills.

Study Skills and the Secondary School Curriculum

In the past, study skills often have been neglected in secondary schools because they do not fit neatly in the subject-based organizational structure. Subject area classes usually focus on content and tend to be isolated from one other. In contrast, study skills such as listening, planning study time, creating a helpful study environment, and taking notes, are relevant to almost all subjects.

Some skills are more subject-specific: i.e., solving word problems in math and science or learning vocabulary in a foreign language. Still other skills proceed from a basic core, but vary somewhat in application by subject. The skills needed to learn from a history textbook, for example, are both similar to and different from those needed for a math text.

The mismatch between the structure of study skills and the secondary organization can militate against their inclusion in the secondary curriculum. To solve this dilemma, principals should initiate and support a *schoolwide* program of study skills instruction.

A Schoolwide Program

Successful study skills programs vary according to the characteristics of different schools, but experience demonstrates that every effective program meets the following needs:

1. *The administrator shows strong, wise, and consistent leadership.* Principals can offer such leadership by being personally involved in initiating, supporting, and evaluating study skills instruction in the school. For a program of study skills instruction to succeed, the faculty must know that the principal believes in its value, cares about its outcomes, understands its work-

---

David Marshak is with the Bureau of Study Counsel, Harvard University, Cambridge, Mass., and the hm Study Skills Group, Newton, Mass.

Study Skills

ings, and actively and consistently supports its implementation.

2. *Teachers "own" the study skills instructional program.* For teachers to change their behavior and teach study skills effectively, they must support and participate in program initiation and organization. One way to promote "ownership" is to begin with a schoolwide study skills needs assessment. The Delphi technique is useful for this purpose. (See article 40).

An important second step is to engage teachers and administrators in a collegial decision-making process about the nature of the study skills program. Pick a representative or two from each department, or ask for volunteers to serve on a planning group. If department chairpersons play important instructional roles in your school, include them as well. The departments may want to make specific recommendations to those planning the program.

3. *The program is as schoolwide as possible, and perceived as fair and efficient.*

In some schools, members of a single department volunteer to teach study skills; in others, principals ask for faculty volunteers. In either case, some teachers participate in the study skills program while others do not.

These limited formats are better than nothing, but the most effective approach is schoolwide, with the entire faculty sharing the work and rewards in ways that teachers perceive as wise and fair.

In one high school, for example, each department agreed to focus on two study skills in the ninth, tenth, and eleventh grades. Social studies teachers chose to emphasize note taking and textbook reading skills; English teachers focused on vocabulary skills and study environment; mathematics teachers dealt with problem solving and test preparation skills; science teachers worked on study behavior and test taking skills; and physical education teachers concentrated on listening skills. Industrial arts, home economics, and foreign language teachers focused on study skills specific to their courses.

A junior high school program went even further: Each department agreed to schedule both initial and follow-up lessons in the study skills its members elected to teach. The schedule was distributed to the entire faculty so that teachers would know when their students would deal with particular skills in other courses.

Teachers then reinforced these skills in their own classes.

4. *The program is a multi-year effort.* Effective change—including the move to a study skills program—demands careful planning and preparation as well as conscientious implementation and evaluation. One high school spent a year assessing needs and evaluating study skills resources. During the summer, a group of teachers and administrators met to draft a plan for a schoolwide program. In September, the faculty reviewed the plan and offered modifications.

From October through December, teachers participated in a series of inservice sessions, preparing themselves to teach study skills in a more organized and effective way. In the second semester, instruction began according to the plan. The faculty evaluated its efforts in May, made adjustments as needed, and initiated a full-scale program in the fall of the following year.

5. *Teacher inservice training is provided.* Many teachers know a great deal about study skills, others do not. For a schoolwide program to be successful, all teachers need information about study skills instruction from their peers, from curriculum leaders in the district, and, perhaps, from outside consultants.

6. *Program evaluation leads to appropriate adjustments.* Evaluation is central to any educational initiative. While study skills capability is extremely difficult to measure quantitatively, it can be evaluated qualitatively in several ways: teacher appraisal of their own work and student gains in learning skills; student assessment of their own learning skills; careful comparison of students' work in September with similar work in May.

Resources for Study Skills Instruction

Several published sets of materials are available to assist with the implementation of a schoolwide study skills program. Three of the best are: *hm Study Skills Programs* (published by the NASSP, Reston, Va.); *Learning to Study: Study Skills/Study Strategies* (published by Jamestown Publishers, Providence, R.I.); and the *Cherry Hill Study Skills Program* (published by the E.I.R.C., Sewell, N.J.). Each of these has strengths and limitations, but all are helpful resources.

Thinking Skills

M. Susan Burns, Victor R. Delclos, and John D. Bransford

Almost all students can improve their thinking and problem-solving skills. These higher level abilities involve much more than basic study skills or the mere learning of content.

Thinking skills training is designed to enhance effective thinking and/or to remediate deficient cognitive processes. Study skills programs usually focus on specific techniques for acquiring content more effectively (i.e., taking notes, using time, and building vocabulary).

Thinking skills training cuts more deeply to build such generalized cognitive skills as problem analysis, categorical elaboration, relational thinking, etc. Thinking skills programs use activities in domains such as analytic perception, spatial orientation, temporal relations, analogies, absurdities, convergent and divergent thinking, sequencing, classification, and the like. Some programs provide figural and verbal sequences of instruction and even strategies to use with those who have little or no functional literacy.

Many people assume that thinking skills develop naturally in the course of learning such subjects as mathematics, history, and science. Research suggests, however, that this is usually not so. Consider the student who must learn about the cardiovascular system. The teacher might require the student to learn the following information: "Arteries are thick, elastic, and carry blood rich in oxygen from the heart; veins are thinner, less elastic, and carry blood rich in carbon dioxide back to the heart." Many students memorize this kind of information and simply rehearse the facts. They find that they can remember the facts but do not understand the significance or relevance of what they know. (For example: Why are arteries elastic? What function does elasticity serve?)

Contrast these rote strategies with a hypothetical, "ideal" problem solver. IDEAL here stands for *identify* the problem, *define* it more precisely, *explore* possible strategies for solution, *act* on the basis of the strategies, and *look* at the effects of using the strategies.

Given the characteristics of veins and arteries in the above example, an IDEAL problem solver would first *identify* the existence of a problem; namely, the statement as given simply lists facts without giving the meaning. The student might *define* the problem as a lack of information about the functional significance of various properties of veins and arteries (why arteries need to be elastic but veins do not). Problem definition, in turn, should lead to the *exploration* of possible strategies for solution, such as: (a) read further ahead in the passage to see if the necessary information is provided; (b) consult an encyclopedia; or (c) ask the teacher. The student would then *act* on a particular strategy (e.g., reading ahead in the passage) and *look* at the effects. If the strategy was ineffective, the learner would again verify the problem and reenter the IDEAL cycle.

Many examples could be cited to illustrate the need for effective problem-solving skills. In mathematical word problems, for example, students often fail to define the problem adequately. Instead, they search for a handy formula and apply it, even though their calculations produce an answer that makes no sense. Often, they stop working on the problem rather than try it again. Similarly, students often accept arguments based on faulty reasoning or limit their creative responses by failing to consider other perspectives. Thinking skills programs are designed to reduce these kinds of shortcomings.

Teaching Thinking Skills

A variety of methods and programs exist to teach thinking and problem solving.

Separate Course. One approach to thinking skills training is a *formal course* in which the skills are taught. Several of these programs have been developed. The *Instrumental Enrichment* (FIE) curriculum of Reuven Feuerstein, for instance, incorporates strategies that enhance problem solving. FIE strategies help the learner specify the nature of the problem; identify the information important to the solution of the problem; and compare the outcomes using particular strategies for different types of problems. The goal of the program is not simply to acquaint students with the strategies, but to assist them in acquiring skills so that they will be able to solve a wide variety of problems in differing circumstances.

The *Analytic Reasoning* program developed by Whimbey and Lochhead is a thinking skills program

---

M. Susan Burns and Victor R. Delclos are research associates, John F. Kennedy Center for Research on Education and Human Development, and John D. Bransford is professor, Departments of Psychology and Education, all at Vanderbilt University, Nashville, Tenn.

Thinking Skills

for high school students. In this program, thinking strategies are taught by a "think aloud" procedure. Students work on problems in pairs. One student attempts to solve the problem while verbalizing each step, the other student constructively critiques the attempts. Later the students switch roles. The "think aloud" procedure helps students to become aware of their own thinking processes and to recognize the importance of care and precision in their analysis of problems.

Other available thinking skills programs are: de Bono's *CoRT Thinking Course;* Lipman's *Philosophy for Children;* and Blacks' *Building Thinking Skills.* Our recommended readings provide more details on these and other programs.

Integrated Approach. Thinking courses do help students develop thinking skills, but the strategies may not be as effective taught in isolation as they would be if coupled with academic content. The integrated approach incorporates a problem-solving orientation and thinking skills with instruction in courses such as geometry, biology, and literature. The approach is more demanding of the teacher because it involves teaching strategies as well as content. If, however, a school/district wants to show significant gains on standardized achievement tests, this may be the more productive approach to adopt.

The integrated approach is used in Palinsar and Brown's work on the development of comprehension and monitoring skills, and Bransford and Stein's work on learning and problem solving. Black and Black's *Building Thinking Skills* workbooks can be used both to support content area objectives or as a separate course.

Palinsar and Brown have successfully integrated comprehension-fostering and monitoring skills such as summarizing (self-review), questioning, clarifying, and predicting with content information on topics as unlikely as the skeletal structure of snakes. Similarly, Bransford and Stein's IDEAL approach can be used to structure teaching in many content areas. Indeed, the most effective application of these approaches is using them in several courses at the same time.

Suggested Readings

Black, H., and Black, S. *Building Thinking Skills.* Pacific Grove, Calif.: Midwest Publications, 1984.

Bransford, J. D., and Stein, B. S. *The IDEAL Problem Solver: A Guide for Improving Thinking, Learning and Creativity.* New York: W. H. Freeman & Co., 1984.

de Bono, E. *de Bono's Thinking Course.* London: British Broadcasting Corporation, 1982.

Feuerstein, R.; Rand, Y.; Hoffman, M. D.; and Miller, R. *Instrumental Enrichment.* Baltimore, Md.: University Park Press, 1980.

Glaser, R. "Education and Thinking: The Role of Knowledge." *American Psychologist* 39 (1984): 93–104.

Lipman, Matthew. *Philosophy for Children* Program. Upper Montclair, N.J.: Montclair State College, 1984.

Palinsar, A. S., and Brown, A. L. "Reciprocal Teaching of Comprehension-Fostering and Monitoring Activities." *Cognition and Instruction,* Vol. 1, No. 2 (1984): 117–175.

Whimbey, A., and Lochhead, J. *Problem Solving and Comprehension: A Short Course in Analytical Reasoning.* Philadelphia, Pa.: The Franklin Institute Press, 1980.

Talented and Gifted Programs

Ray Schrepfer

The talented and gifted student may be this society's most untapped resource. Because growth in our post-technological society will depend on creative solutions to complex problems, the question for administrators is no longer "Should we have a talented and gifted (TAG) program?" but rather, "What type of TAG program should we have?"

Definition

No true consensus has been reached on a definition of giftedness. Definitions range from narrow estimates of intellectual ability as measured by standardized I.Q. tests to broad but highly subjective characterizations of "outstanding performance" in art, science, leadership, etc.

In the past decade, many states and school districts have adopted some variation of the U.S. Office of Education's 1972 definition:

> Gifted and talented children are those identified by professionally qualified persons who by virtue of outstanding abilities are capable of high performance. These are children who require differentiated educational programs and/or services beyond those normally provided by the regular school program in order to realize their contribution to self and society.
>
> Children capable of high performance include those with demonstrated achievement and/or potential in any of the following areas, singly or in combination:
> 1. General intellectual ability
> 2. Specific academic aptitude
> 3. Creative or productive thinking
> 4. Leadership ability
> 5. Visual and performing arts
> 6. Psychomotor ability

This definition broadens the definition of giftedness in a useful way but fails to account for the role of motivation and commitment in superior performance. Further, the six categories are not mutually exclusive. Only "specific academic aptitude" and "visual and performing arts" are distinct performance areas. The other four categories are generalized skills that can apply to many areas of performance. Definition, then, is somewhat of a problem; one that must be settled by the local district or school.

Ray Schrepfer is principal, Mid-Prairie Junior High School, Kalona, Iowa.

Trends and Practices

This writer's personal experience in developing, implementing, and evaluating a local TAG program during the past 10 years reinforces support of the following useful practices:

- *Team Administration.* The formation of a building team to develop and administer the TAG program is a recent trend. Regular staff members are paid for extra time and assume additional responsibilities. They write goals and objectives, design programs, develop strategies for identification and evaluation, and may do some of the teaching or arrange for other staff members to do so.

  Team responsibility has several advantages over single person coordination. The team is more likely than one person to have the time and expertise to supervise all phases of the program; teaming builds a solid core of staff committed to the program; it encourages involvement of other staff and the community; it ensures continuity as team members move to other assignments; in some cases, it is more cost effective than a full-time person.

- *Multi-Source Identification.* All students are rated in the initial screening process, which utilizes information from peers, parents, self, teachers, and standardized tests. Computer programs can collate all this information and print out rank order lists. This initial information is usually sufficient for identification of those gifted intellectually and academically. Giftedness in leadership, creativity, and the visual and performing arts is less easily quantified. "Studio experiences" help to discover those with special talents. Interviews by a selection committee are an effective method of final screening.

- *Programming.* New media and methods are making more personalized forms of education possible. Leading the way, of course, is the computer. Students can do creative writing, compose music, analyze data, and learn basic information from computers. Telecommunication is enabling schools to expose students to learning experiences and courses that could not be offered locally. Industry, in particular, is also very supportive of TAG programs, assisting with mentors, equipment, and money.

Talented and Gifted Programs

Current talented and gifted programs include special projects within the classroom, special classes, and completely separate schools (magnet schools).

• *Individualized Teacher Inservice.* Inservice strategies are being developed around individualized teacher needs. The following model for TAG staff development is designed to move teachers through different stages of commitment to gifted education:
1. Growing in awareness of gifted and talented characteristics
2. Accepting the need to program differently for the various abilities and learning styles exhibited by gifted and talented students
3. Exploring potential methods for differential programming
4. Preparing methods and materials
5. Evaluating the implementation effort. Faculty members move through the model at their own pace, based on previous experience and present needs.

Qualitatively Different Education

NASSP's *Practitioner,* "Lest the Gifted Be Unseen: Qualitatively Different Education" (Pannwitt, 1978), emphasizes that the aim of all gifted and talented education is *enrichment*—providing experiences that replace, supplement, or extend the regular curriculum. Pannwitt cites these qualitative differences in effective programs:

- *Differentiated curricula* embodying a high level of cognitive and affective concepts and processes beyond those normally provided in the regular curriculum.
- *Instructional materials* designed specifically for the G/T and used in an intensive, in-depth manner to accommodate uniquely different learning styles.
- *Learning activities* that require independent research outside scheduled class assignments, are accelerated or self-pacing, and differ otherwise from regular activities for the grade level.
- *Flexible administrative arrangements* for instruction and cultural enrichment both in and out of school.
- *Active parent involvement* in the local school and in national, state, and community councils for the gifted.

The needs of TAG students can be met in many ways, but none will be successful without public and school commitment to program, budget, and inservice. Most importantly, administrators must make a commitment to the needs of TAG students as a regular and continuing element of the school program.

Advanced Placement Programs

Sol Levine

College level or Advanced Placement (AP) courses are offered, under the auspices of the College Board, by one in every 25 American secondary schools. These classes are taught by high school teachers using course descriptions provided by the College Board. Each May, students take locally-administered AP exams that are scored at a national center.

Examinations are graded on a five-point scale, with five as the top score. Nearly two-thirds of U.S. colleges grant advanced placement and/or credit to students earning scores of three or higher. A student may enter college with 12 or more credits; thus, required coursework and tuition costs are reduced. Many colleges award sophomore standing to students with a sufficient number of qualifying scores.

At present, AP courses are available in history (American and European); English; science (biology, chemistry, and physics); foreign language (Spanish, German, French, Latin); mathematics (calculus AB and BC); art (history, studio); music; and computer science.

Why an AP Program?

Among the many advantages of instituting an AP program are:

- AP courses provide an excellent "bridge" or transition to the college experience. Students get a sense of what college work is like.
- AP classes meet the needs of bright and talented students and help combat "senioritis."
- AP adds rigor to the curriculum and raises academic standards.
- AP enables students to receive advanced standing and/or credit in college, saving them time and money.
- Teachers are motivated to higher intellectual pursuits and tend to become more expert in their respective fields.
- Content and method "spillover" occurs from AP classes to other classes.
- AP is excellent public relations for the school.

Sol Levine is principal, Beverly Hills High School, Beverly Hills, Calif.

How To Launch an AP Program

The principal initiates the AP program, and typically needs to confront the following questions:

- Is there a need for the AP program?
- Which staff members have the background and knowledge to teach AP courses?
- Who will coordinate the program?
- How will staff and community support be enlisted for a college level program?
- How will the program be administered and organized?
- Is the program affordable?
- How can the success of the program be evaluated?

Enlisting staff support is essential for the success of any new program. Experienced principals know that change is not easy to achieve. Informal discussions with key faculty members are a good way to begin. Provide time for selected teachers to visit AP schools and/or participate in College Board AP conferences and regional workshops. Knowledgeable teachers can be asked to lead a discussion on the benefits of an AP program or show the College Board film, "AP: Option for Excellence." (The film and other assistance are available from the College Board, 888 Seventh Avenue, New York, N.Y. 10106.)

After sensitizing staff to the benefits of Advanced Placement, create a task force of key staff members to study the feasibility of introducing the program. Some warnings are in order: Clearly define the tasks and goals of the task force. Ask them to study problems as well as benefits. Not preparing teachers for the typical concerns and issues can lead to problems.

Ask the task force to develop a specific timetable for program implementation. Move slowly; start with selected AP classes based on student need and interest and teacher availability. Expand later. Be sure you have the understanding and support of all such key school personnel as counselors and department chairs.

The task force should discuss several issues:

- *Costs.* Examination fees ($46 per test) are usually paid by the student, but indirect staffing costs are associated with the program. The AP coordinator may need additional time (for examination administration), and additional classes may be needed if separate AP courses are created. Class size in these courses is

Advanced Placement Programs

usually small, raising the problem of uneven teacher loads.

- *Program Organization.* AP courses are structured differently in different schools. The College Board says that "alternatives often take the form of special seminars, regular courses supplemented by tutorial work or independent study." Most schools create individual AP classes.

- *Student Selection.* Inasmuch as AP classes are very demanding and require higher level skills, student selection is a significant issue. The task force should review the many approaches to student selection used in AP schools—e.g., past achievement, teacher/counselor recommendation, teacher interviews, standardized test scores. Past achievement and teacher/counselor recommendations are the most significant indicators of student success.

- *AP Examination Policy.* Should all students enrolled in AP classes be required to take an AP examination? Schools vary significantly on this issue. Some require the examination as an integral part of the class; others allow students to opt for the examination if they feel prepared.

- *Teacher Participation and Training.* Teaching AP classes requires a thorough, sophisticated knowledge of the subject matter. Teachers must have the ability and desire to teach these courses. Since essays are used in all AP examinations, more essays must be assigned (and graded). Teachers may even have to take additional university coursework as well as inservice workshops.

- *AP Classes and Grade Point Average.* Students frequently ask, "Why should I take an AP course and risk lowering my GPA?" In addition to the intrinsic educational value of the concept, many schools argue that AP grades should be weighted to address GPA deflation. These schools equate a B in an AP course with an A in a regular class. The issue certainly requires airing and discussion before launching into the program.

Require the task force to present its findings and recommendations to the entire staff (or department). It is impossible to overestimate the importance of keeping the staff informed. A report should also be sent to the superintendent and school board after any program redesign based on staff feedback. Hold a special evening program to stimulate parental interest and support. Discuss the benefits, values, and costs of the AP program. If only one class is being offered initially, meet with the students enrolled and their parents.

Evaluating the AP Program

The AP program can be evaluated by standard techniques. Periodic classroom visitation will establish whether appropriate higher level skills and subject matter are being taught. Visitation will also detect whether new AP teachers are aiming the course *beyond* the undergraduate level. Teacher and student evaluation of the course at year's end is another effective rating tool.

The AP examination, of course, provides a measure of course (or student) quality. (In subsequent years it also serves as an excellent teacher guide.) Each school is provided summary scores (on the 1–5 scale) for each subject area. The percentage of students with scores of 3, 4, or 5 is a good indicator of student success. Formal longitudinal studies or informal contacts are feasible. Graduate follow-up studies can show how students view their AP experience after they have started college.

This type of feedback is particularly valuable to the teacher. Increased AP course demand is a straightforward measure of success, as is interest on the part of additional departments to offer AP classes. The experience in most AP schools is that the demand for AP classes tends to increase yearly until an optimum number is reached.

The many national reports urge schools to raise standards and expectations. Most AP schools would assert that a strong and vibrant AP program is a step in that direction.

Special Education

Robert A. Sedlak and David A. Sabatino

State-of-the-art curriculum development integrates special education with vocational or career goals. Secondary students with special needs, whenever possible, are scheduled into vocational/technical classes. Students who are physically handicapped or who lack some academic skill can be successful in these programs with reasonable accommodation. (See Gugerty's 1981 and 1983 manuals, which explain a large number of modifications to tools, equipment, and machinery that accommodate the disabled.)

Several current practices in special education are of particular interest:

- *Social Studies.* All students are customarily required to take American history or American government to qualify for a high school diploma. These classes can be highly demanding for special students. The Livonia (Mich.) Public Schools have developed excellent adaptations for these courses. The scope and sequence of the major texts were reviewed and a series of modular booklets prepared on the significant content objects. Interested school districts can purchase the modules that are compatible with the series being used locally.

- *Social Skills.* Studies of postsecondary adjustment have shown that social skills are the major deficiency of students graduating from special programs. These skills deal with expressing feelings and aggression, making apologies, responding to criticism, starting and ending a conversation, asking questions, seeking assistance, and planning. Research has demonstrated that many of these skills must be taught directly by the teacher. Typical instructional procedures include the presentation of a vignette or problem situation that focuses on a specific skill; brainstorming with students for appropriate solutions; modeling appropriate response(s) by videotape, filmstrip, or live presentation; and student role playing in identical or similar situations with feedback on individual performance.

- *Reading Materials.* Few, if any, secondary textbooks are written in a high interest/low vocabulary format. Many special educators accept the necessary responsibility of modifying and adapting passages from available texts to appropriate reading levels for the reading disabled student.

Special education students may need vocabulary development that focuses on sight word recognition and comprehension. Most secondary handicapped students require a variety of materials, equipment, and strategies that enhance skill development in sight word comprehension and recognition, linguistic analysis, and reference skills.

Sight word vocabulary can be developed to a satisfactory level through board, track, and tachistoscopic games that reinforce this skill. These games are economical and can be modified to suit the vocabulary needs of any student. Comprehension is also essential to sight word development. Strategies for developing comprehension emphasize arousing interest in words, examining their sensory or emotional power, investigating their semantic features, defining them, and analyzing the structural and contextual cues surrounding them.

- *Problem-Solving Skills.* Curriculum developers have not focused adequate attention on teaching problem-solving skills. Special education students meet their biggest challenges trying to cope with the types of information processing required in problem situations. Sifting out those bits of information needed for solving a given problem is an essential but challenging skill.

At the secondary level, problem-solving activities should focus on socially relevant situations. Some limited research (Lydra and Church, 1964) indicates that helping students find solutions to real classroom and home problems rather than simulated ones is highly effective in developing the needed skills.

- *Measurement Skills.* Handling money and using basic measurement devices (e.g., yardstick, thermometer, bathroom scale, measuring cup, etc.) are essential skills for secondary school students. Functional skill requires the active manipulation and use of these materials. The skills can be broken down for special education students by task analysis into easily learnable steps.

Some aspects of mathematics demand simple memorization—the basic facts and equivalences that most adults use without second thought, such as 12 items make a dozen, 60 seconds make a minute, etc. Special education programs stress these essential skills and provide help for students who have trouble memorizing.

David A. Sabatino is dean and Robert A. Sedlak is professor, School of Education and Human Services, University of Wisconsin-Stout, Menomonie.

Special Education

Media Practices

Special education teachers recognize that effective use of media can enhance the skills of disabled learners. Compressed speech, audiovisual tutoring, and videotaped modeling are particularly effective. Movies, filmstrips, and other audiovisual resources can be used to increase vocabulary and communication skills; videotape and photography can be used to illustrate such positive social skills as responding to criticism, making requests, or initiating a conversation; and computer-assisted instruction is helpful in developing basic math, reading, and leisure skills for the handicapped.

The current emphasis on microcomputer applications has tended to deemphasize the importance of other media in the special education curriculum. All media can benefit handicapped children but a judicious use requires teacher time and planning.

- *Overhead Projector.* The overhead projector offers several advantages over a chalkboard in working with the learning disabled. The light allows the teacher to direct learner attention to a specific location in the room; the images are enlarged, and the teacher can maintain visual contact with the learners throughout the lesson; and with a copy machine, teachers can quickly develop functional transparencies from realistic, everyday materials (i.e., newspapers, notices of public hearings, etc.).

- *Audiotapes.* Audiotapes can help students compensate for poor reading skills. Passages can be taped for students to listen as they read, and resource room teachers can develop libraries of talking books in many subjects. Cassette recorders, variable speed recorders, and devices such as language masters can provide learning alternatives for students who lack note-taking skills.

- *Television and Videotape.* The Supreme Court's latest ruling governing the recording of trials and hearings offers social studies options for the handicapped. News broadcasts, documentaries, and even commercials can provide graphic illustrations for many of the standard social studies topics. Regularly scheduled public television programs in science, health, social studies, and language arts offer teachers excellent ways to teach content outside their competence. Schools now subscribe to public television stations and receive advanced listings and study guides for many of the educational television programs.

Videotape equipment can also be used to develop student social skills through role playing activities.

- *Microcomputer.* The microcomputer is by no means a cure-all in handicapped education, but it can be a useful tool in achieving specific individualized education plan (IEP) goals. Software is the key. A speech synthesizer or a cassette-type recorder under computer control can adjust the readability levels of different materials for the student, and teachers can minimize reading problems by having small groups of students work as teams on microcomputer-directed activities. (Explicit rules are needed, of course, to minimize the probability that the equipment will be misused.) For physically handicapped learners, single-switch operated programs are available from the Minnesota Educational Computing Consortium (MECC).

Minimal software resources for a classroom would include drill and practice programs in math, spelling drill and practice, and a word processing program such as the Bank Street Writer. An authoring program/language such as Pilot also is helpful.

References

Gugerty, John; Rashal, A. F.; Tradewell, M. D.; and Anthony, L. K. *Tools, Equipment and Machinery Adapted for the Vocational Education and Employment of Handicapped People.* Madison, Wisc.: Wisconsin Vocational Studies Center, University of Wisconsin, 1981. (Supplement issued in 1983.)

Lydra, W. J., and Church, R. S. "Direct, Practical Arithmetic Experiences and Success in Solving Realistic Verbal 'Reasoning' Problems in Arithmetic." *The Journal of Educational Research* (1964): 530–533.

Experiential Education

Diane Hedin

Experiential education, or learning through experience, is *the* original educational method. However, a 1980s definition is in order. Today, experiential education is defined as educational programs offered as an integral part of the general school curriculum but taking place outside of the conventional classroom; students are in new roles featuring significant tasks with real consequences, where the emphasis is on learning by doing with associated reflection.

Experiential education is especially valuable today, when a narrow view of academic learning (i.e., scores on standardized achievement tests) has blinded many to other facets of adolescent life. Experiential programs help young people become active, concerned, and involved citizens by encouraging them to take on responsible roles in the life of the community. They allow them to test, stretch, and challenge their sense of who they are, what they believe, and what they can do. They encourage intellectual development, the capacity to solve problems, and to make complex, thoughtful judgments. They allow students to apply what they have learned and to understand their everyday experiences outside the classroom.

Several national studies of experiential learning (Conrad and Hedin, 1981; Newmann and Rutter, 1983) show that a wide variety of students benefit from this approach—those with high and low GPAs, students in inner-city schools and private prep schools, seventh graders and twelfth graders. The most intellectually and psychologically complex thinkers are the most satisfied with these programs, a fact which suggests that experiential learning should not be a "dumping ground" for reluctant scholars.

Program Models

Experiential learning is a grass-roots movement rather than a government or university-based initiative. Individual principals, teachers, students, and parents have started programs to meet their own interests and those of their communities. As a result, programs do not fall into neat categories.

Diane Hedin is associate professor and assistant director, Center for Youth Development and Research, University of Minnesota-Twin Cities, St. Paul.

Some are for credit, others are not. Some are attached to particular subject areas, others are not. Similar kinds of activity may be geared to quite different objectives. We have chosen to categorize programs according to the general nature of the student activity or experience.

• *Community Service Programs.* The most common form of experiential learning involves students serving as volunteers in the school system and in community social agencies. Many school-based programs start here because the needs are already identified, supervision and expert guidance are available, students are genuinely needed, and assigned tasks are significant and responsible.

In Hopkins, Minn., twelfth graders can enroll in a social studies elective entitled "Community Involvement." Students serve as volunteers in elementary schools, day care centers, nursing homes, centers for retarded and/or handicapped children, Meals on Wheels, and within their high schools as peer counselors and teachers. They work in the community for two hours a day, four days a week, and spend one day in a classroom seminar discussing their field experiences, studying psychology, and working on interpersonal helping skills. Students receive two credits in social studies. This very popular course has been in operation for more than 10 years.

• *Internships.* Experiential education students may spend a few hours a week for a semester or full-time for a year exploring an occupation or career of interest. Internships provide a look at the *inside* of an organization, a way to experience an occupation firsthand, to get an in-depth view of how decisions are made, and to test one's competence to fill an adult role.

Students at Joan of Arc Junior High, New York City, and Work Opportunity Center, Minneapolis, learn first-hand about medical careers. Both programs are deliberately designed to develop inner-city youths' interest in the health professions and give them the background and confidence to pursue health careers. In New York, junior high students spend one full day each week as interns with researchers, physicians, and technicians at New York University Medical School. In Minneapolis, senior high students spend half of each day in the program, interning in local hospitals, studying biology with an emphasis on medical health issues, and exploring careers.

A Community Internship Program in Beverly Hills,

Experiential Education

Calif., places eleventh and twelfth graders in stockbroker's offices, law offices, medical centers, TV studios, retail stores, hospitals, government agencies, social service agencies, and other settings. Students, who earn academic credit for their participation, apply for the internships, which typically run two or three hours daily for one school term. No formal class or seminar is required, but some students do write reports and/or have informal discussions with the program coordinator.

- *Community Study.* Community study means the application of social science and scientific research skills to community problems and needs. A survey of community attitudes conducted by a ninth grade civic class in one rural community gave the town council information about citizens' preferences for a new swimming pool *vs.* a new waste management system. A math class did a careful study of the school's energy system efficiency. In a biology class, students checked river water samples to determine the river's safety as a swimming area for residents. Spurred by the success of the Georgia Foxfire Project, many students look into the history of their locale in history or English classes, interview older people, and produce newspapers and pamphlets to preserve the heritage of their area.

Ninth graders in Kirkwood, Mo., can enroll in a program entitled "Community Participation." In this elective program, students take four academic subjects in a block: English, mathematics, citizenship, and science. They spend two hours, twice a week, working on community consumer and ecological projects; taking field trips to courts, government offices, and scientific organizations; and performing volunteer work for social agencies and in political campaigns.

Ingredients for Success

Experiential education can take many forms. It can be integrated into any subject matter, and can be effective with younger and older students, and with the most and least academically oriented. However, three factors are critical to the success of any program:

1. The principal must understand and support the concept of learning through direct experience, in and out of the classroom.
2. Teachers who work with the program must be flexible, energetic, and committed to it.
3. Opportunities must be created for students, with teacher guidance, to reflect and to integrate their field experiences. A weekly seminar or classroom activity, then, is a necessity. Without such reflection, social and intellectual development is greatly reduced.

The logistical and practical problems of scheduling, transportation, insurance, etc., can be solved if the basic ingredients are present. Schools across the country have found creative ways to transport their students, and scheduling the program during the first or last periods of the day eliminates one trip for which the school is responsible. Insurance policies that cover students in work-study and vocational education are applicable to experiential programs as well. Interdisciplinary courses can provide the time needed for students to learn in the community.

References

Conrad, D., and Hedin, D. *Executive Summary: Experiential Education Evaluation Project.* St. Paul, Minn.: Center for Youth Development and Research, University of Minnesota, 1981.

Newmann, F., and Rutter, R. *The Effects of High School Community Service Programs on Students' Social Development.* Madison, Wis.: Wisconsin Center for Education Research, 1983.

Resources

Association for Experiential Education, Box 4625, Denver, Colo. 80204.

The Center for Youth Development and Research, University of Minnesota, 386 McNeal Hall, St. Paul, Minn. 55108.

Institute for Responsive Education, 605 Commonwealth Ave., Boston, Mass. 02215.

National Center for Service Learning, 806 Connecticut Ave., Washington, D.C. 20525.

National Society for Internship and Experiential Education, 1735 I St., N.W., Suite 601, Washington, D.C. 20006.

PLANNING ELEMENTS

Conducting Needs Assessment

Arlene Fink and Jacqueline Kosecoff

Needs assessment is defined by the *Encyclopedia of Educational Evaluation* as the process by which one identifies needs and decides upon priorities among them. In education and training programs, a need is often defined as a condition in which there is a discrepancy between an acceptable state of affairs and an observed state of affairs.

Needs assessment can be done for individuals, groups, or institutions. According to the *Encyclopedia*, you can either measure the discrepancy objectively or estimate it subjectively. If you use the first method you compare the level of measured performance with the level judged acceptable. If you use the second method, you select people whose judgment you trust and ask them whether a need exists in a given area.

A value judgment is necessary in either case. Someone has to decide where the "acceptable" level is, and someone has to rate the degree of need that exists.

Instead of offering more theory, we will describe a needs assessment method developed by David Satcher. His strategy has five steps which we will translate into a hypothetical educational example.

Step 1: Identify Potential Objectives

The first step is to compile a comprehensive list of objectives for the program. Go to the experts, the literature, or the community.

Example: In our hypothetical education needs assessment, we obtained statements of goals primarily from a review of the literature, an analysis of the future job market, and a review of 20 school districts located throughout the country.

After the list was compiled, we gave it to a group composed of two teachers, two representatives from labor/business, two community persons, and a professor of education. We asked them to discuss and refine the findings. They identified 50 goals such as these:

- Communication of knowledge—the skill to acquire and transmit
- Aesthetic—cultural and leisure pursuits
- Consumer — personal buying, selling, and investment.

Arlene Fink and Jacqueline Kosecoff are editors, How to Evaluate Education Programs, *Capitol Publications, Inc., Washington, D.C.*

Step 2: Decide Most Important Goals/Objectives

Next, select the individuals and groups whose interests and views you consider important. Have them rate the objectives and then combine the results.

Example: We identified three groups for participation in our needs assessment—students, teachers, and school administrators. We drew a random sample of 350 students from all the secondary students in the district, representative in terms of sex, ethnicity, and family income. The sample of teachers (n=50) included high school instructors and career guidance counselors. Administrators (n=18) were the principals and vice principals in each of the district's high schools. (In an actual needs assessment, we would also have surveyed parents and the community.)

To decide which goals were the most important, we asked each individual to complete a questionnaire that included the statements and a rating scale with five choices. In rating the goals, we asked people to assign at least two goals to each of the five response categories: 1=least important, 2=below average, 3=average, 4=above average, 5=most important. A Q-sort technique was used, with each goal written on a separate card for easy sorting into the five categories. (People have a tendency to rate *all* objectives either very high or very low, and Q-sort is one way to break that pattern.)

Step 3: Assess Nature, Type of Current Services

Next, you must get information about how well your schools are meeting these goals now. You might find this information in school records or in experimental and evaluation data, or you might try a survey of community experts or ordinary citizens.

Example: We gave teachers and administrators (not students) two additional three-point rating scales on the needs assessment questionnaire. One was for judging *feasibility* (Can we do it?), and the other for assessing *feasibility* (Can we do it?), and the other for assessing *availability* (Are we already doing it?). We wanted to know whether services rated as important are already available, and if they are not, whether they are impossible (or impractical) to provide.

Here are the directions to teachers and administrators for rating feasibility and availability:

Conducting Needs Assessment

Rating Feasibility of Services

Please rate the feasibility of implementing this goal in the school program on a scale that goes from "easy to provide" to "possible to provide, but difficult," to "cannot be provided at this time." Please rate the feasibility with the present resources available to our school district.

Rating Availability of Services

Please rate the availability of each goal or service. How easy is it for the school in which you work to implement the goal at this time? The three-part scale goes from "easily available" to "available, but difficult to get" to "not available as far as I know."

We tried a single 50-goal questionnaire on a small pilot sample (25) of students, teachers, and administrators. In addition to the responses described above, we added "Do not understand" to each rating scale.

After the pretest, we revised goal statements to make them clearer and less confusing, and dropped the ones that appeared difficult to understand. The final questionnaire contained 38 statements. (We also arranged for a Spanish language version of the questionnaire.)

Step 4: Collect Information

Consider using questionnaires (or interviews for small samples) for collecting the needs assessment information. Check the accuracy and completeness of the response.

Example: We used self-administered questionnaires for this assessment. Homeroom teachers distributed the questionnaires to students; teachers and administrators received them in their school mailboxes. The completed forms were returned to a clerk at each high school, who substituted code numbers for names to ensure anonymity.

Step 5: Select Final Goals

In the last step, you must synthesize information in order to set priorities among goals. Although complex mathematical models are sometimes used, relatively simple schemes can produce excellent results.

For our educational needs assessment, we calculated the averages of all ratings of availability, feasibility, and importance. We analyzed the results which enabled us to set appropriate priorities:

- We gave top priority to the goals that were rated highest in feasibility and importance, and lowest in availability.

- For objectives rated *low* in availability and feasibility but *high* in importance, we set up a committee to study whether we might be able to offer these services.
- Finally, we ruled out some goals that were rated highly important and feasible because they were already available.

Delphi Technique

Another useful tool for needs assessment is the Delphi Technique.

1. Each participant contributes information at each stage (there are three or four *before* seeing what others have said).
2. Each participant knows his/her own responses but those of others remain anonymous.
3. The results of each step are shared as part of the *next* step.

The Delphi Technique has the advantage of not requiring repeated meetings, yet provides for systematic information gathering and group priorities by substituting a computed consensus for the usual majority.

A typical Delphi Technique employs a three-stage process. The first questionnaire collects information about personal concerns and priorities. The second consists of items developed from the first-round responses; participants privately rank each item according to their own priorities. The third questionnaire gives participants an average (mean or mode) of second-round responses and an opportunity to reconsider personal choices in light of the group judgments. The result is group consensus.

Other Delphi variations are short questionnaires or charts with statements developed in advance by a planning committee, and computerized versions using Q-sort cards for the ranking process.

References

Anderson, Scarvia B.; Ball, Samuel; Murphy, Richard T.; et al. *Encyclopedia of Educational Evaluation.* San Francisco, Calif.: Jossey-Bass, 1975.

Rasp, Arthur Jr. "Delphi: A Decision Makers Dream." *Nations Schools,* July 1973.

Satcher, David. *A Needs Assessment Study for Family Practice in an Inner City Community.* Los Angeles, Calif.: UCLA School of Medicine, Robert Wood Johnson Foundation, 1977.

Condensed with permission from Capitol Publications, Inc., Washington, D.C. Originally developed for How to Evaluate Education Programs, *Vol. 3, No. 2, February 1979.*

Critical Analysis of the School Program

Kenneth J. Dunn

The principal who is committed to instructional leadership must participate directly in the key operational aspects of program planning, implementing, and evaluating. Planning and implementing decisions should receive particularly high priority because the success of any instructional improvement may well depend on timely leadership. Because no significant program improvement can take place without quality information on the current status of the school program, a critical analysis of that program is essential.

The Process

The principal should *lead* all key planning sessions, *collaborate* in the setting of priorities, and *lend support* to the process of analysis.

Step 1: Inform All Concerned. A critical analysis of the school program should focus on the current state of the curriculum, schedule, teaching strategies, and learning outcomes as viewed against criteria established by the staff, the district office, the state education department, and evaluation agencies such as the National Study of School Evaluation. These criteria should be discussed, revised, and approved by staff, supervisors, and appropriate central office staff. The school board should receive progress reports through the superintendent's office.

Regular bulletins should be sent to all interested groups. Teachers should never feel that "students know more about proposed changes than we do."

Step 2: Select Criteria for Analysis. Appoint a small subcommittee of respected teachers and administrators to review and recommend criteria for the analysis. The criteria might include:
- Current board of education policies and regulations;
- The school philosophy and program handbook;
- State department of education accreditation guides;
- The latest state certification report or an evaluation review by a regional accrediting agency;
- The Secondary School Evaluative Criteria (or Middle School/Junior High School Evaluative Criteria)—particularly the section on Design of Curriculum and Instructional areas.

Step 3: Train for Decision Making. Train staff members in brainstorming techniques, conflict resolution strategies, productive meeting techniques, priority grid development, and the principles of group cohesiveness and commitment. Lead and/or participate in these sessions.

Step 4: Design a Plan for Program Analysis. Clear, concrete, measurable assessment criteria related to the overall goal-setting process are the key elements of the design. Specific questions, rating scales, narrative comparisons, and other techniques should be constructed. The plan should describe how the analysis will be carried out, by whom, in what context, and in what format.

Step 5: Implement the Analysis. Direct the analysis team to complete the task according to a reasonable and flexible time schedule. Set interim report meetings. Communicate the results to all concerned. (See Step 1.)

Some Basic Approaches to Program Analysis

- *National Study of School Evaluation Approach* (NSSE). The evaluative criteria used by various regional accrediting associations offer a basic framework for developing local program analysis instrumentation (i.e., the National Study of School Evaluation; Associations in the Middle States, New England, North Central, and Northwest; the Southern Association; and the Western Association of Schools and Colleges).

The NSSE Evaluative Criteria section on Design of Curriculum provides 15 principles for analyzing a program, a set of questions to describe the nature of the program, and an evaluation component. Key assessment areas are student educational needs, school and community goals, curriculum balance, articulation and flexibility, follow-up studies, continuing evaluation, curriculum sequences, staff organization, and curriculum organization.

The NSSE manual is a useful starting point for schools whose current staff and administration have not yet completed a critical analysis of the program.

- *Organization, Process, and Product Approach.* Ralph Tyler and others who participated in the famous Eight-Year Study (1933–41) used a simple evaluation

---

Kenneth J. Dunn is professor and coordinator of administration and supervision, Educational and Community Programs, Queens College of the City University of New York, Flushing.

Critical Analysis of the School Program

technique that is still practical and very effective. Small working committees of staff members analyze and describe:
- The organization of the school's program
- The process by which it serves the students
- The product or outcomes expected.

The *organization* committee produces concise descriptions of the curriculum and its goals by subject and program. The *process* committee tackles such diverse elements as school scheduling, teaching approaches, academic sequences, class changes, program resources, program flexibility, and the building itself. The *product and outcomes* committee establishes criteria for the assessment of student performance and success goals to be achieved, courses to be required and implemented, and follow-up studies (college and beyond).

- *Behavioral Outcomes Approach.* A behavioral approach would focus directly on the results of the school program as reflected in various behavioral outcomes (Dunn and Dunn, 1977). Faculty (and student) brainstorming groups would develop a list of behaviors and related rating scales. Some of the possibilities are:
1. Individual student diagnostic data on achievement, aptitudes, interests, learning style, and self-concept.
2. Individual student prescriptions with objectives, resources, activities, and testing related to program objectives and student learning strengths.
3. The use of available resources, materials, and media.
4. Changing instructional methodologies, seating arrangements, small-group techniques, etc.
5. Instructional options and structured student choices.
6. Longitudinal studies of program and student performance.

The rating scales simply list objectives by number and the percentage of students/teachers meeting each objective.

- *Indices of Impact Approach.* A fourth approach to program review, and perhaps the most quantitative, was developed by the late Ben Rosner. A series of objective, quantifiable items is listed and coded for each objective or instructional area of the program. The following example on library use illustrates the technique.

Program Analysis: Library

1. What percentage of the student population uses the library on a regular basis?

	% of Students
- Less than 2 times a year	_____
- 2 times a semester	_____
- 2 times a month	_____
- 2 times a week	_____
- 3 to 5 times a week	_____

2. What percentage of the students report to the library?
- each day _____
- each week _____
- each month _____

3. What are the weekly utilization figures?

	Number
- Circulation of books – fiction	_____
- Circulation of books – non-fiction	_____
- Use of non-circulating reference books	_____
- Use of non-print material	_____

Many types of questions can be asked about the library, a course of study, a department, or a program. The objective is to list quantifiable elements of a program, collect data, and assess the results against expectations. The resulting report can offer invaluable baseline data for planned improvement.

These approaches to the critical analysis of school program (*Evaluative Criteria, Organization, Process and Product, Behavioral Outcomes,* and *Indices of Impact*) also can be used to develop goals or to organize for program improvement.

References

Dunn, R., and Dunn, K. *Administrators Guide to New Programs for Faculty Management and Evaluation.* West Nyack, N.Y.: Parker Publishing Co., 1977.

Dunn, R., and Dunn, K. *Teaching Students Through Their Individual Learning Styles: A Practical Approach.* Reston, Va.: Reston Publishing Co., 1978.

National Study of School Evaluation. *Secondary School Evaluative Criteria: Narrative Edition, Middle School/Junior High School Evaluative Criteria: Revised Edition.* Arlington, Va.: NSSE. 1975, 1979.

Goals for the School

David A. Erlandson

Because individuals and organizations tend to continue doing what they have done in the past, formal goal-setting activities often replicate what is currently being done, with the minor adaptations that are necessary for survival. Goals should reach beyond what is presently being done.

School administrators, accustomed to solving immediate problems and putting out fires, sometimes have difficulty in reaching beyond the current experience to set suitable goals for the school. What is needed, rather than problem-solving behavior, is problem-*finding* behavior. The operative questions are: What needs to be done? What are the problems that need to be solved?

Even then, a danger remains that those involved will define problems for which they have convenient solutions. A systematic goal-setting process is needed.

Generating and Ranking Goals

To generate goals that are truly responsive to the needs of an organization and its environment, goal alternatives must be developed. What follows is a three-step procedure for setting and ranking goals that has been used successfully in a number of school settings. Some modifications to this procedure may be appropriate in some local situations (see Articles 40 and 41).

1. *Select a Team.* Choose a representative team to generate priorities and goals. The team should be large (and heterogeneous) enough to be familiar with the primary forces and the range of problems that affect the school. At the same time it should be small enough for effective discussion. If an existing school supervisory-management team exhibits these characteristics it may be the ideal goal-setting team, since its operating procedures already are established. Some principals may wish to augment this team with teachers and community representatives. A workable team should have 8 to 12 members.

2. *Generate Goal Alternatives.* Each member of the goal-setting team should generate a list of what he or she believes should be the chief goals of the school in the forthcoming academic year. This goal-setting exercise should draw heavily on any needs assessment information collected by the school. Approximately two weeks should be allowed for team members to solicit ideas from other persons in the school organization and the community (including parents), and to develop their listing. The team may wish to consult the professional literature and review what other schools are doing.

After the individual lists of goals have been collected, a subcommittee of three team members should examine and combine them into a consolidated list, eliminating duplications. The subcommittee's task is merely to collate the information, not to make judgments about the respective merits of the goal statements.

3. *Rank Goals by Delphi Technique.* The revised list of goals should be resubmitted to the entire team, with instructions to rank them by a modified Delphi technique in terms of their importance to the school. A sample Delphi procedure is given in Figure 1.

The three-member subcommittee should record the ranks assigned to the goals by each team member and figure an average rating for each goal. The goals should then be distributed to the entire team with the data showing individual team members their personal rankings on the first round and the average team rankings of each goal. Team members consider this information and once again rank the goals.

Figure 1. *Sample Delphi Procedure*

Name _____ Date _____

Directions for Ranking the School's Goals

Step 1. From the accompanying list of 24 goals for our school, select the *nine* goals that you consider to be most important for our operation next year. List the numbers of these nine goals in column C below.

Step 2. From the list of 24 goals, select the *nine* which you consider to be least important. List the numbers of these nine goals in column B.

Step 3. List the numbers of the remaining *six* goals in column IV at the bottom of the sheet.

Step 4. Of the nine goals you've listed in column C, select the *four* you consider to be more important and list these in column D. List the remaining *five* goals from column C in column V.

Step 5. Of the nine goals in column B, select the *four* you consider to be less important and list these in column A. List the remaining *five* goals in column III.

David A. Erlandson is associate professor, educational administration, Texas A & M University, College Station.

Goals for the School

Step 6. Of the four goals in column D, select the most important *one* and list its number in column VII. List the remaining *three* goals from column D in column VI.

Step 7. Of the four goals in column A, select the least important *one* and list it in column I. List the remaining *three* goals from column A in column II.

A	B	C	D
___	___	___	___
___	___	___	___
___	___	___	___
___	___	___	___
	___	___	___
	___	___	___
		___	___
		___	

I	II	III	IV	V	VI	VII
_	__	___	__	__	__	_
	__	___	__	__	__	
	__	___	__	__	__	
		___	__	__		
			__			

Least Important ◀──────▶ Most Important

This two-step Delphi process avoids the hazards of the usual group meeting while retaining its principal benefits. The team members individually generate and rank goals without group pressure, but with written feedback after the first stage.

After the second ranking has been tabulated by the subcommittee and distributed, the team should hold a series of meetings to discuss the relative importance of the various goals and the implications of alternative rankings for the school program. During these meetings, the team can rewrite goals to reduce overlapping and redundancy.

Validating Goals

After the team has settled on a final list of goals, they should be validated by the remainder of the staff, by parents, and/or others. Figure 2 illustrates a relatively quick and efficient way to rank goals with a large number of persons. The example assumes that the original list of 24 goals has been reduced to 19.

These goal-setting procedures may be modified to fit the requirements of a particular situation. The essential features of the process are generation of alternative goals, input from individuals, and group judgment. Principals should note that the procedures take a considerable amount of time if they are executed properly. A principal who wishes to use the process for program planning should wait no later than the beginning of the spring semester preceding a new academic year.

Figure 2. *Goal Ranking Process*

Directions for Goal Ranking

Consider the 19 goal statements listed below in terms of their importance to the operation of our school next year.

You have a total of 48 Xs to distribute among these 19 goals to indicate their relative importance.* You may assign from 0 to 5 Xs to a goal statement. Place the Xs in the boxes that follow the statement. The more Xs you give a statement, the greater importance you assign it. It is not necessary to assign any Xs to a goal statement. You must assign 5 Xs to *at least one* goal statement.

Goals	1	2	3	4	5
Improve the Instructional Program					
Improve the Organizational Climate					
Improve Maintenance and Safety Standards					
Develop Student Pride and Feeling of Self-Worth					
Increase Parental Involvement in School Activities					
Develop Student Understanding and Appreciation of Other Cultures					
Develop Moral Standards of Behavior in Students					
Develop Student Health Habits, etc.					

*NOTE: 48 Xs are provided because there are 19 goals in this exercise and 95 possible spaces (19 x 5). The rule of thumb is to allow half as many Xs as there are spaces, thus providing for considerable variance in sorting out the statements.

Goal Indicators

David A. Erlandson

Goals are established to be achieved, but observable criteria (i.e., indicators of goal achievement) are needed to determine the level of goal achievement. Reasonably precise indicators, such as standardized and criterion-referenced tests, are available for many instructional goals. However, school goals not directly related to instruction have not been the target of much evaluation. These goals often are stated so nebulously and cover so many unrelated activities that they cannot readily be measured. Goal indicators are almost impossible to construct if goals are not clearly stated. Thus, establishing clear goals is the essential prelude to selecting goal indicators.

Generating Initial Goal Indicators

Article 42, "Establishing Goals for the School," recommends that the principal select a team to identify and rank goals. That same team can generate goal indicators and strategies for tracking goal performance.

First, the team should decide which goals will be evaluated. Ideally, it would be useful to set indicators and track performance for all goals. Practically speaking, however, a long list of goals is cumbersome and more difficult to analyze. Initially, keep the number of goals manageable (perhaps 8 to 10). Other goals can always be added to the evaluation list later.

After the goals to be evaluated have been specified, each team member should be given primary and secondary responsibility for at least one goal. Depending on the number of goals and team members, it may be necessary for some individuals to have primary and secondary responsibility for more than one goal. (Avoid this if possible.) When the number of team members is more than the number of goals, two or more persons may have primary responsibility for the same goal. This overlapping responsibility is particularly valuable in the early stages of the process.

Each team member should be asked to develop a list of observable events and behaviors that may be used to judge the performance of the goals. Team members should be given a week or two for this task, and should be encouraged to be creative and to obtain the insights of others in and outside the school organization.

David A. Erlandson is associate professor of educational administration, Texas A & M University, College Station.

Indicators should focus on different aspects of goal performance:

1. The *resources* (inputs) of money, time, materials, and energy allocated to a goal. These indicators assess cost effectiveness. If certain disciplinary procedures are draining excessive amounts of faculty energy from other goals, for example, they may not be justified even if discipline problems are minimized.
2. The *processes* by which goals are accomplished. These indicators promote understanding of why certain results are achieved. They may suggest changes in operation.
3. The observable *products* (outputs) of goal attainment. These indicators are the most objective measures of goal effectiveness.

The following example illustrates goal indicators for a school mathematics program:

Goal: The mathematics program will prepare all students to live in a highly technological society.

A. *Input Indicators* (Resources)
   - Percentage of mathematics teachers with advanced degrees or certain skills
   - Percentage of mathematics teachers competent in the use of the microcomputer
   - Integration of computers and calculators in core mathematics courses
   - Age of instructional materials and textbooks used in mathematics

B. *Process Indicators*
   - Percentage of students, by race and sex, enrolled in mathematics courses
   - Performance objectives written for each course in the mathematics curriculum
   - Application of skills/concepts and problem solving in all mathematics courses
   - Articulation of mathematics with other subjects taught in the school

C. *Output Indicators* (Products)
   - Teacher grade distributions in all mathematics classes
   - Scores on statewide mathematics assessment tests
   - Demonstrated student skills in using microcomputers for basic operations
   - Projects in science fairs and other programs using mathematics as a base or an operation.

Goal Indicators

After the initial lists of goal indicators have been prepared, team members should hold a series of meetings to review, critique, and modify them. These meetings help each team member develop a broad view and become knowledgeable about the data that will be important for measuring performance.

Tracking Goals and Refining Indicators

The team should meet periodically (perhaps every two months or once a quarter) to review goal achievement. Between meetings, each team member should collect data on the primary and secondary goal indicators that he or she is tracking.

- *Summary Sheets.* Data summary sheets should be divided into two columns. The goal indicators assigned to a team member should be listed in the first column. The indicators should include resources supporting the goal, processes used to implement the goal, and products achieved. The team member's observations of what actually occurs should be listed in the second column. Observations should be keyed to the specific indicators whenever possible, but any useful comments about goal performance should be included. The latter information can help in developing additional goal indicators.

- *Data Collection Procedures.* Team members should progressively develop systematic data collection procedures. These procedures should support various ways of looking at the goals. A commercially prepared school climate inventory might be administered to the staff and student body, for example. A series of interviews might follow with key personnel in the school, a schedule of observations be arranged, and a log/journal of observations kept. An outline of faculty, parent, and student perceptions of goal achievement might be developed. Analysis of specific goals should take place from enough points of view to control for individual bias.

Team members who have primary and secondary responsibilities for the same goals should share information on the indicators. Dialog among team members can lead to refinement and broadening of the indicators. At total group meetings, team members with primary responsibility should discuss the indicators and data collected on each goal. Time spent reviewing and critiquing goal indicators and goal achievement is well spent, even if several sessions are required for a single review. The group sessions give greater precision to the goal statements and indicators, and thereby enhance future data collection efforts.

In the largest sense, the process of refining goals and indicators is continual. For some comprehensive goals (i.e., "Improve the Instructional Program") the process literally has no end. For lesser goals, a satisfactory precision may be achieved rapidly. When this occurs, energy can be directed to other goals not on the original list.

Determination of goal indicators and the evaluation of goal performance should never become perfunctory. Done properly, the process can provoke excitement about the mission of the school and create effective alternatives for achieving it.

Subject Area Goals

Robert French

Statutes calling for student achievement standards were enacted by nearly all state legislatures during the late 1970s and early 1980s. Generally these standards focused on reading, writing, and mathematics, and were tied to high school graduation. Seldom was the idea of competency extended to other subject areas or related to specific courses. Competency became nothing more than a testing program that neither represented the total achievements of a school/district nor had much effect on the instructional program.

Subject area goals provide a way to analyze the curriculum, to decide whether the instructional program is on target. Goal setting in the content fields, whether by subject area, individual courses, or specific student competencies, can be a worthwhile staff-student-parent activity and can provide standards for curriculum development.

Most schools or school districts already have a structure for promoting instructional improvement or curriculum development, whether through department chairs, a superintendent's cabinet, a curriculum committee, or a supervisory-management team. This is a good starting point for program development.

The Sequence of Program Development

Defining subject area goals continues a process of program development that starts with articulation of a philosophy of education, and culminates in a set of educational expectations differentiated as learning goals, instructional goals, and achievement goals. Figure 1 outlines this sequence.

The distinctions between philosophy, goals, and expectations must be understood before subject area goals can be developed. Unfortunately, many secondary schools have a plethora of courses that have little to do with the school board-adopted philosophy of education and district educational goals.

Setting Subject Area Goals

Subject area goals are broad statements of expected student competency. Identifying subject area goals

---

Robert French is superintendent, Piedmont Unified School District, Piedmont, Calif.

helps clarify present and future instructional needs. Subject area goals should:

- Be global in nature
- Represent the ultimate skills for the subject in question, regardless of specific course content
- Be general in scope
- Relate to all courses in the subject area
- Contain several subsumable skills
- Be limited in number (usually 3–7)
- Be written as "student will" statements, but without specific standards of achievement
- Be stated clearly so that students and teachers will know what is expected.

Each subject area has unique content, but the process for setting the goals is quite similar. Start by asking this question: What general skills should a student master in completing a course in this subject area? Goals should be general enough to allow each course to contribute to the goal achievement.

One of the most difficult secondary school subject areas in which to develop goals is *science*. Following are some sample subject goals for this content area:

1. The student will demonstrate mastery of the principles of scientific problem solving. From a stated problem the student will be able to:

    - Form an hypothesis
    - Set up a controlled experiment
    - Make observations and organize data into usable form
    - Interpret data and draw conclusions based on the data.

2. The student will demonstrate knowledge of career opportunities in scientific fields, including employment opportunities, benefits, and specific career requirements.

3. The student will identify contributions that science or scientists have made to the world around him or her.

Whether a student takes a course in chemistry, physics, or biology, each with its own specific course of study and objectives, the three subject area goals apply.

Some subject areas may require more specific goals. The first four goals below fit all social studies courses, but goal five refers to a specific course. (This "basic facts" goal could be written for many courses.)

Subject Area Goals

Figure 1. *Sequence of Goal Development*

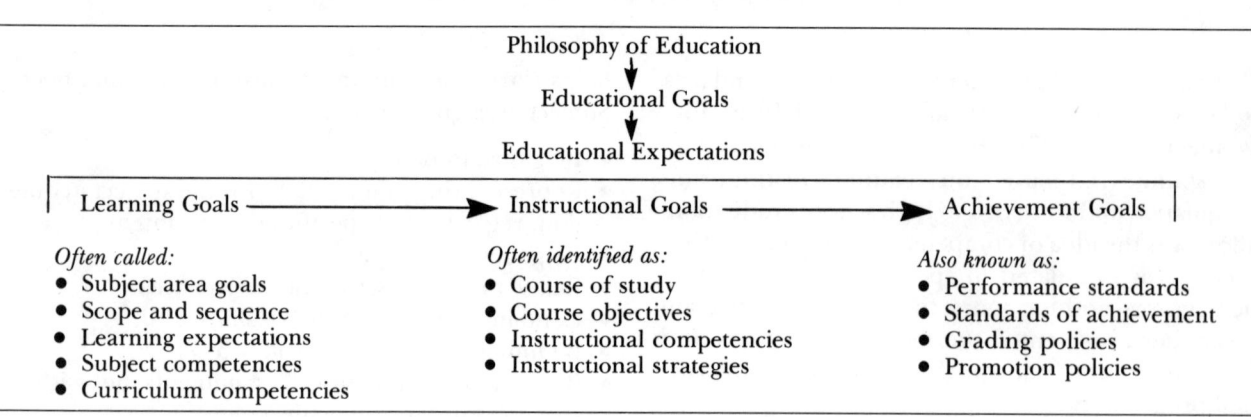

Philosophy of Education
↓
Educational Goals
↓
Educational Expectations

Learning Goals ⟶ Instructional Goals ⟶ Achievement Goals

Often called:
- Subject area goals
- Scope and sequence
- Learning expectations
- Subject competencies
- Curriculum competencies

Often identified as:
- Course of study
- Course objectives
- Instructional competencies
- Instructional strategies

Also known as:
- Performance standards
- Standards of achievement
- Grading policies
- Promotion policies

1. The student will be able to use social studies analytical skills (i.e., distinguish fact from opinion, establish frame of reference, and formulate hypotheses).
2. The student will be able to identify values implicit in social, political, or economic issues.
3. The student will be able to apply specific conceptual schemes to a given situation.
4. The student will be able to analyze social or economic trends using specific social studies concepts (e.g., inflation, using the laws of supply and demand).
5. The student will demonstrate a knowledge of basic facts in United States history and government.

Critiquing the Curriculum

Subject area goals can be used to critique the curriculum (either existing or proposed courses). Develop a grid or matrix listing the goals horizontally and the courses vertically. Determine, in an appropriate group, which goals are met in various courses.

Interesting patterns can arise in this exercise. You may find that one or more of the goals is included in all courses, but that some goals are not treated in any. Should you throw out these goals? Probably not, as long as they are defensible. It is better to modify one or more courses to include them. Are you teaching what you agree is important? Are the scheduled courses the appropriate ones to offer? Are some courses just current fads? And so forth.

After completing a matrix of subject area goals by courses, develop a matrix listing basic skills such as reading, writing, and mathematics against the various subject area courses. Where are you teaching basic skills? Are skills such as main idea, inference, sequence, and vocabulary taught in U.S. history, chemistry, woodshop? If not, why not? Teachers can infuse basic skills into any course once they perceive the vital relationship between philosophy, subject goals, and the related educational expectations.

Student Competencies

Robert E. Blum and Jocelyn A. Butler

State or district competency requirements can effectively establish a schoolwide framework of basic goals for all students in the curriculum content areas. In a more general sense, competency statements give definition to the credit requirements typically associated with high school graduation.

What Is a Competency?

A competency is a statement of an intended student outcome. Competency outcomes have several common elements. They are:

- Generally accepted as desirable for all students.
- Stated in a uniform format: "The student can . . . (verb) . . . (object)." (The student can write a complete sentence. The student can compute the cost of living using local sources of information.)
- Written as applications of knowledge, skills, or attitudes judged necessary to function successfully in adult life.
- Written in clear and concise language so all persons understand the meaning.
- Measurable. Assessments are plausible and practical.

Types of Competencies

Competencies define some degree of student proficiency in knowledge, skills, behaviors, or attitudes.

Knowledge and skill competencies include: school subject skills, outcomes required for successful achievement in typical subject areas such as art, business, and English; basic skills that most people agree are necessary for daily functioning (e.g., reading, writing, computing, decision making); and/or adult life role skills, the ability to apply knowledge, skills, and attitudes to specific adult tasks in everyday life.

Attitude and behavior competencies describe student conduct expected in school, or such factors as willingness to try new tasks, persistence, citizenship, and others. Many attitude/behavior competencies model adult roles in the community.

Robert E. Blum and Jocelyn A. Butler are with the Goal Based Education Program, Northwest Regional Educational Laboratory, Portland, Oreg.

Content of Competencies

Determining the scope of a set of competencies is the first step in competency development. This definition process entails specifying the types of student outcomes that will be included in the competencies.

Several sources can be used to define the content of competencies:

- *Public opinion.* A state legislature or board of education may mandate competencies; the community served by the local school may suggest areas of concern or identify specific competency statements.
- *Existing competencies.* A school or district might adopt the competency framework developed by another system or use that system's competencies as a starting point.
- *Descriptions of life role skills.* A school or district might conceptualize: the different roles of adult life (worker, citizen, consumer); the cognitive, affective, and psychomotor categories of the major taxonomies (i.e., Bloom, Krathwohl); curriculum program areas (English, business, education, science, etc.); the objectives of such national assessment programs as the Adult Performance Level Test, and the National Assessment of Educational Progress.

When general competency categories have been established, specific competencies are developed in each category. Competencies such as "comprehending the main theme in a paragraph" or "writing a compound sentence" or "computing the time interval between two points on a map" are familiar to any principal whose state or district has a minimum competency program. These competencies cut across subject matter lines and are usually evaluated by some type of criterion-referenced test once or twice a year.

The idea of minimum competencies can be extended to include subject matter areas required for a diploma or for credit in a course. A school or district might decide that no student will receive credit in ninth grade English who cannot write a persuasive essay that is free of mechanical errors; or credit in twelfth grade physical education who cannot improve his or her personal time by two minutes in the mile run during a two-month period. This kind of approach takes the mystery out of earning credit, and can bolster parent and community confidence in the schools's operation.

Student Competencies

Some competencies are intended for all students, but special students may require special consideration. Competencies may also reflect the norms and interests of a given school or district.

Writing Competency Statements

Competency statements should be clear and succinct, and follow a consistent format.

The level of generality is always a concern. Specific competency statements communicate the exact nature of what a student is required to do. They make it easier to set standards of achievement and to design instructional activities and materials. On the other hand, general statements allow greater flexibility in performance, making it possible to require the same competencies of all students. Fewer, more general competencies simplify record keeping and are easier to communicate to school board members, parents, and community members. Some trial and error may be necessary to achieve balanced statements that are both clear and equitable.

Competencies typically are presented with other information that relates the competency to instruction, measurement, and instructional management activities and procedures. Information about the courses to which competencies have been assigned, suggested measurement procedures (specific outcome statements), instructional resources and activities, and related instructional goals are usually printed on the same page with the competencies. A uniform format is necessary here to ensure clarity.

Testing for Competence

Methods to check competence must be planned and developed carefully.

- Tests must really measure the desired competence. Skill in "addition and subtraction" is not the same as "balancing a checkbook," even though addition and subtraction are needed to balance a checkbook.
- A variety of measures should be formulated, ranging from paper and pencil tests to performance assessments. The method should suit the competency being measured.
- Measures should have good technical qualities, such as validity and reliability.
- The measures should be practical, not take extraordinary amounts of time and resources, and preferably, be embedded in regular classroom assessments.
- Records of competency attainment should be maintained for each student. Microcomputers can be very helpful in maintaining these records.

Steps in Establishing a Competency-Based Program

Careful planning is essential to the development and implementation of a successful program. The following seven steps outline a process for establishing workable competencies:

1. *Inform people about the effort.* People who know are likely to support and participate.
2. *Collect information.* Plan, prepare instruments, and undertake the data collection activities needed to identify competencies; organize and analyze the collected data.
3. *Draft an initial set of competencies.* Transform the data into a set of simple, easy-to-read competencies.
4. *Validate the competencies.* Have various constituencies review initial competencies to ensure that the statements are clear and include those things that matter.
5. *Prepare a final set of competencies.* Complete the final editing and formatting of the competencies, reflecting the review process. Delete, rewrite, and reorder the statements as necessary.
6. *Communicate the competencies widely.* Inform constituents and other interested parties about the process used to develop competencies and the content of the competency set.
7. *Update competencies periodically.* Competency sets should be reviewed and updated at least every three years.

Performance Standards

James M. Monasmith

In the past, when parents asked, "What are you teaching?" principals and teachers dusted off the latest curriculum guides and showed scope and sequence charts with arrays of objectives. Today's parents are more sophisticated. Products themselves of the electronics age, they often want to probe deeper than the typical curriculum guide permits. They are apt to want answers to the following questions:

- Exactly what is it that my son or daughter must master in each subject at each grade level?
- What are my responsibilities as a parent to assist the school in achieving its goals for my child?
- What evidence do you have that students in this school are mastering basic skills?
- What evidence do you have that students in this school are behaving responsibly?

Implicit in these questions are performance standards for the school.

Concerned parents want to know, in specific terms, what is expected of students. They want standards that challenge learners, and they expect schools to provide evidence of individual and group progress toward these standards.

In Support of Standards

The classic study of teacher expectations for student performance was reported in *Pygmalion in the Classroom* (1968). Rosenthal, a Harvard psychologist and Jacobson, a school principal, found that student achievement scores were related directly to the expectations that teachers had for students. The authors explained their findings in terms of a teacher "self-fulfilling prophecy." Many studies confirm that teacher expectations do indeed affect how they act toward students, and this in turn affects how students achieve.

Among the more salient findings are these:

- Teachers demand less of students who are not expected to perform well
- Time-consuming but effective teaching methods are used less frequently with students not expected to achieve

James M. Monasmith is principal, Colville High School, Colville, Wash.

- Students not expected to achieve well receive less feedback on the questions they ask
- Higher level comprehension questions are less likely to be asked of these students
- "Wait time" after questions is shorter when teachers expect less
- More criticism is directed at students when expectations are low
- Students expected to achieve well receive more praise.

These findings represent only a part of the research (1968–1973), but the trend is clear. How teachers perceive their students influences how they act toward them. More recently, Rutter et al. (1979), in a study of inner-city London, England, schools found that higher achievement was associated with higher expectations for students. Other studies in the United States (Austin, 1979; Brookover and Lezotte, 1979; Edmonds, 1979) reveal that effective schools have a sense of purpose and convey that purpose to the students. In these effective schools, students tend to achieve more because more is expected of them.

Setting Higher Standards in the Classroom

The most practical way to foster high expectations in the classroom is to develop performance standards for each subject. Criteria must be spelled out in advance so that students and parents can know what is expected. One state recently passed legislation that mandates performance standards in all high school courses by July 1, 1985. Rather than wait for the legislature or parent action groups to press the issue for performance standards, principals can work with teachers to develop local expectations for each course.

Most principals are familiar with standard course descriptions. The performance approach carries the description a step further and sets a level of expected performance for students to earn credit. Performance indicators outline the behaviors necessary for competence.

Teachers in district or school teams write the performance indicators using criterion-referenced assessment strategies. Performance indicators close the loop that started with development of the district/school philosophy. (See Figure 1)

Performance Standards

Figure 1. *Development of Performance Standards*

District/School Philosophy
↓
Educational Goals
↓
Student Competencies
↓
Performance Indicators

Some samples may be helpful:

Competencies
- Ability to write letters for practical purposes.

- Capability of developing and implementing a personal health and fitness plan.

Indicators
The student writes a letter ordering a product advertised in a newspaper. The letter is rated on clarity, format, spelling, punctuation, and grammar.
Develop a personal health and fitness plan; participate in planned activities for one quarter; collect various measures (e.g., weight, endurance, strength) as determined by the instructor; review progress with the instructor.

Sensitizing Staff

Making performance standards explicit and holding students accountable for learning can have a profound impact on student achievement. What seems like a perfectly good idea for most students, however, can result in harsh treatment for some. Learning is a highly personal matter. Higher expectations must be tempered by good sense, careful judgment, and appropriate decision making. It is simplistic to think that higher standards mean higher performance for all students.

An important role of the principal is systematically sensitizing teachers to the meaning of higher standards and expectations:

1. Have teachers observe their students in other teachers' classrooms (especially those not doing well). There is no more compelling message than to see a student doing well in another setting. Usually the teacher leaves the observation trying to think of ways to help the student achieve in his or her own classroom.
2. Share research findings on expectations. Publish the findings in the daily or weekly bulletin, discuss them at faculty meetings, talk about them in one-to-one conferences.
3. Help teachers understand that failure can be combatted. Manipulate time constraints to allow teachers to work more with students who do not achieve as well. "Problem" students may require reteaching or more personalized methods of instruction.
4. Organize the curriculum so that students are not confused by inconsistencies. Expectations should be the same in similar areas of the program.

References

Austin, G. R. An analysis of exemplary schools and their distinguishing characteristics. Paper presented at the meeting of the American Educational Research Association, San Francisco, April 1979.

Brookover, W. B. and Lezotte, L. *Changes in School Characteristics Coincident with Changes in Student Achievement.* East Lansing: Institute for Research on Teaching, Michigan State University, 1979.

Edmonds, R. Effective schools for the urban poor, *Educational Leadership*, 1979, 37, 15–27 (a).

Rosenthal, R. and Jacobson, F. *Pygmalion in the Classroom: Teacher Expectations and Pupils' Intellectual Development.* New York: Holt, 1968.

Rutter, M., Maughan, B., Mortimer, P., Ouston, J., and Smith, A. *Fifteen Thousand Hours: Secondary Schools and their Effect on Children.* Cambridge, Mass: Harvard University Press, 1979.

School Improvement Plans

Fred W. Skoglund

A program improvement plan (PIP) is a structured process having specific short and long-term goals and objectives that focus on the improvement of instruction. Review and evaluation plans are established to share ideas and evaluate the results.

Without a structured plan for improvement, schools find it difficult to develop a sense of purpose and direction. A fair and consistent improvement plan promotes good school climate, increased opportunities for teacher professional development and student educational growth, and more effective evaluation.

Ownership, simplicity, consistency, and inherent value are the foundations of a successful improvement plan. How a school responds to a set of objectives and goals depends on the behavior of the administration. Writing about management in *Theory Z*, Ouchi (1981) states:

> The basis of Theory Z approach to management is quite simply that involved workers are the key to increased productivity.... The first lesson of Theory Z is trust. Productivity and trust go hand in hand.

Formulating the Plan

Develop a PIP packet for each teacher, containing:

- School/district philosophy, goals, and learner priorities.
- Three planning forms.

1. *General School Goal:* Ask teachers to complete Planning Form I about the major focus of the school for the year, such as, "an increase in student literacy skills." Determine by consensus the general goal for the year.

2. *Specific Curriculum Objectives.* Every year, each teacher team or department should target specific areas for improvement that are concerned with student outcomes. Have teachers complete Planning Form II, focusing on the newly chosen general goal for the year.

Fred W. Skoglund is principal, Thunderbird High School, Phoenix, Ariz.

3. *Personal Improvement Objectives.* Professional growth, classroom discipline, methods of instruction, and other outcomes of teacher activity should be targeted and assessed using the district/school performance appraisal form. These objectives should be incorporated into the teacher's formal performance evaluation.

Name: _____

Department: _____

Planning Form I

GENERAL SCHOOL GOAL

1. State below the 1984 goal for _____ _____ School.

2. State, in terms of teacher activities, what will be done to achieve the goal.

3. What will be offered as evidence of the effort extended to accomplish this goal?

Name: _____

Department: _____

Planning Form II

SPECIFIC CURRICULUM OBJECTIVES

1. What area(s) of the curriculum will receive emphasis this year?

2. What student outcomes will be targeted for improvement? (Write behavioral objectives for these target areas.)

3. What teaching strategies will be used to accomplish the targeted objectives?

4. What will be accepted as evidence of successful performance and how will it be measured?

School Improvement Plans

Orientation, Implementation, and Feedback

Hold a faculty orientation meeting to review the school philosophy and goals, introduce and discuss the PIP packet, and present a rationale for implementing the improvement plan. Allow department or curricular teams to meet to discuss possible general goals, to develop related curriculum objectives, and to share ideas for personal improvement.

After the department or subject area meetings, each teacher should complete the three planning forms and submit them to the principal. The principal should assign each supervisory-management team member to work with several departments. The administrative team as a group should review the reports to get an overview, and then meet separately with assigned departments.

PIP progress reports should be a regular part of all meeting agendas. During departmental and department chair meetings, individual and group "success stories" can offer positive reinforcement. The administrative team should discuss PIP progress reports at its regular meetings. This process allows all administrators and department chairs to exercise instructional leadership, reviewing plans in progress, encouraging success or improvement, and providing assistance as needed.

Principals should monitor teacher efforts, measure the rate and effectiveness of improvement, and demonstrate a sincere interest in the processes being used. It is good practice to report to the faculty on a regular basis about overall progress in meeting the general school goal for the year.

Conduct an orientation at the beginning of each new school year to review the philosophy, modify the improvement plan if necessary, share success stories from the previous year, and encourage teachers to continue their commitment to instructional and program improvement.

Reference

Ouchi, William G. *Theory Z*. Reading, Mass.: Addison-Wesley, 1981.

Staff, District, and Community Support

Arthur W. Steller

Exemplary high schools have a common commitment to developing standards and objectives that are responsive to staff interests and community goals and that are visible to all concerned. In successful schools, parents and other community members know what the school believes to be instructionally important because they have helped with its determination. Students know what they are expected to learn because teachers make their expectations clear.

Central office staff need a clear idea of what resources and help are needed. Both district and school-based personnel need benchmarks to judge effectiveness.

Effective schools research cites strong leadership at the school level as the most consistent characteristic of outstanding schools. Principals interested in legitimizing their role as instructional leaders must generate staff, central office, and community support. The ability to orchestrate forces in the community and the school is essential to any real instructional improvement.

Working with Staff

Principals should develop strategies that encourage and sustain staff ownership of the school program.

1. Release teachers from noninstructional supervision. Hall, bus, and cafeteria duty can be handled by others with less training. The time saved can be used for instructional improvement.
2. Do not try to treat all teachers equally. Some teachers, by virtue of their ability and experience, should have more to say about what happens in the school.
3. Get out of the office and on the "front lines" with the other teachers. As principal teacher, you should be the model. Teach a class, meet with students, be visible on the campus, serve as a teacher adviser.

Arthur W. Steller is superintendent, Mercer County Public Schools, Princeton, W. Va.

4. Emphasize teaching and learning. Listen to what teachers have to say about class loads and the other conditions of teaching.
5. Encourage faculty preparation in goal setting, planning, evaluation, and decision making. Create the organizational structures that make teachers your colleagues in a learning community (e.g., collaborative staff planning; goal-oriented faculty meetings).
6. Give recognition to faculty members for their accomplishments. Let them know that you appreciate what they have done and are doing.

Working with District Personnel

Each school is a part of a total school system. School autonomy within the system may differ depending on the amount of central control required by district philosophy or by supervisory personnel. The actual degree of autonomy usually flows from the perceived competence of the principal and program success as measured by the performance of students.

Principals can both enhance district relationships and help their schools achieve their goals.

1. Pursue instructional improvement goals within a context that recognizes district concerns. Drawing support from the district is far easier when school goals correspond with system directions.
2. Keep school district personnel informed about what the school is doing instructionally. Once or twice a year, invite board members, the superintendent, and other district staff to a special review of school programs. Involving teachers, students, and parents during these visits tends to strengthen commitments to the school.
3. Invite district staff to assist in the improvement efforts. Encourage school personnel to serve on district committees and task forces and establish regular channels of communication with them.
4. Utilize the services of district supervisory personnel to assist individual teachers who may be having difficulty, to serve as consultants for curriculum writing teams in the school, or to assist in planning and executing staff development activities.

Staff, District, and Community Support

Working with the Community

Parents have a vested interest in the quality of the school's instructional program, but so do others in the community. Parents should be involved in identifying school priorities and in supporting the instructional program. Other community members can be invited to participate on school committees or task forces.

Some specific suggestions for enlisting community support are as follows:

- Ensure that citizens advisory committees and other parent support groups are representative groups.
- Prepare an annual report on instructional goals and progress for distribution to parents and community. These reports should be attractive, short, concise, and written in readable style.
- Establish a school-based speakers' bureau of teachers, support staff, and students to present the school's accomplishments. A one-page flier giving the presenter's name, position, and topic should be mailed to civic groups.
- Open the schools to visitors on a "come when you can" basis. Show that you have nothing to hide—that you are open to constructive criticism as well as to praise.
- Invite the public to join the instructional team. Cooperative education programs have long served schools and appear to be on the increase; mentorships are increasing as ways to challenge able and motivated students; tutorials benefit students who need the undivided attention of an adult for 30 to 60 minutes at a time.

Budgeting for Instructional Improvement

James R. Larson

While many of the current calls for excellence have large price tags, financial support continues to be in limited supply. Because principals seldom have much to do with increasing district revenues, the chief priority is clear: Making the existing budget work for program improvement.

Leadership during a period of declining resources is more difficult than during a time of growth. Attention must be paid to the pitfalls associated with operating on less:

Trap 1: Considering the budget as just an accounting system. A budget is not a list of expenditures; it is a catalog of priorities and an invaluable aid to decision making. The building budget is one of the best ways to communicate to the public what you and your staff consider important.

Trap 2: Thinking that budgeting has a beginning and an end. The process really never stops: planning and allocations, consideration of priorities, a "final" plan, administration and coordination, review and appraisal. Budgeting is not a once-a-year task.

Trap 3: Funding old priorities with new money. Some things cannot be done now, given the financial resources. Do not tie up a large portion of your limited funds year after year in projects that are no longer realistic. Declining resources should alter priorities.

Trap 4: Figuring automatic (percentage) increases for all of your departments. Incremental budgeting is a trap. This "no decision" method assumes that your budget was perfect last year, that all programs grow at the same rate, and that all are of equal value. Automatic increases tend to perpetuate old priorities.

Trap 5: Asking for twice as much and hoping for half. This old game is self-defeating. Require your department heads to plan their needs as small pieces of the whole, with back-up information. To request exactly what you need and in priority order requires faith that the superintendent or board will not cut everything in half. Assign a priority number to all of your budgetary requests: 1 = "an absolute must for our program"; 2 = "this will keep us going another year as is"; or 3 = "when our ship comes in."

Trap 6: Being imprecise in your budgeting directions. Open-ended directions such as "What do you need for next year?" can result in unsatisfactory results. Teachers have in mind some new classroom space; you give them some new textbooks. Obviously, this leads to disappointment, frustration, and feelings of lack of support.

Trap 7: Keeping the process to yourself. If you feel that budgeting is some dark, mysterious process that requires an administrative certificate, everyone is in trouble. Budget making must be open and everyone must understand the timeline and the process.

Trap 8: Answering requests for funds with vague truisms. Some projects or ideas should never be funded, even if money is available. Some are bad, some are unworkable, and some are simply not needed. If you consistently respond to requests with a "lack of resources" answer, teachers will stop, or at least slow down, their dreaming and planning. Staff members deserve a reasonable assessment of a project's chances for success; an honest evaluation of their ideas, not stock answers.

Trap 9: Using "soft" money for "hard" items. A "hard" item is a budget item that will always be with you. "Soft" money comes and goes. A rule of thumb: If you cannot do without it, do not support it with disappearing funds.

Trap 10: Implementing outside (mandated) projects with inside funds. Insist that state or district mandates (e.g., new graduation requirements) include supporting funds for curriculum planning, staff development, and start-up materials. Do the same thing for new programs at the building level. Support what you think is important with continuing funds.

The Possibilities

The other side of the budgetary coin offers things that can be done to make the most of a less than perfect fiscal environment.

- *View the budget as a statement of educational priorities.* The budget makes public what school personnel be-

---

James R. Larson is assistant superintendent/instruction, Sylvania City Schools, Sylvania, Ohio.

Budgeting for Instructional Improvement

lieve to be important. Develop the budget as a set of instructional objectives.

- *Invest in long-range programs for school improvement.* If the school budget is a reflection of instructional planning it should acknowledge the value of research and development and provide incentives. The budget should support more than the day-to-day, year-to-year program. Program improvement commitments are investments in long-term gains. Take the risk. Offer teachers grants. Remodel instructional areas. Set up planning groups and task forces.

- *Establish a contingency fund.* No matter how many times you prepare a school budget, you undoubtedly overlook something. Emergency requests arise: unplanned or unanticipated expenses, and just plain not-to-be-missed opportunities. Save something. You never know when you might need to support a teacher's attendance at a summer workshop, publish an anthology of student writing, or purchase a new piece of computer software.

- *Be knowledgeable about national, state, and district financial trends.* Stay up-to-date on new budget issues and sources of funding. Federal and state programs sometimes bury dollars in obscure places. Read the fine print of current legislation and ask questions.

- *Look for ways to expand your budget base.* Grants money from public agencies and private foundations has decreased over the past two decades, but it has not evaporated. Evidence exists that some areas are staging a comeback. Ask for help from district personnel who are knowledgeable about outside funding sources. The Carnegie Foundation, for example, is interested in learning styles projects at the secondary level. The National Science Foundation wants to improve student achievement in science and mathematics.

Budgeting for program improvement is one of the principal's most important instructional responsibilities. No school improvement plan can be successful without careful and systematic commitment to this task.

IMPLEMENTATION ELEMENTS

Organizing the Program

Selecting Staff

John M. Jenkins

With fewer able young people being attracted to teaching and with the attrition of qualified women and minorities from the profession, the need for effective teacher selection methods is especially acute. Probably no other decision a principal makes is more important than the selection of teachers. An old maxim reminds us that when good teachers are selected, school problems are reduced, if not eliminated.

The manner in which positions are announced and the procedures for screening and interviewing are particularly important, and there is a growing need to look beyond the teacher education institutions for candidates, even if only for partial assignment.

Getting Started

1. *Know what you want.* The principal must be clear about the nature of a position, the job expectations, and any special qualities required of applicants. Knowing what you want is crucial to the final selection process. Committing one's thoughts to writing and then sharing them with significant others in the school helps with this process. Remember: clarity is contagious.

2. *Communicate your needs to others.* In most large school systems, advertising for a position is managed by central office personnel. The principal must provide information about the vacancy and the unique qualities, if any, of the person who is sought. This process is even more important if the personnel office will screen the first wave of applicants. Remember: No one knows the needs of your school better than you, despite the amount of experience personnel workers have in the selection process.

3. *Attracting appropriate candidates.* The wise principal builds the school's image as a good place to work and learn. How prospective teachers view a school may determine the number and quality of applicants who apply. Maintain an active file of applicants at the school level. Review their applications periodically, and request updated information as appropriate. When a vacancy exists, you can contact any promising applicants and suggest they apply through the district personnel office. Remember: Good schools have a way of attracting the better teachers, and good schools don't happen by accident.

Information Gathering

The literature notes a number of characteristics of effective teachers that contribute to their effectiveness. Experienced principals can intuitively validate such qualities as competency in one's teaching field, good judgment, a sense of responsibility, variable teaching skills, organizational ability, a sense of humor, ability to work well with students and parents, a wide array of interests, and good physical and mental health. Gathering information from which to make judgments on each of these dimensions is not always easy, but some strategies enhance the process:

- Ask each applicant to submit a written statement of philosophy as part of or as a supplement to the application. The written statement should contain ideas, beliefs, and values related to education. Each assertion should be supported with appropriate evidence. This written statement provides information about the applicant's ability to organize thoughts and to think and communicate in writing (as well as the ability to spell, punctuate, and use good syntax).

- Review transcripts and credentials for each of the applicants. Give particular attention to overall GPA and to grades in the academic major. Inspect the transcript for the applicant's depth of study in a particular subject field. An applicant may have earned good grades but completed a less rigorous curriculum.

- Check for academic awards received at college or university. Honor graduates in particular have demonstrated exceptional ability to perform in an academic setting. Given an acceptable personality, these persons can serve as excellent models for students, and probably will adjust well to the myriad contingencies of teaching.

- Make direct contact with the candidate's personal and professional references. Telephone the references of applicants you wish to consider seriously. Conversing with such persons enables you to ask specific questions about the applicant's judgment, problem-solving ability, and sense of responsibility.

John M. Jenkins is director of the P. K. Yonge Laboratory School, University of Florida, Gainesville.

Selecting Staff

The Interview

1. Establish a school screening committee for each vacancy to reduce the number of applicants to be interviewed. Even if a similar procedure is used at the district office, it is still helpful at the building level. The committee should include staff members with a vested interest in ensuring that an appropriate candidate is chosen. Some schools also involve parents and students.
2. Whether the applicants are interviewed initially by a committee or directly by the principal, the interview can provide an opportunity to learn much about various traits:
   - *Dress and appearance* are clues to good sense and modeling potential for students.
   - *Distracting mannerisms* can be observed.
   - *Ability to communicate orally* can readily be assessed.
   - *Ability to think on one's feet* can be weighed by posing challenging and divergent questions.
3. Interviews should be structured to begin with easier questions and progress to more challenging ones. Start, for example, with "Tell me something about yourself—your interests, leisure time activities, and professional goals." As the interview proceeds, questions about specific classroom situations and knowledge of educational trends can uncover the applicant's ability to explain his or her pedagogical knowledge base.
4. Use the interview to measure the candidate's enthusiasm for joining the faculty. Your second or third selections may be candidates for future vacancies.
5. All persons who apply for a position have a right to know the final outcome. Each unsuccessful candidate should receive a communication from the principal. Word processing equipment now allows us to communicate quickly and efficiently, without stereotypic form letters and even with a personal note or two for applicants you wish to consider for future openings.
6. Contact the successful candidate immediately, and personally when possible. Good candidates may be in line for several positions. You do not want to lose your first choice because you failed to make the first offer.

Some Promising Trends in Staffing

Recent reports on the status of high school education signal the need for more cooperative endeavors between education and the private sector. Business and industry can assist schools by providing temporary or part-time personnel to fill vacancies where available candidates are in short supply.

Three practices are prominent in the literature:

- With fewer qualified applicants in mathematics and science, some states are relaxing certification requirements to allow the employment of adjunct teachers from business and industry.
- The endowed chair is a practice from higher education that has promise for public and private secondary schools. An electronics firm might endow a chair in science; a computer company, a chair in mathematics; a parent support group, a chair in any area critical to a local school.
- Independent research projects are attractive to some high school students. Volunteers from the community might work with these students on a one-to-one basis to extend the resources of the school.

Scheduling the School

Henry R. Traverso

Scheduling is an important vehicle for implementing a school's philosophy and objectives. While the scheduling choices are numerous, a variety of tested models are documented in the literature on secondary school administration and can be seen in operation in schools.

Dealing with the Basics

Decision making about scheduling involves an understanding and consideration of a number of restrictive factors. Regardless of the local philosophy of education or the degree of budgetary flexibility, scheduling constraints will exist and must be identified and accommodated.

Among the restrictive elements principals must include in schedule planning are:

- State and local regulations (length of school day and year, minutes per subject per week, etc.);
- Graduation requirements, including the number of required versus elective courses;
- Student course-load patterns (minimum and maximum number of courses taken each semester or year);
- Length of courses—whether quarter, trimester, semester, or year-long;
- Period or program modifications, including double periods for laboratory courses, early release for work study or other vocational experiences;
- Variable staff assignments (reduced classroom loads for department heads, work study supervisors, etc.);
- School plant limitations (overcrowded enrollment, lack of general purpose rooms, specialized room usage);
- Staffing impact from declining enrollments (increase in dual-subject teaching assignments);
- Negotiated teacher contract arrangements (total number of classes and preparations that can be assigned to teachers).

Choosing the Right Fit

When principals have identified the variables described above, specific choices can be made, in consultation with the total school community, about a number of scheduling options:

Henry R. Traverso is director of curriculum, Regional School District #10, Burlington, Conn.

- Periods in the school day—possibilities range from 4 to 40
- Days in the cycle—from the usual 5 or 6 to 10 (See *NASSP Bulletin,* December 1980, pp. 87–91)
- House plans—school-within-a-school concept, as old as this century
- Schools without walls—the use of facilities in the community
- Scheduling models—conventional schedules, flexible modular schedules, and their many variations. (See Figures 1 and 2.)

Figure 1. *Traditional Schedule*

	Monday	Tuesday	Wednesday	Thursday	Friday
1	A	A	A	A	A
2	B	B	B	B	B
3	C	C	C	C	C
4	D	D	D	D	D
5	E	E	E	E	E
6	F	F	F	F	F
7	G	G	G	G	G

These topics may not be familiar to all teachers, and the principal may need to provide some inservice training before implementation can begin.

Choices at the Buffet

Throughout the history of secondary education, administrators have modified the school schedule. From the "schedule of recitations" of colonial days to the flexible-modular alternatives of recent vintage, countless efforts have been made to devise appropriate schedules to match the instructional objectives of schools. If the periodic introduction of new scheduling models is indicative of either dissatisfaction or progress, then someone has yet to invent the "perfect" schedule.

A variety of schedule models are explained in the NASSP publication, *Scheduling the Secondary School* (Dempsey and Traverso, 1983), including: conventional, conventional modular, flexible period, flexible-modular, rotating, block, fluid block, pontoon-transitional, daily demand, and individualized. The monograph also gives detailed instructions in schedule building and conflict matrix preparation.

Scheduling the School

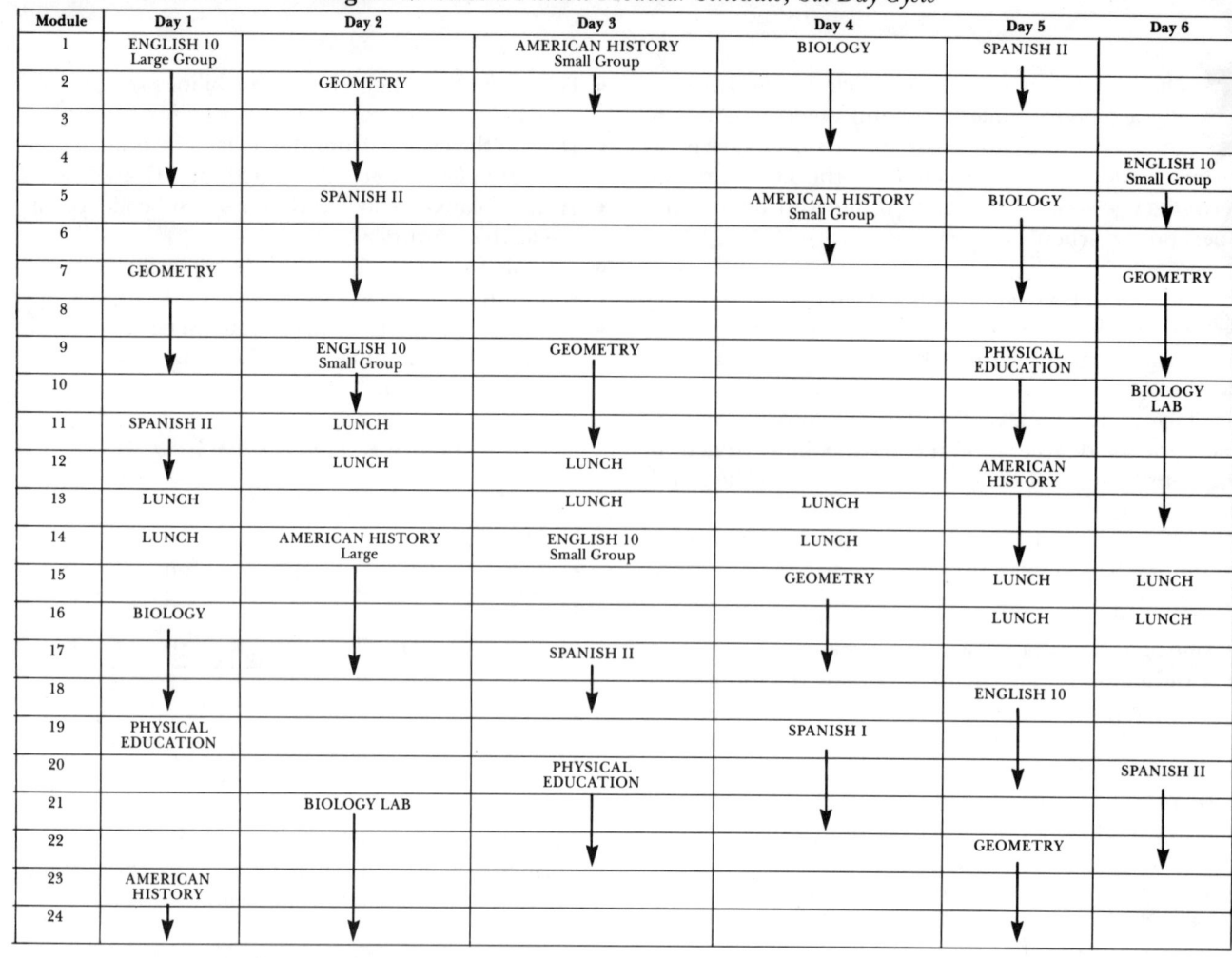

Figure 2. *Student Flexible Modular Schedule; Six-Day Cycle*

Module	Day 1	Day 2	Day 3	Day 4	Day 5	Day 6
1	ENGLISH 10 Large Group		AMERICAN HISTORY Small Group	BIOLOGY	SPANISH II	
2	↓	GEOMETRY	↓	↓	↓	
3	↓	↓			↓	
4	↓	↓			↓	ENGLISH 10 Small Group
5		SPANISH II		AMERICAN HISTORY Small Group	BIOLOGY	↓
6		↓		↓	↓	
7	GEOMETRY	↓		↓	↓	GEOMETRY
8	↓					↓
9	↓	ENGLISH 10 Small Group	GEOMETRY		PHYSICAL EDUCATION	↓
10	↓	↓				BIOLOGY LAB
11	SPANISH II	LUNCH				↓
12	↓	LUNCH	LUNCH		AMERICAN HISTORY	↓
13	LUNCH		LUNCH	LUNCH	↓	↓
14	LUNCH	AMERICAN HISTORY Large	ENGLISH 10 Small Group	LUNCH	↓	↓
15		↓	↓	GEOMETRY	LUNCH	LUNCH
16	BIOLOGY	↓	↓	↓	LUNCH	LUNCH
17	↓	↓	SPANISH II	↓	↓	
18	↓	↓	↓	↓	ENGLISH 10	
19	PHYSICAL EDUCATION			SPANISH I	↓	
20	↓		PHYSICAL EDUCATION	↓	↓	SPANISH II
21		BIOLOGY LAB	↓	↓	↓	↓
22		↓	↓	↓	GEOMETRY	↓
23	AMERICAN HISTORY				↓	
24	↓	↓			↓	

Process Selections

The rapid progress of technology makes it difficult to predict with any precision the future methodologies that will be available for performing the two essential tasks of scheduling: constructing a master schedule, and preparing individual student schedules. Diminishing costs of hardware and software, as well as the miniaturization of the equipment, suggest that most scheduling in the near future may be accomplished at the administrator's desk with a microcomputer. Even if large computers are employed at the district office or through a service bureau for conflict matrices or schedule printing, entry of data and the updating of individual schedules likely will be processed at a terminal in the school office.

Additional Resources

Since the turn of the century, only a handful of books have been written which deal exclusively with the entire spectrum of secondary school scheduling. Some books written in the '60s and '70s provide well-documented and highly descriptive accounts of flexible-modular scheduling incorporating variable cycles, team teaching, large and small-group instruction, and independent study. Principals who have not had formal experience in scheduling need only look to the *NASSP Bulletin* and the scheduling monograph to fill whatever gap exists in their training. Several computer-related magazines regularly report on available software for scheduling and other administrative purposes.

Reference

Dempsey, Richard A., and Traverso, Henry P. *Scheduling the Secondary School.* Reston, Va.: NASSP, 1983.

Staff Development/Inservice

Joseph F. Rogus and Elizabeth Shaw

Teacher openness to instructional improvement is related directly to the school's commitment to organizational improvement. If the school administration is committed to accomplishing its educational goals and to improving the quality of life for the school staff, then instructional improvement efforts will have a healthy chance of being effective. Because of the close relationship between individual and organizational strength, the concepts of staff development, inservice, and organizational development must be viewed as a group.

Staff development is first and foremost an attitude, a commitment to help individuals grow personally and professionally in a supportive climate. Staff development involves a broad range of activities designed to promote staff self-renewal and, indirectly, more effective learning for youngsters. Staff development activities are long-range in orientation and place the individual staff member at the heart of the growth planning process.

Inservice is one activity, or a series of planned program activities, designed and carried out to promote participant competence. Inservice activities are short-range in orientation; i.e., they occur at a specific place and time, and, to enhance the probability of success, they usually involve participants in the planning process.

Organizational development is a change strategy to improve organizational effectiveness. It is a systematic process for improving the ways in which an organization or institution functions and is managed, especially in response to change. It involves the entire staff in the identification of group goals, the development of group skills, the appropriate restructuring of the organization, and the evaluation of the results. Organizational development addresses itself to improving communication skills, developing mutual working relationships, and making useful structural changes in the organization.

The attitude brought by staff members to all these programs is colored by how positively they view themselves. This self-perception, in turn, is conditioned by the extent to which a "development" attitude permeates the day-to-day operation of the building. In essence, maximum productivity and satisfaction are dependent on positive growth both in individuals and the organization itself. Fortunately, processes exist which foster such growth. The challenge to the principal is to internalize and project a growth perspective, and to instill this spirit in the activities associated with staff and organizational development.

The following sections contain several suggestions for strengthening staff development, inservice programming, and organizational development activity. While each subsection is treated separately, it is important to emphasize that the different sets of activities would be integrated in time in order to facilitate both individual and organizational growth.

Helpful Steps for Informal Staff Development

A spirit of staff development begins with the day-to-day routines that affect the individual's perspective toward self and the organization. The following starter questions are a useful way to assess administrative behavior in a given school:

- Are teachers greeted as they come to work each day?
- Are staff involved in the decision-making process on problems of importance to them?
- Are administrators available to talk with staff at convenient times?
- Do staff meet socially on a regular basis?
- Are teachers rewarded for positive performance?
- When criticism is appropriate, is it offered constructively?
- Is on-site assistance provided when staff need it?
- Are administrative staff members engaged in furthering their own growth?
- Are staff responsibilities fairly distributed?

A positive response to these items simply assures that staff are personally valued and provided a positive climate in which to pursue their personal growth. How a person views him/herself as a result of daily interactions strongly influences the predisposition he/she brings to formal staff development, and in particular, to specific efforts at fostering instructional improvement.

Helpful Steps for Formal Staff Development

Formal staff development requires at least three commitments from the principal: to state in policy and administrative regulations the commitment of the or-

Joseph F. Rogus is professor of education and Elizabeth Shaw is administrative assistant in the Department of Educational Administration, University of Dayton, Ohio.

Staff Development/Inservice

ganization to staff development; to set aside funds for staff development programming (even if the amount is small, establishing a real budget is a significant symbol of commitment); and to involve staff in program planning.

Staff participation is crucial to both individual and organizational growth. By sharing power in the planning process, administrators are saying that accountability will be collegial. No one is going to "do it" to anyone. Historically, much staff development, and particularly inservice programming, has been remedial in character and geared (as teachers view it) to giving answers to questions "no one asked." Ownership in the planning process is absolutely essential to establishing a collaborative thrust.

Formal staff development activity can take many forms:

- Curriculum development and evaluation
- Individual-personal growth planning (a job-target approach apart from the formal assessment process)
- Conference participation
- Informal conferencing with other teachers
- Peer clinical supervision activity
- Faculty inquiry into significant school problems
- Joint problem solving
- Inservice programming.

These activities take on a staff development character only if a commitment exists to assist individuals to grow while organizational goals are addressed.

Helpful Steps for Inservice

Inservice is one of the many types of staff development that warrants special note because so much time and energy are spent in organizing it, frequently with minimum impact. Inservice efforts are more likely to be effective if they are conducted in a positive climate, involve staff in the planning, and deal with needs perceived by the staff to be important.

For effective inservice programs, the following factors, at minimum, need attention:

- Program objectives should be clearly stated and disseminated to participants.
- Planned activities should be congruent with stated program outcomes.
- Planned activities should have a "learning by doing" emphasis.
- Staff must understand how inservice fits the big picture.
- If the purpose is to develop new skills or refine existing skills, provision must be made for staff to:
  —Observe the modeling of the desired skills
  —Practice the skills with peers
  —Receive feedback
  —Obtain coaching of the desired behavior in the classroom.
- Data must be collected on whether session objectives have been achieved, and whether staff have found the session worthwhile.
- The learning setting must be comfortable.
- Participants must receive reinforcement for participation.
- Follow-up arrangements must be clear to participants.

Organizational Development

The concepts of staff development, inservice, and organizational development are interrelated. Organizational development cannot occur apart from a staff development perspective, and inservice is an important part of that perspective. While staff development generally emphasizes maintenance programming, personal enhancement, and program institutionalization (all important components of organizational development), organizational development itself has the distinctive function of defining and addressing improvement outcomes for the organization while making it possible for individuals to meet their personal and professional objectives. The organizational improvement function implies the need for staff to be competent and self-assured in their own right and to understand and contribute to mutually acceptable organizational outcomes.

Activities which are effective in enhancing organizational (as well as individual) growth include:

- Establishing clear, two-way, open communications.
- Building trust and understanding by creating close, personal communication so that hidden agendas and painful feelings can be dealt with openly.
- Involving as many persons within the organization in decision making as practicable, particularly for outcomes that are directly relevant to them.
- Encouraging information sharing.
- Helping groups identify problems that confront them and developing collaborative plans for addressing those problems.
- Helping groups analyze their own group behaviors.
- Valuing problem identification behavior and helping groups develop/refine procedures for bringing conflict into the open.

School Learning Climate

Lawrence W. Lezotte

Schools, complex, goal-oriented organizations, can be productive and satisfying places for those who are associated with them. For this to occur, however, a number of factors must be present. Two emerge as essential: a positive school learning climate, and a principal who influences the establishment and maintenance of such a climate.

Recent studies of schools that are effective in teaching basic skills provide valuable information about what constitutes a positive school learning climate. The studies also describe effective practices employed by principals of those schools.

Defining School Learning Climate

Effective schools research uses the term "school climate" in a specific sense. "Climate" frequently has been associated with physical attributes of the school environment (e.g., temperature, lighting, noise level), or characterized as the level of satisfaction in the school or classroom (e.g., morale, trust, openness, cooperation).

Effective schools research relates climate to productivity (that is, a businesslike atmosphere, commitment to achievement of goals and to student engagement in academic tasks). Because of this specialized focus, researchers use the term "school learning climate," rather than school climate. The addition of the word "learning" centers attention on those aspects of climate that are related to the productivity levels of the school.

In this context, school learning climate is defined as the norms, beliefs, and attitudes reflected in the school's institutional patterns, and behavioral practices that enhance or impede student achievement.

The Role of the Principal

■ *The Mission of the School.* One of the primary responsibilities of the principal is to communicate the school's mission and curricular priorities to teachers, students, and parents. The principal must answer the question: "What *is* the role and function of a school in our society?" In effective schools, the answer includes these beliefs:

- Schools exist primarily for the purpose of teaching and learning
- A core body of knowledge or set of skills exists which the school cares about more than anything else
- The staff is willing to be held accountable for teaching these essential skills.

As the instructional leader of the school, the principal must ensure that the school's mission is widely known, well understood, and (ideally) accepted by all who work in the school.

Try this exercise: Assume that a visitor arrives at your school asking, "What does your school care most about?" Would the visitor hear a similar answer from each staff member, or would the replies show disparity? Staff responses should exhibit a *shared* understanding of what the school cares most about.

To promote a wide acceptance of the school's mission, principals should:

- Involve staff in developing the mission statement of the school
- Prepare a written document which clearly states the mission, curricular goals, and educational priorities
- Widely disseminate the document or its content to teachers, parents, and students
- Formulate and maintain a management system which, when implemented, ensures that all members are working toward the agreed-upon mission.

■ *High Expectations for Student Achievement.* A critical dimension of learning climate centers around the beliefs about the learning potential of students served by the school. The staff in effective schools believe that all students can learn and should be expected to do so. This belief is clearly articulated in the school's mission statement and accountability system. The principal can lead the way in fostering high expectations for student learning, and, by carefully monitoring and guiding progress, move with teachers toward implementing these expectations.

To create a school learning climate that communicates high expectations, principals should:

- Clearly and consistently communicate the belief that all students can learn and are expected to do so
- Develop a management system that facilitates frequent and close monitoring of student achievement
- Utilize a process of instructional supervision to review teacher practices and instructional strategies that promote mastery outcomes for all students

---

Lawrence W. Lezotte is professor and chairperson, department of administration and curriculum, College of Education, Michigan State University, East Lansing.

School Learning Climate

- Plan inservice programs that reinforce staff belief that all students can learn
- Constantly review and revise school policies that communicate anything other than high expectations for student achievement.

■ *Teacher Instructional Effectiveness.* The school learning climate must convey the expectation that all teachers can instruct effectively and are expected to do so. Teachers, to be effective with students, need a clear sense of their own ability.

To ensure that teachers develop and maintain a personal sense of efficacy, principals should:
- Communicate through action and involvement the belief that all teachers can teach well and are expected to do so
- Develop and maintain an instructional supervision system that promotes each teacher's sense of efficacy
- Plan inservice programs to assist teachers in improving their instructional skills and expanding their knowledge of content necessary to teach all students.

■ *Teacher Collaboration.* Too frequently teacher training programs emphasize autonomy as both a desirable and inevitable characteristic of teaching. The effective schools research offers a straightforward, alternative interpretation of what this autonomy should mean. An effective school prizes teacher collaboration and creates structures that encourage this outcome. Teachers do not relinquish their professional autonomy; instead they embrace practices that promote the "interconnectedness" of learning goals and events—from grade to grade and teacher to teacher. Working closely together as colleagues ensures that individual as well as group efforts are appropriate to the long-term goals of the school.

To promote collaborative relationships in the school, principals should:
- Encourage collaborative teacher planning
- Structure the school environment and curricular tasks so that staff members work in teams
- Communicate to teachers that "doing one's own thing" can never compromise the school's agreed-upon goals and curricular priorities
- Coordinate, through systematic instructional management, the coverage of course content from grade to grade and teacher to teacher.

■ *Leadership.* Teachers in effective schools recognize the need for direction, coordination, and support from the principal as instructional leader. The principal must develop a keen sense of responsibility to fulfill teacher's expectations of this leadership role.

Principals attempting to improve their own leadership of the school learning climate should:
- Recognize that complex organizations need to be led toward goals
- Be present, active, and visible within all school settings
- Regularly raise questions about student achievement
- Provide systematic feedback to teachers on goal attainment throughout the school year
- Closely monitor pupil progress and teacher performance.

Leadership in complex organizations such as schools is an essential first condition for organizational productivity and satisfaction. Commitment and energetic leadership from the principal are necessary if the essential attributes of a positive school learning climate are to be systematically established in the school.

Change Facilitator Style

Gene E. Hall and Shirley M. Hord

Leadership by principals is vital to the improvement of schools and to their effectiveness for students. The principal's leadership style in change and improvement—or "change facilitator style" varies; three particular styles can be observed. These change facilitator (CF) styles are referred to as Responder, Manager, and Initiator.

Change Facilitator Styles

The Responder. Responder principals place a great deal of emphasis on allowing teachers and others the opportunity to express opinions about school activities. These principals believe that their job is to maintain a smoothly operating school by attending to the traditional administrative tasks, following up on teachers' requests, and treating students with concern. Responders view teachers as strong professionals who require little support or assistance in improving their instructional practice. They emphasize the personal side when relating to teachers and others.

They allow everyone to provide input into decisions in order to weigh feelings and to facilitate ownership of decisions. They often delay decisions to the last possible moment. They have a tendency to make decisions in terms of short-range needs rather than long-term instructional or school goals.

The Manager. Manager principals are characterized by a wider array of behaviors. They are responsive to people and situations. Manager principals defend teachers from excessive demands, and when appropriate, become very involved with them in implementing changes. Yet, they rarely initiate beyond the minimum of what is imposed. Their behavior seems to spring from their rapport with teachers and other school and district staff.

Managers provide support and help to teachers who wish to modify classroom practices to improve instruction. They maintain open lines of communication, both to keep teachers informed and to increase their own knowledge and sensitivity through teacher reaction and feedback. Teachers say these principals are always open and understanding and can be counted on to provide assistance.

Gene E. Hall is director and Shirley M. Hord is co-program director at the Research and Development Center for Teacher Education, The University of Texas, Austin.

The Initiator. These principals are committed to long-range goals that are clear and decisive, and they "push" teachers and students to achieve them. Their school goals typically transcend current improvement efforts. Their vision is based on strong beliefs about what school and teaching should be like. They make decisions based on their goals, on what they believe is best for students, and on their knowledge of what is currently happening in classrooms.

Initiators have clear expectations for students, teachers, and themselves. They articulate and monitor their expectations through frequent contacts with teachers. They make clear how the school is to operate and how teachers are to teach. When necessary, they reinterpret district policies and adapt programs to better suit the needs of their schools. These principals are determined but not unkind.

The Relationship of CF Style to Climate and Implementation

What are the consequences of the three facilitator styles? The answers depend on the specific questions asked. Teachers reported in nine study schools administered by principals with differing styles little difference in the degree of satisfaction with their schools. Manager-led schools had slightly more positive climates than Initiator-led schools. Responder-led schools had lower, but still positive, climates. Manager-type principals seem to protect their teachers against great demands, in contrast to Initiators, who push for high expectations. Responder's lack of coordination and consistency may contribute to teacher frustration and job ambiguity, and hence to lowered perceived climate.

The degree of teacher implementation of new practices was also measured. The relationship between principal's style and teacher implementation was calculated. Implementation took place in all schools, but more quality and quantity was achieved in classrooms of Initiator-style principals than in Manager-style or Responder-style schools. The correlation between implementation success at the classroom level and Initiator principal change style was .74.

Second Change Facilitators

A surprising and significant finding of our research on principals was the role of the Second Change Facilitator (Second CF/Consigliere). In each school,

Change Facilitator Style

Indicators of Change Facilitator Style

Dimensions/Behaviors	Responder	Manager	Initiator
Vision and Goal Setting	Accepts district goals as school goals	Accepts district goals but makes adjustments at school level to accommodate particular needs of the school	Respects district goals but insists on goals for school that give priority to this school's student needs
Structuring the School as a Work Place	Responds to requests and needs as they arise in an effort to keep all involved persons comfortable and satisfied	Expects all involved to contribute to effective instruction and management	Insists that all persons involved give priority to teaching and learning
Managing Change	Sanctions the change process and attempts to resolve conflicts when they arise	Maintains regular involvement in the change process, sometimes with a focus on management and at other times with a focus on the impact of the change	Directs the change process in ways that aim toward effective innovation use by all teachers
Collaborating and Delegating	Allows others to assume responsibility for the change effort	Tends to do most of the intervening personally, but will share some responsibility	Will delegate to carefully chosen others some of the responsibility for the change effort
Decision Making	Decisions are influenced more by immediate circumstances and formal policies than long-term consequences	Decisions are based both on the norms and expectations that guide the school and the management needs of the school	Decisions are based on high expectations of what is best for the school as a whole, particularly learning outcomes and long-term goals
Guiding and Supporting	Relies on teachers to report how things are going and to share any major problems	Maintains close contact with teachers and the change effort in order to identify actions needed to assist teachers with the change	Collects and uses information from a variety of sources to monitor the change effort and to plan interventions that will increase the probability of quality implementation

(Reprinted with permission.)

Excerpted from Hall, Rutherford, Hord, and Huling. "Effects of Three Principal Styles on School Improvement." *Educational Leadership*, vol. 41, no. 5.

one or more persons was nearly as active (even more active) than the principal. This Second CF often was an assistant principal, a teacher on special assignment, or a district or area level curriculum specialist/coordinator.

Second CFs acted in complementary fashion with their principals. When Responder principals made few facilitating actions, the Second CFs made more. When Manager principals made large numbers of interventions with teachers, the Second CFs made fewer. Interestingly, Initiator principals and their Second CFs were equally active.

Because the principal and a Second CF can divide facilitating roles, parts of the role that may not be comfortable for the one can be implemented by the other. If the principal is not a "nudger" or "pusher" for change, the Second CF might accept this responsibility. In any case, the complementary responsibilities are best identified in advance and the team trained to facilitate as a unit.

What Does Change Facilitation Mean in Practice?

Change facilitator stylistic differences are apparent in the set of descriptive behaviors developed from our analyses of principal behaviors. These style indicators for the three types of principals, presented in the figure, show how the three styles differ.

Principals *can* make a difference through facilitative leadership. An important aspect of instructional leadership is facilitating change in classroom practice. The characteristics of CF styles and the behaviors associated with their success can be utilized by instructional leaders. Initiator and Manager CF styles appear to be most effective.

To what extent principals can change their facilitating styles is a question that has been raised by our findings. Additional discussion and research are needed, however, before we can suggest any useful answers.

Supervising Classroom Management

School Attendance

Clarence L. Stone

School attendance at the high school level is a long-standing problem affecting student achievement in many school districts across the nation. Fights, vandalism, and a rash of other negative behavior can be traced to truancy and the habitual skipping of classes.

Schools are a microcosm of the communities in which they are located. The attitudes, feelings, and behaviors of students mirror the values and customs of adults in the same locale.

The research cites a number of reasons for student truancy and absenteeism:

- Poverty (inadequate clothing)
- Boredom
- Peer group influence
- Poor academic background and daily preparation
- Apathy of parents, students, community, teachers, and administrators
- Poorly constructed policies on discipline and attendance
- Inconsistent enforcement of rules by administrators and teachers
- Lack of support from central administration and board
- Poor curriculum
- Poor parent-teacher communication
- Lack of pride and sense of responsibility on part of students and staff.

What Can Be Done?

1. Local school boards have the responsibility and authority to establish reasonable and enforceable rules to govern student conduct. For rules to be enforceable, community support must exist. The building principal, with central office support, must involve all who are affected by attendance rules in their examination, revision, and/or construction.
2. Principals must see that well-developed rules and regulations governing attendance are in place and consistently enforced. Rules should be regularly examined by staff, parents, and students to ensure fairness and appropriateness.
3. Teachers are the key to any improvement effort. Principals must assist teachers to become better classroom managers. Effective classroom management facilitates effective teaching and good student attendance.
4. Teachers with good student attendance and punctuality records should be used as mentors for teachers who are having difficulty. Teachers should receive recognition for motivating students to attend class and to be on time.
5. Principals should conduct regular inservice for students, staff, and parents on attendance procedures. Ensure that everyone knows the rules.
6. Principals and teachers should examine successful attendance programs in the district or area. Adopt those features that will be useful in your school and community. Consider automatic dialing systems to contact homes. Check first with schools using these systems before purchasing them.

Strategies for Better Attendance

Students will go to class if they experience good classroom management and good teaching. Students want structure if it is positive and supportive. The following are reasons students regularly cite for punctual class attendance.

- The class is interesting; I don't feel lost; I can keep up; it's not boring.
- There is something for you to do when you get to class; you don't have time to sit and talk with friends.
- My parents insist that I go and that I be on time.
- The teacher makes the class special; you learn something new every day; you can't afford to miss it.
- My teachers care about me; they want me to learn.
- The teachers are strict and consistent; they insist that you be on time and that you attend daily.
- Teachers enforce rules without favorites; rewards and punishment are given as appropriate.
- Teachers give impromptu quizzes.
- Teachers mark attendance promptly and consistently.

Principals can have a significant impact by supporting strategies that encourage a high level of class attendance and punctuality:

1. Teachers should establish reasonable rules and apply them consistently.
2. Teachers should check attendance promptly each day.

Clarence L. Stone is director of state and federal projects, School District of the City of Highland Park, Mich.

School Attendance

3. Teachers should greet each student daily in a personal way.
4. Classroom instruction should be appropriate for student capabilities.
5. Teachers should establish a reward system for "good" attendance.
6. Principals and teachers should get to know parents. Letters should be sent to parents at the beginning of the year reinforcing concern for good attendance.
7. Teachers should make follow-up calls to parents when students are frequently absent.
8. Students with habitual attendance problems should be referred to counselors, attendance staff, or administration promptly enough for positive interventions.

No quick fixes or panaceas solve vexing attendance problems. Many schools throughout our nation have developed and are maintaining quality attendance procedures that have dramatically reduced truancy and tardiness. Research on effective classroom management and time-on-task has strengthened the quality of teaching and given practitioners new insights for maintaining a quality learning environment. In particular, school policies and regulations must protect instructional time, and principals must work for a school climate that is positive, supportive, and productive.

Student Discipline

Paul R. Graff

Good discipline is a by-product of good instruction. When schools make student achievement a priority and organize the learning environment to support successful teaching and learning, discipline also benefits. Discipline, then, is not an end in itself but a tool to facilitate learning.

A number of researchers have documented that disciplinary problems most regularly occur among students with unresolved learning problems (Bloom, 1976; Duke, 1976; Glasser, 1969). A program of effective discipline builds on a program of effective instruction and classroom management.

Discipline is a structure or framework that provides people with the skills and processes required to manage themselves and to be responsible for their actions. Regardless of what rules are in effect at a point in time, a school needs a systematic behavioral program that is understood and adhered to by most participants. Discipline is not intended to fix something, but to prevent unacceptable occurrences.

Philosophy

Behavior is the result of decisions made by individuals. Many actions of young people that are viewed by adults as disciplinary problems are in reality socialization behaviors that seem quite acceptable to the student.

A disciplinary problem is created when a rule is broken and/or a conflict between people arises. Rules are broken because the offender is unaware, has misunderstood what is expected, or is in defiance of a rule. Conflict occurs when those who establish, enforce, or are protected by the rules clash with the violator. When an individual believes he or she has few or no behavioral options, disciplinary problems can occur.

The management of school disciplinary problems often is complicated by the misperceptions of those involved. Parents and students look for exceptions or allege that an offense is atypical. A general disciplinary philosophy and process is needed.

What To Try

A total "bag of tricks" for school or classroom discipline is almost beyond the imagination. Some savants have proposed a hierarchy of disciplinary events tied to specific occurrences: for each crime, a specific punishment. In practice, this approach is difficult because of the many conditions that can affect a disciplinary situation.

Certain fixed elements need to be a part of any effective disciplinary structure. Discipline is an ongoing process, the result of daily encounters among people. School rules can give direction or cut off opportunities for students and staff. Discipline should be a way of showing students that someone cares about them.

1. A basic notion is to keep the framework simple. Put into place those rules that are most necessary for daily functioning—i.e., classroom conduct, lunchroom code, and rules for student activities. Everyone in the school should know that certain behaviors are expected, and that inappropriate behavior will result in certain consequences. For staff, this means setting the example. The most effective discipline is preventive rather than vindictive. Beyond these basics, few general rules are necessary or workable.

2. A second key element is the provision of options. Offenders frequently act as they do because they think they have no other choices. The wise disciplinarian makes offenders aware of their choices and of the consequences if the misbehavior continues. Prompt staff response to negative behavior usually means improved behavior. Generally, more options are available when problems are few.

3. Flexibility is as important as consistency. Double standards should not be tolerated, but a great amount of flexibility is necessary in developing the disciplinary plans for a building and in administering the consequences after behavior problems occur. Always handling a problem in the same way has a tendency to set a precedent; a given punishment is associated with a specific crime which may result in students being dealt with unfairly. As you administer consequences for misbehavior, you are also choosing from options. In those instances where behavior is never appropriate, a series of consequences that increase in severity usually cures the problem.

4. Effective discipline is a function of time and place. What works well in one school at one time may not be effective elsewhere at another time. Each setting is unique and must be dealt with in a unique way. In

---

Paul R. Graff is principal of Raytown (Mo.) High School.

Student Discipline

many situations, an effective way to deal with unacceptable behavior is to point out what is appropriate, when it is appropriate, and where it may occur. The offender is given an opportunity to exhibit acceptable behavior in a proper setting.

A School Plan for Discipline

Brookover and his colleagues (1983) recommend a school plan for discipline that is communicated clearly to students and parents and carried out by *all* teachers. The plan must reflect three distinct ways of responding to inappropriate behavior:

Preventing misbehavior by:
- Thorough planning for instruction
- Appropriate instruction which meets student educational needs
- Positive reinforcement to motivate students toward useful goals
- Setting procedures to streamline daily organizational activities (attendance procedures, passing periods, etc.)
- Contingency planning for rainy days, assemblies, schedule changes, etc.
- Effective supervision in the classroom, halls, and other areas
- Consistent rules in all classrooms, in accordance with the school plan.

Responding to misbehavior by:
- Setting limits by consistent enforcement of the boundaries of acceptable behavior
- Emphasizing the consequences of student choice in continuing disruptive behavior
- Establishing consequences (negative reinforcement) in advance that are both reasonable and workable (e.g., loss of privilege, calling parents, making up lost time, isolation)
- Establishing incentives (positive reinforcement) that reward students for acceptable behavior
- Providing additional follow-through for students who need extra attention (e.g., counseling, remedial work)
- Setting up in-school suspension for flagrant offenses as an alternative to outright suspension.

Obtaining help for nonconforming students: Problem students satisfy their needs for social, emotional, and academic recognition in unacceptable ways. The few students with serious behavior problems should be referred to professional personnel in the school or specialized agencies in the community.

How Does Discipline Affect Instructional Leadership?

Discipline involves staff and students in a daily experience together. A solid disciplinary framework tends to produce increased morale, positive human relationships, and consequently, improved achievement. Administrators and teachers need to help young people recognize that the most important purpose of self-discipline is to understand and to take responsibility for one's actions.

References

Bloom, B. S. *Human Characteristics and School Learning.* New York: McGraw-Hill, 1976.

Brookover, W. B.; Beamer, L.; Efthem, H.; Hathaway, D.; Lezotte, L.; Miller, S.; Passalacqua, J.; and Tornatzky, L. *Creating Effective Schools: An Inservice Program for Enhancing School Learning Climate and Achievement.* Holmes Beach, Fla.: Learning Publications, 1982.

Duke, D. L. "Who Misbehaves? A High School Studies Its Discipline Problems." *Educational Administration Quarterly* 12 (1976): 65–85.

Glasser, W. *Schools Without Failure.* New York: Perennial Library, 1969.

Classroom Management

Hilmar Wagner

Effective classroom management should be consistent with schoolwide disciplinary policies, and should sustain instructional strategies that improve student achievement.

Brookover and his colleagues (1982) discuss a series of techniques that are at the heart of a successful classroom management program. The following strategies have been shown to improve the efficiency of instruction, increase useful time-on-task, and prevent behavior problems from occurring.

- *Planning and Preparation.* Careful planning improves instructional quality and prevents boredom.
- *Fluency of Transitions.* Switching smoothly from one topic to another facilitates student time use and eliminates distraction.
- *Monitors.* Student helpers assist with clerical tasks and free the teacher for instruction.
- *Routines.* Students learn acceptable classroom routines for entering and leaving class, changing groups, etc., early in the year.
- *Traffic Patterns.* Learning areas are arranged to facilitate both access to learning materials and acceptable movement.
- *Enrichment Activities.* Alternative activities are available to students who finish their work early.
- *Attendance Taking.* Students have standing assignments or projects to work on during routine administrative tasks.
- *"Tired" Time.* The time before (and after) lunch is often less productive. Group activities and hands-on tasks are used at these times.
- *"With-it-ness."* The "with-it" teacher knows what is going on in the class, and intervenes to prevent misbehavior.
- *"Overlapping."* The skilled teacher can handle more than one activity at a time (i.e., assist an individual while supervising a group).
- *Group Focus.* Effective classroom managers establish a single focus for any group activity and work to reduce cross purposes.
- *Smoothness and Momentum.* Effective managers strive for a deliberate, orderly pace, with continuity of thought and action. (See Kounin, 1970, for more on tired time, with-it-ness, overlapping, group focus, smoothness, and momentum.)

Hilmar Wagner is coordinator of teacher education at the University of Texas at El Paso.

School Scheduling

The 1983 Carnegie Report recommends that school schedules be arranged more flexibly to permit larger, more efficient blocks of instructional time. Teacher control of the use of available time is the key. Consider scheduling in blocks of time rather than traditional 50–60 minute periods. Some subjects (science, art, shop, band) simply take more time to set up and to put away, decreasing useful instructional time. On the other hand, elective subjects should not be allowed to dictate the schedule for a building. The key issue here is careful planning and organization.

Instructional Planning

Teaching can be more effective when it is monitored. The principal might periodically monitor lesson plans. Some teachers allow too much unsupervised or seatwork time during a class period (e.g., reading the text, studying for a test, or using the entire period for a quiz).

Teachers must plan to match the difficulty of their material to student abilities. If a student lacks skill or ability for a certain activity, alternatives should be available. Then the student will not disrupt the regular learning environment. Students should be rewarded for what they do well, not punished by activities they cannot possibly accomplish. In this vein, teachers should not be too dependent on the textbook, which may stress only one instructional approach.

Teacher Observation

Recall when you were a teacher and the principal or supervisor dropped in on you while you were teaching. Your demeanor and behavior probably changed somewhat, regardless of how effective a teaching job you were doing. The principal should set aside definite blocks of time to observe instruction in his or her building. Unannounced observations for several short periods of time may be more effective than two formal announced observations a year.

Tell your teachers in advance what your plans for observations will be (frequent, unannounced), what you will be looking for, and how they will be evaluated. Follow-up procedures for those not up to standard should include a conference and suggestions for im-

Classroom Management

provement. Bring in master teachers or district supervisors to assist in offering specific content and process suggestions.

Some principals have been extremely successful with a "buddy system," pairing a new or marginal teacher with a proven master teacher to assist in classroom management and instructional planning. Above all, teachers need many positive "strokes" for a job well done and reasonable noninstructional duties so that they will have time for preparation.

References

Boyer, E. L. *High School: A Report on Secondary Education in America.* New York: Harper and Row, 1983.

Brookover, W. B., Beamer, L., Efthim, H., Hathaway, D., Lezotte, L., Miller, S., Passalacqua, J., and Tarnatzky, L. *Creating Effective Schools: An Inservice Program for Enhancing School Learning Climate and Achievement.* Holmes Beach, Fla.: Learning Publications, Inc., 1982.

Kounin, J. *Discipline and Group Management in Classrooms.* New York: Holt, Rinehart and Winston, 1970.

Instructional Planning

Hilda Borko and Jerome A. Niles

One must plan successfully to teach successfully. Planning is structured into most teachers' day; they are often allocated a daily planning period. School calendars mark certain days during the contract period as special planning days. Many principals require that teachers plan, and collect teachers' written plans on a regular basis.

Despite its importance to teaching, planning has received little attention in programs to improve the quality of instruction. Most teachers agree that planning is an important component of teaching, but many do not see the need for personal growth in this area. Yet, teachers can learn much about planning that will help them improve the quality of management and instruction in their classrooms.

Principals can help by providing guidance in the use of planning techniques. To this end, principals need information on two broad questions: What suggestions about planning are useful to teachers in each phase of their professional development? How can an environment be created within the school that encourages teachers to improve their planning and recognize its potential for improving instruction?

The Beginning Teacher: Planning in the Induction Year

The first year of teaching has a character of its own. It is different from a teacher's preservice preparation and is likely to influence subsequent years in the profession.

- A recurrent theme in accounts of first-year teachers is their attempt to establish a level of classroom control that will allow them to teach. Perhaps the most important planning advice that first-year teachers can receive is help in establishing and maintaining control in their classrooms. Several studies have shown that plans made at the beginning of the year are particularly important. The system of routines, rules, and procedures typically in place by the end of the first month of school serve as a structural framework for instructional activities throughout the year. Teachers who fail to install these classroom systems are much more likely to experience difficulty in managing their classrooms.

- Good day-to-day planning minimizes management problems by helping to maintain the flow of classroom activity. Since beginning teachers typically complete their preservice experience with some sense of the importance of planning, we might expect their first question to be, "What do experienced teachers do when they plan?" Field-based descriptions of planning cast light on the question. From the research, we know that experienced teachers typically focus planning on subject matter content and the corresponding activities, with relatively little attention to objectives or evaluation.

 Experienced teachers usually do not specify objectives because purposes are directly stated or implied in the instructional materials or curriculum guides they use. Beginning teachers have not yet had many opportunities to work with the curricular materials and are not as familiar with the goals and objectives they address. They need to focus more on the instructional objectives, their relationship to content, and ways to evaluate them. Again, experienced teachers are better diagnosticians because they know the material and the students.

 The differences between experienced and novice teachers suggest that the objectives-based, means-end model of planning, first proposed by Tyler in 1949 and still used in many teacher preparation programs, may be useful to the first-year teacher. This model outlines lesson planning as a four-step process: specifying behavioral objectives, choosing appropriate learning activities, organizing and sequencing the appropriate activities, and selecting evaluation procedures.

- The concept of overplanning is an important one for the beginning teacher. Experienced teachers and supervisors typically urge their student teachers to overplan. Overplanning does not imply detailed scripts that can actually hinder the flow of a lesson and depersonalize teacher-student relationships. Rather, overplanning means that the teacher develops more activities than are needed, under the assumption that to run out of good activities is to run out of order in the classroom.

Hilda Borko and Jerome A. Niles are associate professors, College of Education, Virginia Polytechnic Institute and State University, Blacksburg.

Instructional Planning

Planning in the Early Years of Teaching

The early years of teaching have been described as a time of consolidation. Teachers' growing confidence and mastery of basic teaching skills enable them to concentrate less on survival techniques and more on teaching itself. Teachers begin to see the positive effects associated with a thorough knowledge of subject matter and appropriate instructional activities. Teachers in their early years, then, concentrate on mastery of the subject matter and development of related learning activities. Given these priorities, the Tyler model is less appropriate and is usually replaced by a more general planning model.

Journeyman teachers are ready for planning changes. They should be encouraged to engage in more long-range planning, moving the focus from individual lessons or class periods to entire instructional units. They should also begin to differentiate instruction for subgroups within the class, based on variation in content and the performance capabilities of students.

Experienced Teachers: Planning for the Attainment of Mastery

Most successful teachers have achieved mastery in the activity flow and associated management skills that are preconditions for effective learning. Many feel they have achieved their goals and have no need of improved planning.

Planning, however, can serve as a tool for experienced teachers to build their teaching repertoires. The cyclic model of planning recently proposed by Yinger illustrates this possibility. The model sees planning as a three-stage problem-solving process in which the teacher: (1) defines the planning problem based on considerations of content, goals, personal knowledge, and experience; (2) designs instructional activities by repeatedly cycling through a process of elaboration, mental testing, and adaptation; and (3) implements and evaluates the activities in the actual classroom setting. Through this process, activities are rejected, modified, and incorporated into the teacher's repertoire of knowledge and experience.

To be maximally effective as a developmental tool planning must, at least occasionally, include other teachers. Group planning sessions offer an ideal opportunity for teachers to learn from each other as they discuss the practice of teaching. Planning is a time to explore together, to brainstorm, and to mentally test alternative teaching methods and solutions. Cooperative planning also provides a setting for curriculum review and materials evaluation.

The Principal's Role: Facilitating Planning

Planning can make a unique contribution to the professional growth of teachers. Principals can encourage staff development and growth by creating an environment in which planning serves a developmental function. Principals should recall that planning fulfills different purposes at different phases of a teacher's development.

Beginning teachers should be encouraged to plan instructional experiences that will maintain the flow of activity in the classroom. Their plans should include objectives, evaluation procedures, and more than enough activities to address the selected content; perhaps even take the form of written "lesson plans." Planning in the early years of teaching should reflect more differentiation for subgroups of students and attention to larger instructional units. Experienced teachers should use planning to expand their repertoires of teaching strategies and activities, and to facilitate the match between the learner and the instructional content.

Principals should provide planning time within the school day, scheduled so that teachers have the opportunity to plan together. Restructuring the schedule in this way may be inconvenient, but the potential payoff for teachers and the instructional program is enormous. Planning, then, becomes a staff development activity in which teachers are encouraged to share ideas about teaching and to jointly design and evaluate instructional activities and materials.

References

Tyler, R. W. *Basic Principles of Curriculum and Instruction.* Chicago: University of Chicago Press, 1949.

Yinger, R. J. "A Study of Teacher Planning." *Elementary School Journal,* Vol. 80, January 1980, pp. 107–127.

Development of Curriculum Guides

Gerald D. Bailey

School/district curriculum guides frequently go unused. A number of reasons account for this: Curriculum guides frequently are developed with little or no input from potential users. Certainly if a guide is viewed as irrelevant, disorganized, or impractical, it will be ignored or will make little contribution to school improvement.

Not all schools see the value in curriculum guides. For some, the development is viewed as too costly or time consuming. But curriculum guides can be a valuable tool for improving instruction, clarifying purposes, and communicating school programs.

What Type of Curriculum Guide Is Needed?

The first task in the development of a curriculum guide is to determine its purpose. Unless teachers see a reason for preparing a guide, they will not give serious attention to the task.

Administrators and teachers must first decide why they need a guide and who will benefit from its use. Guides can serve different purposes, and may be written for different consumers.

Curriculum guides may serve the following purposes:

- To provide direction or goal focus for school programs
- To use for planning the scope and sequence of the school curriculum
- To serve as a basis for selecting, planning, and evaluating instructional units
- To provide coordination within a department or between attendance centers
- To establish a focus for developing sets of competencies
- To serve as a criterion for selecting, developing, and evaluating instructional materials
- To identify topics for classroom or districtwide action research
- To inform the public about curriculum issues
- To inform professionals outside the community about the school/district curriculum.

Once the purpose has been determined, administrators and teachers must decide what type of curriculum guides they wish to develop.

Gerald D. Bailey is professor of education, Kansas State University, Manhattan, Kans.

The curriculum guides most frequently produced by school districts include:

1. General curriculum guides concerned with school goals and the school experiences that lead to these goals.
2. Scope and sequence charts for subject areas.
3. Instructional guides to aid teachers in planning (a) the entire instructional program of a school district or several grade levels; (b) a specific subject area; or (c) topics which cut across several subject areas (safety education, career education, etc.).
4. Instructional guides for planning and designing teaching units.
5. Guides for action research projects.
6. Informational guides to interpret the curriculum for parents or outside professionals.

What Should the Curriculum Guide Contain?

No single curriculum guide format meets the needs of all school districts. The contents of a guide depend on the intended purpose. The following elements are generally incorporated in comprehensive curriculum guides:

1. Foreword: a narrative that indicates the purpose of the guide and how it is to be used by teachers and administrators.
2. School Philosophy and Goals: a series of statements that identify the school/district's purposes and long-range student outcomes.
3. Subject Goals: a listing of goals for each subject content area, related to the general school goals.
4. Competencies: a listing of specific behaviors that learners must demonstrate at some point in the curriculum. Competencies detail how learners are to fulfill the subject goals.
5. Scope and Sequence Charts: displays specifying what is to be taught (scope) and when it is to be taught (sequence)—K-12 outlines of major concepts to be taught by all grade or proficiency levels.
6. Topic (Content) Outlines: the content or concepts in the various subject areas. These outlines show what is to be taught on a weekly or day-to-day basis.
7. Instructional Objectives: a series of specific statements about the conditions, types of activity, and evaluation of student learning. They show how the competencies are to be achieved.

Development of Curriculum Guides

8. Bibliography: a listing of the various texts available for teacher use; the resources housed at the district office that can be used at the various grade levels.
9. Media: a listing of media that are available for use in the various subject areas.
10. Evaluation Strategies: identification of testing strategies in the various subject areas; the evaluation guide should identify but not prescribe specific testing methods.
11. Instructional Methodologies: a listing of the methods that teachers are currently using at the various grade levels and in different subject areas (lecture, small-group instruction, contract learning, etc.).
12. Learning Styles: the identification of strategies for addressing typical student learning styles. Inventory forms for diagnosing learning styles should be included.
13. Community Resources: a listing of speakers, materials, and community locations that can be used to enhance classroom instruction.

How Can the Use of the Curriculum Guide Be Promoted?

Curriculum guides should encourage daily or weekly use. Each section should have space after the printed material to allow teachers to write pertinent comments or to include additional material. Ideally, the guides should be printed in loose-leaf format.

Principals can promote the guides by using them during classroom observations. If clinical supervision is employed, observation can focus on teacher implementation of the various elements of the guide. Teachers should keep a record of how they use the guide and for what purposes. The principal should schedule periodic departmental or staff meetings to discuss the strengths and weaknesses of the various guides.

How Can the Curriculum Guide Be Evaluated?

Developing a curriculum guide is a time-consuming process. The development time is justified only if the guide is helpful to the people for whom it was written. The initial evaluation of a guide should focus on these elements:

- Does the guide have a foreword which explains its purpose?
- Does the statement of school philosophy or goals identify broad student outcomes?
- Does the guide identify goals for each of the subject areas? Are they tied to the school goals?
- Does the guide identify competencies for each of the subject areas? Are they tied to the school goals?
- Does the guide have scope and sequence charts? Do they illustrate what is being taught in the K-12 curriculum?
- Does the guide have a comprehensive listing of topics (content) for each of the subject areas?
- Does the guide identify instructional objectives for each of the subject areas? Are they tied to the competencies?
- Does the guide have a comprehensive teacher and student bibliography?
- Does the guide have a comprehensive listing of media available to teachers for the respective subject areas?
- Does the guide identify evaluation procedures used by teachers in the different subject areas?
- Does the guide have a comprehensive listing of instructional methods used in each subject area?
- Does the guide list strategies for identifying and addressing different student learning styles?
- Does the guide have a comprehensive listing of community resources for each subject area?

Additional long-term evaluation may include district criterion-referenced lists, student follow-up, regional accreditation, and self-evaluation. Many school districts allow curriculum guides to fall into disuse. Principals should know why:

1. The guides were developed with little or no input from intended users.
2. The guides were based on materials from other school districts rather than on the specific needs of local students and teachers.
3. The guides were designed by consultants without adequate involvement of teachers.
4. The guides are keyed to specific subject texts rather than a comprehensive scope and sequence.
5. The guides were written for only one segment or subject area in the K-12 curriculum.
6. The guides include irrelevant, disorganized, or impractical materials.

References

Bailey, Gerald D., and Littrell, J. Harvey. "A Blueprint for Curriculum Development: Establishing a Systematic Design." *NASSP Bulletin,* March 1981.

Littrell, J. Harvey, and Bailey, Gerald D. "Eight Step Model Helps Systematic Curriculum Development." *NASSP Bulletin,* September 1983.

Supervising the Diagnostic Process

Developmental Traits

Donald C. Clark

If teachers are to effectively diagnose instruction, they must have a good understanding of adolescent developmental traits. Principals should take the lead in assisting teachers to acquire a general knowledge of adolescent characteristics and the implications for the school program, as well as the physiological, psychological, and sociological characteristics of the school population. Before this process can be initiated with the staff, however, principals need to understand several concepts. They include:

- Physical development and maturation as it relates to self-concept/esteem
- Psychological development as it relates to learning and self-concept/esteem
- Sociological development as it relates to peer groups, feelings of anonymity, and victimization.

Assessing Developmental Traits

Physical Development. A good source of information about physical development is *Adolescent Life Experiences* by Gerald Adams and Thomas Gullotta (1983). These authors list the following major physical growth and development factors:

1. The age when children begin to mature has dropped from 14.2 to 12.5 from 1900 to the present.
2. Girls mature approximately two years earlier than boys.
3. Adolescents are given little preparation for impending changes.
4. The psychological consequences of physical development may be more dramatic for those adolescents who begin maturing early, are obese, or start dating early.
5. Variations in the growth process create many social and personal adjustment problems for the atypical adolescent.
6. Normal and atypical patterns of physical growth in adolescence affect body image and influence social relations and personality development.

Physical development traits and levels of sexual maturation are difficult to assess in the school setting. But because of the close ties with social development and self-concept/esteem, regular weight and height measurements should be collected in physical education classes to monitor periods of rapid student growth; and physical education/health teachers and counselors should be alert to detect early and late maturing youngsters.

Readiness for learning is the issue. Special activities such as group counseling, adviser/advisee programs, and recognition projects can be planned for students who may have a higher problem potential.

Psychological Development. The early adolescent faces psychological challenges to intellectual growth and self-concept/esteem. Teachers and administrators should carefully weigh the following factors:

1. Most youngsters progress from concrete thinking to formal thinking during the ages 11 to 14.
2. Self-concept becomes increasingly complex as the individual develops toward adulthood.
3. All perceptions shape self-concept and the affective component of perception shapes self-esteem.
4. Individuals with good self-esteem see themselves as persons of worth; they respect themselves but do not necessarily feel superior to others. Individuals who lack self-esteem consider themselves unworthy, inadequate, or deficient.
5. Low self-esteem is related to many undesirable social consequences. Moderate to high self-esteem appears to be the optimal level for effective functioning.

Adolescent cognitive levels can be assessed with one of several test instruments. These include: *Concrete-Operational Reasoning Test* (Ankney and Joyce, 1974); *Logical Reasoning Test* (Burney, 1974); and *The Language Arts Test of Cognitive Functioning* (Brazee, 1981).

Many instruments have been developed to measure self-concept/esteem. They include: *Self-Consciousness Scale* (Simmons, Rosenberg, and Rosenberg, 1973); *Content of Self-Image Scale* (Simmons, Rosenberg, and Rosenberg, 1973); *Self-Esteem Scale* (Rosenberg, 1965); *Perceived Self-Image* (Simmons, Rosenberg, and Rosenberg, 1973); *Self-Esteem Scale* (Savin-Williams and Demo, 1983); and *Self-Esteem Inventory* (Coopersmith, 1959).

The organization and sequence of content and instructional strategies should be appropriate for the cognitive functioning levels of students. Expecting students to function at higher levels when they are not yet ready can be frustrating for both teachers and

---

Donald C. Clark is professor of secondary education, University of Arizona, Tucson.

Developmental Traits

students. Appropriate assessment can guide instructional planning (see Article 64), and support sensible prescription and placement decisions (see Article 65).

Self-concept/esteem is important to success both in and out of school. Adams and Gullotta (1983) point out that, "Helping youths to do well in school, establishing positive peer relations, and maintaining a supportive home environment seem to be very important aspects of assuring moderate to high self-esteem." Identification of students with low self-esteem allows school personnel to design intervention programs to encourage self-acceptance, self-regard, and perceived competence.

Sociological Development. Peer groups are very important to the adolescent. Peer influence increases during adolescence while the influence of parents, teachers, and other significant adults decreases. Several social development factors should be considered:

1. Peer groups do not replace parental or adult influence, but supplement it.
2. Peer relationships progress from groups of all girls and all boys to mixed groups.
3. Peer relationships are disrupted at periods of transition (elementary to middle level, middle level to high school) with increased perceptions of anonymity and victimization.
4. Peer groups provide highly reinforcing settings for specific adolescent behaviors.

Through careful observation, teachers and administrators can monitor the many peer group influences in the school. In classrooms, teachers can note which student friendships influence classroom climate, behavior, and learning, and the degree to which adolescents feel isolated, unknown, and victimized by their fellow students. The following instruments are recommended for this kind of assessment:

- *Anonymity Scale* (Blyth, Simmons, and Bush, 1978)
- *Victimization Scale* (Blyth, Simmons, and Bush, 1978).

A wise principal involves peer groups in building school spirit and a positive social climate. Teachers can harness peer group influences through small-group strategies and collaborative decision making.

School personnel concerned with lessening the impact of student transitions (as indicated by anonymity and victimization scores) can promote better relationships through adviser/advisee groups, big brothers/sisters, and athletic and social activities. Adviser/advisee groups are very useful in helping students feel a part of the larger school environment. Multi-age-grouping allows students to develop social skills such as welcoming new students, practicing assembly behavior, and helping other students with problems. Teacher and administrator visibility in the halls and on the grounds before and after school, during class breaks, and during the lunch hour can also reduce the student's sense of victimization.

Diagnosis of student traits is an important but often neglected task in secondary schools; developmental readiness remains a relatively unimportant consideration in general program planning. If secondary schools are going to become more responsive to the needs of the adolescent learner, appropriate assessment procedures must be initiated and developmental data collected as a continuing element of program planning and implementation.

References

Adams, Gerald, and Gullotta, Thomas. *Adolescent Life Experiences.* Monterey, Calif.: Brooks/Cole, 1983.

Ankey, P., and Joyce, L. "The Development of a Piagetian Paper and Pencil Test for Assessing Concrete Operational Reasoning." Doctoral dissertation, University of Northern Colorado, Greeley, 1974.

Blyth, D.; Simmons, R. G.; and Bush, D. M. "The Transition into Early Adolescence: A Longitudinal Comparison of Youths and Two Educational Contexts." *Sociology of Education* 51 (1978): 149–162.

Brazee, Edward H. "Student Responses to a Language Arts Test of Cognitive Functioning." *Journal of Early Adolescence* 1 (1981): 373–384.

Burney, G. "The Construction and Validation of an Objective Formal Reasoning Test." Doctoral dissertation, University of Northern Colorado, Greeley, 1974.

Coopersmith, S. "A Method for Determining Types of Self-Esteem." *Journal of Abnormal Social Psychology* 59 (1959): 87–94.

Rosenberg, M. *Society and the Adolescent Self-Image.* Princeton, N.J.: Princeton University Press, 1965.

Savin-Williams, R. C., and Demo, D. H. "Conceiving or Misconceiving the Self: Issues in Adolescent Self-Esteem." *Journal of Early Adolescence* 3 (1983): 121–140.

Simmons, R. G.; Rosenberg, F.; and Rosenberg, M. "Disturbance in the Self-Image at Adolescence." *American Sociological Review,* October 1973.

Learning Style

James W. Keefe

Learning is an internal process. We know that learning has taken place only when a more or less permanent change is observed in learner behavior. Similarly, we can recognize individual learning style only by observing a student's behavior. Learning style tells us *how* a student learns best. Style characteristics reflect genetic coding, personality development, and environmental adaptation. They are relatively persistent qualities in the behavior of individual learners.

Although learning style and cognitive style have often been used synonymously in the literature, they are not the same. Learning style, in fact, is the broader term and includes cognitive as well as affective and physiological style factors.

Elements of learning style appeared in the literature as early as 1892, but research findings were plagued with methodological problems. Specific research on cognitive styles was greatly expanded in the United States after World War II at Brooklyn College, the Menninger Foundation, and the Fels Institute. Much learning style research is traceable to the instructional improvement projects of the 1960s.

Current research reflects two lines of inquiry. One group continues to show interest only in the cognitive dimensions of style. The other is concerned with applied models of learning and teaching and a multi-dimensional analysis of style. School diagnosis of student learning traits demands attention to both approaches.

What Is Learning Style?

The NASSP Learning Styles Task Force (1984) defines learning style as "the composite of characteristic cognitive, affective, and physiological factors that serve as relatively stable indicators of how a learner perceives, interacts with, and responds to the learning environment. It is demonstrated in that pattern of behavior and performance by which an individual approaches educational experiences. Its basis lies in the structure of neural organization and personality which both molds and is molded by human development and the learning experiences of home, school, and society."

Learning style can be categorized in cognitive, affective, and physiological domains.

James W. Keefe is director of research, NASSP, Reston, Va.

1. *Cognitive styles are "information processing habits . . . which represent a person's typical modes of perceiving, thinking, remembering, and problem solving"* (Messick, 1969).

The vast majority of research on personality-related learning variables has dealt with cognitive style. Each learner has preferred ways of perception, organization, and retention that are distinctive and consistent. These characteristic differences are called cognitive styles.

Messick (1976) lists more than 20 cognitive factors that are derived from experimental research. Perceptual modality, for example, characterizes learner preferences or capability for using the various senses. The conventional modes are auditory, visual, and kinesthetic. Development seems to evolve from kinesthetic in childhood to visual and (eventually) verbal in adulthood.

Field independence versus dependence is another cognitive trait, measuring a continuum of analytic as opposed to nonanalytic ways of experiencing reality.

Other cognitive factors are complexity versus simplicity, reflectiveness versus impulsivity, leveling versus sharpening (memory traits), etc. The newest factors founded on brain behavior research are cognitive (i.e., hemispheric function).

2. *Affective styles are motivational processes—attention, expectancy, incentive—viewed as the learner's typical modes of arousing, directing, and sustaining behavior* (Keefe, 1979).

The second domain of learning style encompasses the motivational traits of attention, application, and valuing. Motivation is the product of a wide variety of influences: the cultural environment, parental and peer pressures, school practices, and personality factors.

Values are involved. Not every student can be successful in every learning environment, because personal or ethnic values may run counter to school expectations. Most teachers think of students as motivated if they do what the teacher wants done; as unmotivated if they do not. Because of the subjective component here, affective factors require very careful diagnosis.

Locus of control is an affective style factor that characterizes the forces within an individual's personality that direct or motivate action. A person with an "internal" locus of control thinks of himself as responsible for his own behavior. The "external," on the other hand, sees forces beyond his control as responsi-

Learning Style

ble for what happens. Internality is a highly desirable learning trait.

Other affective factors include need for structure (conceptual level), persistence, achievement motivation, imitation or modeling behavior, and social motivation.

3. Physiological style describes the impact of various biological or environmental factors on the learning behavior of the human body. *Physiological styles are biologically-based modes of response that are founded on sex-related differences, personal nutrition and health, and reaction to the physical environment.* (Keefe, 1979).

Physiological factors are among the most obvious influences on school learning. The student who is hungry or ill behaves differently than the healthy youngster. Bodily (time) rhythms influence individual learning readiness. Males and females learn differently in certain situations.

All learners are affected by the physical environment of the school. Environmental elements that influence learning are light, sound, and temperature.

School Applications

School programs and research in learning style have mushroomed in the past decade. The key questions to be answered are "How does a given learner best learn?" and "What do we do about individual differences among learners?" If we wish students to have optimum learning experiences in our schools, we must make some changes in the educational delivery system. But do we change the learning environment or try to change the learner?

Some believe that we need more responsive instructional environments based on stylistic and skill differences among learners. Most recent innovative teaching methods reflect this point of view. Others feel that we should help the student become more responsive to the *existing* learning environment. If a youngster is not very adaptable or cannot cope well in a conventional classroom setting, they say we should and can enhance his or her cognitive style to increase achievement.

The work of Charles Letteri of the University of Vermont typifies the therapeutic approach. Letteri has taken the assessment of cognitive style a step further by combining several existing information processing factors in a profile that predicts student achievement on standardized achievement tests. His multidimensional "Cognitive Profile," showing a student's position across seven cognitive style continuums, reveals three types of profiles: Type I scores well on standardized tests, Type II shows average scores, and Type III is a low achiever. Of greater significance, Letteri's continuing "augmentation" research indicates that less responsive cognitive traits can be modified with careful, nondirective training.

The majority of practitioners and researchers have concentrated on changing the learning environment rather than retraining the learner. Style instruments such as the Myers-Briggs Type Indicator, Cognitive Style Mapping, and the Learning Style Inventory of Dunn, Dunn, and Price assess more than one style domain and several of the factors. The information can help teachers design more effective instruction or place students in more appropriate learning situations.

School administrators interested in more specific information about the various learning style instruments should contact the NASSP Research Department or the Learning Styles Network, St. John's University, Grand Central and Utopia Parkways, Jamaica, N.Y. 11439.

State of the Art

No currently available learning style instrument provides a truly comprehensive assessment of all the important factors of style. Several of these instruments are designed to measure only a single element or domain, and do so admirably. Others are broader, but in practice focus on two of the domains. The time is ripe for a workable second generation instrument. NASSP has initiated such an effort through its Learning Styles Task Force, which is now field testing a new instrument (available 1985).

Learning style diagnosis is unquestionably a primary component of the teaching-learning cycle. Viewed alone, it is merely an interesting assessment technique; but, as a diagnostic tool, it is a foundation for the edifice of personalized education.

References

Messick, S., et al. *Individuality in Learning.* San Francisco, Calif.: Jossey-Bass, 1976.

National Association of Secondary School Principals. *Student Learning Styles—Diagnosing and Prescribing Programs.* Reston, Va.: NASSP, 1979.

National Association of Secondary School Principals. *Student Learning Styles and Brain Behavior—Programs, Instrumentation, Research.* Reston, Va.: NASSP, 1982.

Learning History

Lorin W. Anderson

Research suggests that what or how well students learn in a particular situation depends to a great extent on previous experience and learning.

More than one-half of the achievement differences among students at any grade level can be attributed to differences already present when the students enter that grade level. Furthermore, these differences increase substantially with time to the point where they are more than 10 times as large among high school juniors as among first grade students.

As currently practiced, schooling is far less influential than prior learning (learning history) on subsequent learning. What, if anything, can be done to balance these influences? To answer this question we must first address an intermediate question.

Why Is Learning History So Important?

At least four reasons give substance to the importance of student learning history. First, much of what is learned in schools is sequential in nature. To develop a 1,000-word vocabulary, students must begin with a 10-word vocabulary. To operate on fractions, students must understand how to operate on whole numbers. When students are assigned learning tasks which far exceed their present level of knowledge and skills, they have great difficulty learning, if they do so at all.

Second, even in the most homogeneously grouped classroom, differences in learning history exist. Typically, the teacher assigns a single learning task to all students in a class. Because of prior learning differences, the task will be too easy for some, appropriate for others, and too difficult for the rest. Those students who begin better prepared have less difficulty with the assigned task.

Third, much of what is learned in schools is transmitted verbally. The two main sources of learning in classrooms are teachers and textbooks. Students learn either by listening or reading. Thus, students with larger vocabularies and better language skills are likely to benefit from the way learning occurs, independent of what learning tasks are assigned. Students with more verbally-oriented learning histories (e.g., middle class students) and auditory and visual learning style preferences are at an initial advantage in a wide variety of subject areas.

Lorin W. Anderson is professor, College of Education, University of South Carolina, Columbia.

Fourth, student learning histories are at least partly psychological in nature. Successful or unsuccessful learning experiences over time have profound consequences for the ways that students approach (or avoid) new learning situations. Students who have been successful in school tend to approach new situations with a certain amount of confidence, interest, and positive emotion. Those who have experienced a great deal of failure tend either to avoid new situations or approach them with anxiety, trepidation, and negative emotion.

It is hardly surprising that highly verbal students with good knowledge and skills and a self-assured, positive approach to new learning do very well in school. Conversely, students who have few verbal skills, or have acquired little useful knowledge and skills, or have experienced little in the way of school success, do very poorly. A student's learning history is an important determiner of future learning. Put simply, both learning and failing to learn are cumulative.

What Can Be Done?

A first step in compensating for disparities in prior learning is careful diagnosis of existing learning histories. At present, we have reasonably good information about student verbal abilities from general intelligence tests and standardized achievement batteries. The strong correlation between student performance on these types of tests is likely due to their heavy dependence on verbal abilities.

These tests, unfortunately, present an incomplete picture and are subject to misinterpretation or overinterpretation. Issues of intellectual capacity, genetic predisposition, and learning potential are frequently raised in discussions about general intelligence and standardized achievement test results. While the issues are interesting, tests results only describe the present state of affairs (not the potential) and are incapable of establishing the causes of performance (e.g., genetic predispositions). Additional evidence about student learning history is sorely needed.

Pretests provide one source of evidence. They focus on the prior knowledge and skills that students possess before they learn the specific content of a particular segment of a course or program.

A task analysis is frequently conducted to identify the knowledge and skills to be included in a pretest. Task analysis begins by identifying what is to be learned. This learning is often described in terms of

Learning History

the mastery of a particular instructional objective (e.g., finding the main idea of a paragraph) or acquisition of some particular content (e.g., atomic structure).

The next step in task analysis focuses on the question, "What must students know and/or be able to do to master these objectives or acquire this content?" A list of specific knowledge and skills can be developed in response to this question. Questions keyed to this knowledge and these skills are then included in the pretest.

A great deal of testing seems necessary to assess specific knowledge and skills, but the amount can be reduced somewhat by following a few guidelines.

1. Knowledge and skills common to a fairly wide variety of instructional objectives and content can be identified. A set of short tests on this common core can be developed for teacher use.
2. Comprehensive records of the specific knowledge and skills acquired by students can be maintained and made available to teachers at different levels of schooling.
3. In sequential subjects, the tests administered at the end of each unit can be viewed as pretests for each subsequent unit.

Various types of "affective knowledge" can also be assessed. Students know whether they like a subject or not. They know how well they do in that subject. They know how important they (and others) perceive the subject to be. Affective knowledge helps to explain the motivation, enthusiasm, and perseverance of students when they encounter a particular subject in a particular classroom. Affective knowledge may help to identify students who are unmotivated, easily distracted, or who give up easily. Instrumentation is available from several sources, including the *School Attitude Measure* (Scott, Foresman and Co.) and *A System for Assessing Affectivity* (University of Alabama Press).

Once evidence on learning history is gathered, it must influence instructional planning if improved learning is to occur. A number of appropriate uses have been documented in recent research.

- Instruction can be more variable and flexible through showing, doing, and telling. Learning styles research tends to indicate that when instruction is matched to preferred style, attitudes toward learning improve, as does student achievement.
- Appropriate learning tasks can be assigned to larger numbers of students. After a lesson is taught to the whole class, for example, students might be given varied homework assignments based on their understanding of the group lesson. The emphasis here is on the appropriateness of an assignment for an individual student.
- Reasonable success can be ensured for many students early in any course or curriculum. Less demanding (but not boring) lessons and activities can be assigned at the beginning to facilitate success. Early success results in self-confidence and a willingness to approach new tasks and activities in a more enthusiastic fashion.

Supervising Prescription and Placement

Advisement

James W. Keefe

Understanding the meaning of advisement involves sorting out the various definitions of guidance and counseling. These terms mean different things to different people, and in practice are often used interchangeably.

Guidance is usually viewed in a broader way and is defined as the process of helping students understand themselves and their school. Counseling is used to describe specific one-to-one guidance techniques. Advisement, another guidance function, is the "helping link" between group guidance and professional counseling. The major guidance services are:

- *Career Information*—Vocational and college materials made available in special centers through resource persons, college nights, career days, etc.
- *Instructional Units*—Teaching materials on school orientation, career/college planning, and student concerns or problems.
- *Registration and Placement*—Registering students for the coming term/year, assisting in class assignment, completing college/job recommendations and employment referrals.
- *Records Maintenance*—Establishing personal counseling files for each student.
- *Testing*—Administering and supervising individual and group tests, and standardized, criterion-referenced, and competency tests.
- *Counseling*—Personalized, one-to-one contact for planning, problem solving, or placement.
- *Referral*—Therapeutic referral to district psychologists and specialists, community agencies, and outside professionals.

Advisement focuses on the instructional end of the guidance continuum. It includes several of the guidance functions that do not require specialized professional preparation.

Certainly some guidance activities require high levels of professional training and unique competence. But not all services traditionally provided by school counselors require special training. Teachers, for example, are well-qualified to assist students in academic program planning and placement decisions.

James W. Keefe is director of research, NASSP, Reston, Va.

What Is Advisement?

Advisement is a function of the school guidance program in which teachers, administrators, and sometimes paraprofessionals join professional counselors to help students (advisees) plan and achieve appropriate educational, career, and personal-social goals.

Students are asked to make many important educational, career, and personal-social decisions, generally without much guidance. In advisement, a team of professionals and paraprofessionals works together to help students on an ongoing basis—the kind of assistance counselors do not have time to provide.

Advisement Programs

Programs emphasizing the role of the teacher as a key guidance person have increased in number and sophistication during the past 20 years. These programs are variously termed *expanded homeroom, advisory period, home-base, advisory base, student assistance, teacher adviser,* or *adviser-advisee*. Although the plans vary from district to district and by level of schooling, they generally call for the teacher to assume guidance functions that are narrowly defined and limited to academic program planning, career/college informational assistance, school adjustment help, and personal-social guidance.

Adviser-advisee (AA) or teacher adviser (TA) programs cast the role of the adviser in five broad categories:

1. *Virtually all certificated personnel are responsible for a group of 15–30 students.* Each group is small enough for advisers to work personally with advisees. This is not a conventional homeroom responsibility, but a real guidance responsibility.

2. *Teacher advisers ordinarily retain the same group of advisees during their entire school career.* Each student either chooses an adviser when first entering the school or is randomly assigned a vacant slot in an advisory group. In practice, both methods work satisfactorily.

3. *Teacher advisers collect information about advisees* from the students themselves, from parents and teachers, and from outside sources, and store the information in a cumulative folder for reference. Some schools keep master files in the counseling

Advisement

office; advisers only maintain summary profiles.

4. *Teacher advisers help students recognize their personal talents and interests and plan career goals accordingly.* TAs use background and test information to advise students about their subject matter strengths and weaknesses, and to help set goals.

5. *The adviser functions as the home-base teacher and chief in-school contact for all persons and agencies concerned with the student.* In middle level schools, TAs conduct home-base programs on such topics as getting along with teachers, and study skills. They prepare college or job recommendations for advisees in high school. At both levels, they mediate disciplinary problems and take calls from parents and community persons.

Advisers meet with parents during each reporting period to discuss student progress. They refer specialized problems to professional counselors or administrators and act as advocates for their advisees.

A Cooperative Effort

Professional counselors serve as consultants to teachers, administrators, and others in the adviser-advisee program, conduct inservice training on advisement techniques, and act as resource persons to grade-level or departmental teams. They have time to handle the kind of referrals for which they are professionally trained.

The relationship between teacher adviser and professional counselor is a cooperative one; the functions are distinct but complementary. Teachers handle academic advisement and ordinary school adjustment problems; counselors supervise the guidance program and handle referrals.

Teacher Adviser
Someone for students to talk with about:
1. Grades and credits
2. The use of time
3. Study techniques
4. Educational and vocational plans
5. Life in and out of school
6. Attendance and discipline
7. Problems with students or teachers
8. Employment forms or college recommendations
9. Withdrawal from school

Professional Counselor
Someone for students and teachers to talk with about:
1. Social and emotional problems
2. Problems involving conflicts
3. Test scores, aptitudes, learning problems
4. Contacting school specialists and out-of-school agencies
5. Getting technical help on educational or vocational planning
6. Any change of teacher adviser
7. Referral of any problem by teacher advisers.

Implementing the Program

Schools approach advisement in various ways. Different types of programs can be successful with the proper support and commitment. Middle level schools seem to favor a guidance/activities format; high schools, an academic advisement approach. Some schools schedule short advisory group meetings each day: attendance is taken, announcements made, instructional units carried out, and individual conference appointments scheduled. Other schools alternate group meetings and conferences with regular classes (usually physical education or specialized electives). Still other schools schedule four to six students with the adviser each day.

Adviser-advisee programs are rarely initiated or successful without strong backing from the principal. Most schools have very informal lines of communication and information scarcely travels up or down the line without distortion. In schools with functioning teacher adviser programs, however, the entire school staff acts as a guidance team. Useful ideas are communicated more readily and implemented more willingly because the student is the focus of activity.

The principal's commitment to advisement can be demonstrated by openness to teacher initiative and a willingness to be supportive:

- Providing time in the school schedule
- Arranging for advisement space and materials
- Assigning competent program coordinators
- Organizing and encouraging inservice activities
- Bringing the program to the attention of the community, the superintendent, and the school board.

References

Georgiades, William; Keefe, James W.; Lowery, Robert E.; et al. *Take Five: A Methodology for the Humane School.* Los Angeles, Calif.: Parker and Son, Inc., 1979.

Jenkins, John M. "The Teacher-Adviser: An Old Solution Looking for a Problem." *NASSP Bulletin,* September 1977.

McEwin, C. Kenneth. "Establishing Teacher-Advisory Programs in Middle Level Schools." *The Journal of Early Adolescence,* Winter 1981.

Educational Plans

J. Howard Johnston

The large number of students each teacher must serve have caused individualized programs to falter at the secondary level. Planning for 25 or 30 students in the average elementary class seems reasonable, even with the wide range of abilities found in those classes. But developing plans for the 125 students a middle level or high school English teacher must see each day is quite another matter.

Evidence suggests, however, that the use of student instructional plans improves learning and achievement. The dilemma, then, is that a personalized approach to instruction works best, but secondary schools are organized in such a way that teachers find individualized instructional planning to be nearly impossible.

In fact, individualized planning is possible and workable in secondary schools. Its success depends on certain central elements:

1. *An adviser* who plans with the student, communicates with parents, and monitors student progress.
2. A *plan for academic progress* that focuses student attention on essential skills and content.
3. *Monitoring of student progress* and feedback on achieving the goals in the plan.

In schools with adviser-advisee programs, planning is central to the function of the teacher adviser. In schools without such programs, some type of advisement role must be developed for planning to function effectively. (See Article 63.)

The Adviser

The adviser is a teacher or other school professional who helps an individual student set and achieve appropriate personal, academic, educational, and career goals. The adviser:

- Meets regularly with each student advisee
- Reviews past achievement with the student
- Helps the student set appropriate goals
- Assists the student in meeting established goals
- Monitors the student's progress toward the goals and provides feedback.

J. Howard Johnston is professor and associate dean, College of Education, University of Cincinnati, Ohio.

The adviser acts as liaison between the student and other teachers by communicating the student's goals, asking for help in reinforcing, and monitoring the student's progress.

The Plan

The plan is developed by the student and the adviser and is shared with parents, counselors, and other teachers. The plan must be succinct; that is, it should focus on a few major goals rather than a long list of specific objectives.

Goals may be written in several domains, depending on the needs of the student and the objectives of the school.

- *Work habits:* completion of homework and other assignments, planning of study time, use of resources, etc.
- *Grades and academic performance:* planning for a specific assignment like a term paper, raising test scores, improving grades in a given subject.
- *Skill development:* improving writing/reading skills, building study skills, improving library and research skills, learning typing and/or computer skills.
- *Personal behavior:* reducing tardiness, improving school attendance, entering a contest, participating in a school activity, building confidence with peers.

The list of possible goals is nearly endless, so planning must be selective. The sample planning form shows how major goals might be developed for one student. The model illustrates two important aspects of a well-thought-out academic plan (Figure 1):
- It is brief and to the point.
- The goals yield "observable" products so that both student and adviser know when they have been achieved.

Monitoring and Feedback

Monitoring is crucial to the success of individualized academic planning. Monitoring and feedback must be focused specifically on the goals in the student's plan and utilize evidence from a variety of sources: observations of the adviser, student self-assessment, memos from other teachers and counselors, grade reports, anecdotal records, and letters from parents.

Educational Plans

The feedback sessions should concentrate on three items:

1. A review of the evidence
2. Judgment about how much progress has been made toward achieving the goals
3. Goal setting for future growth.

Individualized educational plans can work in secondary schools if advisement procedures are established and staff members have a strong commitment to individual student welfare.

Figure 1. *Academic Plan*

Student: Steve R.　　　　　　Adviser: Mr. Jones
Period Covered: Fall 84
Grade: 11　　Homeroom: 19B
Date of plan: 9/17/84　　　　Reviewed: 11/21/84

I. Subject Area Goals
  A. English: Keep journal to improve writing for college admission. Write one full page a day.
  B. Math: Practice word problems for SAT test.
  C. Social Studies: (etc.)
  D. Biology:
  E. Fine Arts:

II. Personal Goals
  A. Learn to use word processing program on school microcomputer.
  B. Learn to use a scientific calculator.

III. Educational Goals
  A. Select five colleges for application.
  B. Meet with counselor to discuss career choices in business management.

Student Placement

Robert E. Lowery

Quality schools are places where students achieve and enjoy learning, where a systematic effort is made to place students in programs and courses aligned with their aspirations and their developmental needs.

The principal, as the school's instructional leader, supports these placement procedures and encourages instructional practices that maximize each student's chances for success.

In a typical school, students are placed in courses on the basis of selections made during spring registration. The scenario is common: A descriptive booklet is prepared and distributed to help students select their courses for the coming year. Counselors, teacher advisers, teachers, and parents assist with advice and encouragement. In some schools, teachers validate course selections by signature or stamp. A tabulation is run. Undersubscribed courses are dropped and new choices are made. Finally, a schedule is published based on the "demand" of students. During the summer, students are placed in course selections by hand or by computer, and on their return in the fall, they are given their individual course schedules.

Once initial scheduling is completed, however, follow-up to affirm effective placement is minimal, except in special circumstances.

Some Basic Considerations

Student placement into courses or programs should be based on adequate information about the learner and the nature of the options available.

Students' career aspirations are usually rudimentary, but clear enough for decisions to be made about how their time should be spent in school. Because of the tenuous nature of their aspirations, students need help in deciding which courses to take, in what sequence, and for how long. These decisions are best made cooperatively by the student, a counselor, a teacher adviser, and a parent.

Student placement decisions should consider the developmental characteristics and the prior learning necessary to succeed in courses and programs. The sheer size of the counselor-counselee ratio in most schools prevents meaningful one-to-one conferences in which background information, previous achievement, aspirations, and other relevant data can be carefully reviewed. More often, students are left to their own resources in choosing which courses are best. As one student aptly put it, "It's the blind leading the blind."

Nested within the concept of appropriate placement are several factors overlooked in traditional scheduling procedures, factors such as teacher interest, appropriate grouping, and the availability of instructional materials. Traditional placement can be quite impersonal and mechanical. The real test of any student placement process is the degree of achievement and satisfaction experienced by individual students.

Sharpening the Process

Fortunately, principals can take steps to improve student placement. These steps are neither radical nor far removed from what already exists in many schools.

1. Define school curricula in terms of performance standards and competencies to be achieved. Courses in a subject area should be carefully articulated so that the successful completion of one course prepares the student for the next.

2. Prerequisite learning for each course or cluster of courses should be spelled out. Typically, prerequisites are listed as courses completed rather than as competencies mastered. In a sequential program such as mathematics, the successful completion of one level of math should prepare a student for placement in the next (if sufficient motivation exists).

3. Develop ways to identify learner characteristics and aspirations. (See Articles 60–64). The four-year plan is a good tool. Plan cards can be filled out when students enter the school and should be periodically updated. Current computer technology allows schools to use microcomputer spreadsheet software to assemble information about student academic performance in courses and on tests as background data for placement decisions.

4. Organize an advisement program. An adult who knows the student well can play a major role in appropriate placement and monitoring. In some schools, teacher advisers work with a small number of students to help them make decisions about present and future programs. Teacher advisers

Robert E. Lowery is associate professor and chairman, Department of Educational Administration, School of Education, Seattle University, Wash.

Student Placement

monitor student progress and provide classroom teachers with useful information to facilitate student learning.

5. Involve classroom teachers in placement decisions. Even though the teacher adviser may know an individual advisee best, placement decisions are complex and benefit from other input. Classroom teachers know what is needed to succeed in their courses, and they can evaluate the student's performance in a specific subject better than the teacher adviser.

6. Design a system for monitoring progress that does not permit a student to get hopelessly behind in a course or bored because the work is not challenging. Consider the following: Classroom teachers send reports to teacher advisers about students having difficulty; monthly reports from teacher advisers alert counselors to any unresolved placement problems; a school referral team considers placement of students outside the school setting in special circumstances.

Supervising Instruction

Teaching Styles

Paul F. Kleine

Teaching styles are definitely "in style" (Cornett, 1983). The number and variety of teaching styles, however, can be overwhelming to anyone not immersed in the literature of the field.

Most teachers argue that they vary their teaching style greatly depending on content, learner characteristics, and class objectives, and that their teaching is not reducible to a particular pattern or style. This contention contradicts research evidence and the experience of many instructional supervisors.

Ayers (1983), using supervisor ratings, student evaluations, and interaction analysis data, tracked 133 teachers over a four-year period and found marked consistency in teaching behaviors (correlations ranging from .40 to .60). Brophy and Evertson (1974) and others have also reported teacher consistencies over time and across class groupings.

We will examine the concept of teaching styles more carefully by looking at five components: definitions, learning styles, teaching styles research, problem issues, and suggestions for administrators.

Definitions

Teaching style definitions vary along a continuum from a narrow listing of specific behaviors on one end to a description of global personality characteristics on the other.

Dunn and Dunn (1978), for example, posit a broad definition of teaching style that includes the following nine elements: instructional planning, teaching methods, student groupings, room design, teaching environment, evaluation techniques, educational philosophy, teaching characteristics, and student preference. The Dunns have developed a self-report instrument to assist in identifying individual teacher's style of teaching.

Joyce and Weil (1979) also take a broad perspective. They use the term "model of teaching" to mean "a pattern or plan, which can be used to shape a curriculum or course, to select instruction materials, and to guide a teacher's actions." They go on to identify some 80 defensible models of teaching, grouped in four families:

Paul F. Kleine is director, Bureau of Research Services, College of Education, University of Oklahoma, Norman.

- Social Interaction Models (e.g., social inquiry, role playing)
- Information Processing Models (e.g., inquiry, cognitive growth)
- Personal Models (e.g., nondirective teaching, classroom meetings)
- Behavior Modification/Cybernetic Models (e.g., programmed instruction, simulation).

Keefe (see Article 29) describes teaching styles as "characteristic instructional behaviors reflective of teacher personality and educational philosophy." In this discussion we will define teaching style as the set of behaviors, methods, and strategies that a teacher tends to use consistently over time and in different settings to affect student learning. This conceptualization recognizes that teacher styles do vary from time to time and setting to setting, but that a pattern of behaviors can be recognized and assessed.

Learning Styles

As a prelude to discussing teaching styles, a word needs to be said about teachers' preferred learning styles. Theory and practice both suggest that people tend to teach in a manner similar to the way they prefer to learn. Stensrud and Stensrud (1983) found correlations ranging from .47 to .78 between teachers' preferred learning modalities and preferred teaching styles. Everyone exhibits variations in learning style, but most people tend to show a preference for one or the other 'pure' type. (See Gregorc, 1979; Dunn and Dunn, 1978.) Further examination of learning styles is beyond the scope of this treatment, but readers may consult Article 61 of this handbook for more information.

Teaching Style Research

Cotterell (1982), in reviewing 10 years of research on matching teaching and learning style, found considerable support for matching when teacher and learner satisfaction were both considered, less when student achievement was the major factor. Of the 23 studies reported, 16 showed low to moderate gains for matched conditions, and seven studies showed no differences at all. These findings are consistent with the larger body of research indicating that style matching

Teaching Styles

produces inconsistent achievement gains but solid evidence for affective and attitudinal outcomes.

Another important perspective is evident in the research. Teachers do utilize various styles, but in grades 6 to 12, they prefer to teach in only one style. Middle level and high school teachers tend to favor a reflective, academic learner. This type of learner prefers an intellectual approach and likes to process information reflectively. Research indicates that more than half of all teachers use a "reflective thinker" approach to teaching, while only about one-fourth of the students fall in this category.

Problem Issues

No discussion of teaching styles should neglect a careful review of the limitations inherent in matching or mixing styles.

- *Functional vs. developmental matching.* Should one fit the teacher's style to the learner or stretch the learner to accommodate the teacher? Some researchers and practitioners feel that young children are best served by exposure to a variety of styles and strategies, while older students with strong preferences may require an adaptation of teaching style. Others argue that learning is best served by deliberately matching teaching and learning styles at all developmental levels. Cronbach and Snow (1977) observe: "In education, the time has come to vary the track conditions so that more runners can finish strong."

- *Degree of Mismatch.* If you decide to mismatch styles, the question, then, is to what degree? A small mismatch may be uncomfortable but challenging. A large mismatch may be stressful and, if sustained, contribute to student frustration and even teacher burnout. The decision should be made with care.

- *Preferred vs. Required Matching.* Who decides? Should students, particularly at senior high school age, be allowed to choose teaching styles? Should matching decisions be made by teachers or guided by school policy?

Suggestions for Administrators

- Study and analyze your own dominant learning style so that you know how it might affect your view of teachers' styles.
- Utilize existing instruments (e.g., Dunn and Dunn, 1978; Cornett, 1983) to assess the teaching styles of your faculty and yourself.
- Encourage teachers to recognize and accommodate the different student learning styles. Students rarely understand that there are legitimate alternative patterns of learning, that what may appear to be a difference in learning ability may simply reflect a difference in learning preference.
- Organize staff inservice activities to help teachers stretch or flex into other instructional methodologies suited to differing learning styles. (See Mosston, 1977.)
- Encourage diversity rather than conformity by accepting different teaching styles during supervisory sessions. Begin observations by trying to discern a teacher's style and evaluate the instructional approach accordingly.

References

Ayers, Jerry B. "Consistency of Teacher Behavior Across Time." *Education* 4 (1983): 375–377.

Brophy, J. E., and Evertson, C. M. *Process-Product Correlations in the Texas Teacher Effectiveness Study: Final Report.* Research Report No. 74-4. Austin, Texas: Research and Development Center for Teacher Education, University of Texas, 1974.

Cornett, Claudia E. *What You Should Know About Teaching and Learning Styles.* Bloomington, Ind.: Phi Delta Kappa, 1983.

Cotterell, John L. "Matching Teaching to Learners: A Review of a Decade of Research." *Psychology in the Schools* 19 (1982): 106–112.

Cronbach, L. J. and Snow, R. E., *Aptitudes and Instructional Methods: A Handbook for Research on Interactions.* New York. Irvington, 1977.

Dunn, Rita, and Dunn, Kenneth. *Teaching Students Through Their Individual Learning Styles: A Practical Approach.* Reston, Va.: Reston Publishing Co., 1978.

Gregorc, A. F. "Learning/Teaching Styles: Their Nature and Effects." In *Student Learning Styles: Diagnosing and Prescribing Programs.* Reston, Va.: National Association of Secondary School Principals, 1979.

Joyce, B., and Weil, M. *Models of Teaching,* 2d ed. Englewood Cliffs, N.J.: Prentice-Hall, 1979.

Kleine, P. F. "Teaching Styles and Teaching Role." In *Encyclopedia of Educational Research,* 5th ed., edited by H. E. Mitzel. New York: The Free Press, 1982.

Mosston, M. *Teaching Behavior: Change with Dignity.* Highland Park, N.J.: Center on Teaching, 1977.

National Association of Secondary School Principals. *Student Learning Styles and Brain Behavior: Programs, Instrumentation, Research.* Reston, Va.: NASSP, 1982.

Stensrud, Robert, and Stensrud, Kay. "Teaching Styles and Learning Styles of Public School Teachers." *Perceptual and Motor Skills* 56 (1983): 414.

Supervision Models

James M. Cooper

The primary purpose of supervision is the improvement of instruction, according to most writers. A review of the literature, however, reveals virtually no research suggesting that supervision has made an appreciable difference in the way teachers conduct their classes. Furthermore, teachers see little benefit in supervision as it is currently practiced.

Supervisor observations of teachers and follow-up conferences are few and of short duration. Interactions between supervisors and teachers tend to be on "safe" topics that are not threatening to either party. A "cold war" relationship exists in which little of significance happens in face-to-face interactions between supervisors and teachers.

Clinical and peer supervision are two models that attempt to generate more significant interactions between teachers and supervisors by altering some of the basic assumptions upon which supervision is based.

Clinical Supervision

Clinical supervision is based on the proposition that the supervisor and teacher work together as colleagues rather than in a superior-subordinate relationship. Clinical supervision respects the integrity and individuality of teachers; its psychological tone is consistent with McGregor's Theory Y. The supervisor does not coerce, demand, or evaluate, but instead encourages, explores, and collaborates. Clinical supervision presumes the teacher's professionalism.

A specific, cyclical methodology is characteristic of clinical supervision:

1. Establishing the supervisor-teacher relationship
2. Agreeing on the focus of the observations
3. Observing and collecting descriptive (not evaluative) data of teaching behavior
4. Analyzing the data and discussing the meaning and implications for the teacher's behavior
5. Planning for long-term professional development and future observations.

Real clinical supervision occurs when the form and spirit of the model are integrated. Implementation of the cycle without the underlying spirit or philosophy usually results only in the principal executing the "inspector" role of supervision more effectively.

In the traditional inspector model, the supervisor has sole responsibility for gathering whatever data seem important, making judgments about the teacher's effectiveness, and deciding what changes should be made. The purpose is to monitor teacher performance. The teacher's role is a passive, powerless one.

The clinical model, on the other hand, assumes that if behavioral change is to take place, the teacher must be convinced that change is needed. Sometimes teachers change their behaviors in response to external threat (such as administrative evaluation), but these changes are usually temporary.

To make clinical supervision work, principals must be willing to spend considerable time working with individual teachers on classroom issues and problems about which the teachers want more information. Ideally, the principal and the teacher should meet before the actual classroom observation to discuss the lesson to be observed; to identify the teacher's purposes, concerns, and areas of interest; and to decide what kind of information or data are needed. The principal must be skilled in using different observational techniques (e.g., anecdotal records, verbatim note taking, interaction analysis), and in developing appropriate observation instruments when they are not already available.

After the observation, the principal and the teacher meet again to examine the data, analyze their meaning, and determine what actions the teacher wants to take. In this process the principal must demonstrate knowledge and skill in human relations, interpersonal communication, motivation, leadership, and planning.

In a recent telephone survey, the executive directors of various national education associations and selected practitioners from those groups[1] were asked. "What should be the activities of instructional supervision?" Forty-nine of 63 suggestions involved the techniques and practices of clinical supervision.

James M. Cooper is dean, School of Education, University of Virginia, Charlottesville.

1. Associations surveyed were the American Association of Colleges for Teacher Education, American Association of School Administrators, American Federation of Teachers, Association for Supervision and Curriculum Development, National Association of Elementary School Principals, National Association of Secondary School Principals, and National Education Association.

Supervision Models

Peer Supervision

Instructional improvement requires considerable time and effort, with no easy shortcuts. Berliner, Joyce, and Showers all argue that for teachers to change their teaching behaviors, someone must "coach" them as they try out new teaching practices in their own classrooms. Without coaching, efforts to change teacher behavior are by and large doomed to failure.

The clinical supervision model appeals to many principals, but finding time for coaching is difficult. In this event, principals may wish to consider a peer supervision or "colleague consultation" model to supplement their own efforts. Peer supervision recognizes that teachers can be valuable resources to one another. The research suggests that when teachers are skilled in the observation, collection, and analysis of data, peer supervision can be a promising approach to instructional improvement.

The principal must be the catalyst for peer supervision in the school. Initially at least, the process demands time and effort. Peer supervision calls for new patterns of interaction among teachers, and between teachers and the principal. It requires that the principal work with teams of teachers, not just individuals. Peer supervision's potential can be realized only if the principal strongly supports the program by providing teachers with training, offering them released time to visit one another's classrooms, and separating these efforts from formal administrative evaluation.

A Context for Successful Supervision

The principal controls the context in which supervision occurs. How the school is organized for instruction, the degree of autonomy given to teachers, and the extent to which teachers participate in the important processes of the school influence their reactions to supervision and supervisors. Implicit in clinical and peer supervision is a view that people are valuable individuals but at the same time capable of contributing to institutional goals and objectives.

Job enrichment research proposes three job factors that positively affect employee satisfaction and productivity: meaningfulness, responsibility, and knowledge of results. In the school setting, *meaningfulness* involves teachers being able to use a variety of talents and abilities and seeing their efforts contribute to the success of the school. *Responsibility* is related to the degree of teacher collaboration in organizing classrooms, determining instructional practices and, to the degree possible, developing schedules. *Knowledge of results* implies that teachers receive direct and clear feedback on the effects of their performance (Hackman and Oldham, 1976).

Supervision is helping teachers in ways that improve their productivity and increase their job satisfaction. Productive and satisfied teachers perform better, are more highly motivated, are less likely to be absent from school, and view personal and institutional goals as compatible.

References

Berliner, David. "On Improving Teachers Effectiveness: A Conversation with David Berliner and Ron Brandt" in *Educational Leadership,* Vol. 40 #1, October 1982, pp 12–15.

Hackman, J. R., and Oldham, Gray. "Motivation Through the Design of Work: Test of a Theory." In *Organizational Behavior and Human Performance,* 1976.

Joyce, Bruce and Showers, Beverly. "Coaching of Teaching" in *Educational Leadership* Vol. 40 #1, October 1982, pp 4–8, 10.

Class Size

Glen Robinson

Class size is but one of the many factors that combine to create an effective climate for learning. Existing research does not support the contention that smaller classes, in themselves, result in greater academic gains for learners, nor does it provide clear guidelines on "optimum" size for all types of students at all grade levels. Rather, efficient class sizes are the product of many variables, including grade level, subject area, student characteristics, learning objectives, materials and facilities, teaching skills, instructional methods, support staff available, and budget.

Although research studies show mixed results on the relationship of class size to achievement, both the Educational Research Service (ERS, 1979) and Glass and Smith (1978) report similar findings about the mid-range of class size.

- Within the mid-range of about 25 to 34 pupils, class size seems to have little if any decisive impact on the academic achievement of most students in most subjects above the primary grades (ERS).
- Within the wide range of 20 to 40 pupils, class size makes little difference in achievement (Glass and Smith).
- Smaller classes are important to increased achievement in reading and mathematics in the early primary grades (ERS).
- Students of lower academic ability tend to benefit more from smaller classes than those of average ability. Smaller classes also can positively affect the achievement of economically and socially disadvantaged pupils (ERS).
- Smaller classes are better than larger classes regardless of grade level, subject taught, or student ability, provided that class size is 20 or fewer (Glass and Smith).
- Few benefits could be expected from reducing class size if teachers continued to use the same instructional methods and procedures in the smaller classes. The research indicates that many teachers do not change their teaching techniques to take advantage of smaller classes (ERS).

Some evidence suggests that certain teaching procedures and practices perceived by some to be conducive to learning (i.e., individualization, creative activities, group processes, and use of interpersonal regard) occur more frequently in smaller than in larger classes. John Goodlad reports in *A Place Called School* (1983) that goals in his sample schools frequently called for varied teaching techniques, but that the range of actual practices was narrow—mainly lecturing, monitoring seatwork, and activities requiring rote learning.

Opinion polls consistently show that most teachers believe large classes have a negative influence on morale and job satisfaction. Polls also reveal that the majority of the public and teachers believe small classes are important for learner achievement and progress. The available but limited research is divided about the relationship between class size and student attitudes toward learning.

Implications for Educational Policy

Research on class size suggests that emphasis should be placed on methods and quality of instruction rather than on numbers of students. Findings to date fail to justify small overall reductions in class size or student-teacher ratio as a matter of general policy. Rigid and inflexible limits on class size can be counterproductive to the effective utilization of scarce resources and to grouping flexibility.

More experimentation is needed on optimum class sizes for various types of students, grade levels, and subject areas. Some educators and researchers believe that smaller classes allow teachers more choice in teaching strategies, which could be beneficial for learning. Goodlad recommends changes in instructional methods to engage students in active learning. He reports that barely 5 percent of instructional time in the schools is spent in encouraging students to respond, and less than 1 percent in responses involving reasoning or student opinion. Ernest Boyer, in *High School: A Report on Secondary Education in America* (1983), recommends that basic writing should "have no more than 20 students in each class, and no more than two classes should be included within the regular teacher's load."

Glen Robinson is president, Educational Research Service, Arlington, Va.

Class Size

Class size has a major impact on school budgets. Even small systemwide changes in student-teacher ratios can have a substantial effect on a school or system's budget. Decisions about class size and related ratios demand careful consideration of the potential learner and teacher benefits, utilization of facilities, actual costs, and the political consequences.

Factors Mitigating the Influence of Class Size

Regardless of actual class size, certain program characteristics directly or indirectly affect the learning process. The following interacting variables can influence the impact of class size on student learning.

- *Program Goals*—Clearly stated goals and objectives that are shared by teachers, students, administrators, board members, and parents.
- *Competent Staff*—A staff that believes students can achieve and works together collaboratively to see that they do so.
- *Supportive Environment*—A school climate that supports teacher efforts in the classroom and minimizes outside factors that can disrupt the learning process.
- *Adequate Resources*—Appropriate resources used to support the learning objectives of specific groups of students.
- *Diagnostic Systems*—Processes to allow for instructional planning, grouping for instruction, assessing and monitoring student progress, and feedback to students.
- *Teacher Involvement*—Collaborative procedures for involving teachers in decision making about the school program.
- *Instructional Techniques*—Teaching techniques and strategies for achieving specific learning objectives for specific students.
- *Range of Student Abilities*—Limiting the range of student abilities to lessen the effects of large class sizes, or widening the range in small classes to increase the challenge.
- *Classroom Management*—Helping teachers effectively manage available instructional time (more important than the actual number of minutes allocated for instruction).
- *Support Personnel*—Providing support personnel needed to meet program goals and to maintain a cooperative work environment.
- *Modifying Instruction*—Helping teachers to modify their instructional techniques to take advantage of small classes or to lessen the undesirable effects of increased class size.
- *Reducing Clerical Work*—Reducing the time teachers must devote to routine paperwork and other clerical functions.
- *Training Programs*—Inservice training activities to assist teachers in improving their teaching skills and adapting their instructional techniques to the needs of students in various sized classes.

Asking the Right Questions

Research provides few guidelines for determining the "best" class size. Students at different levels of personal and academic development require different learning conditions for achievement gains to occur. Confronting the class size issue really demands going beyond the usual generalities to address some specific questions:

1. What are the educational goals and objectives for the target group of students?
2. What are the personal and academic characteristics of these students?
3. What teacher, with what class size, using what instructional methods and teaching skills, will be most effective in helping these students achieve their goals and objectives?

Class size should vary according to the answers to these questions.

References

Educational Research Service. *Class Size: A Summary of Research.* Arlington, Va: ERS, 1978.

Educational Research Service. *Class Size Research: A Critique of Recent Meta-Analyses.* Arlington, Va.: ERS, 1980.

Educational Research Service. *Effective Schools: A Summary of Research.* Arlington, Va.: ERS, 1983.

Glass, G. V., and Smith, M. L. "Meta-analysis of Research on the Relationship of Class Size and Achievement." *Educational Evaluation and Policy Analysis* 1 (1978): 2–16.

Grouping Practices

Stephen K. Miller

Homogeneous grouping for instruction is widely accepted in American schools, but the practice is based more on tradition than research. Advocates favor grouping because it is efficient: a response to diversity, generally acceptable to the public, easier to teach. Critics respond that an equal education is vital to social mobility and that the effects of labeling are experienced disproportionately by the disadvantaged.

Defining Terms

Considerable confusion exists here. *Ability grouping* separates students according to capabilities, usually based on aptitude, achievement tests, and teacher evaluations, but most often on a single test score combined with teacher judgment. *Curriculum grouping* (tracking) provides students with different educational experiences, both in content and level of challenge, based on future career goals. Ability grouping is found in grades 1–12; tracking in senior high schools and, to a lesser degree, middle level schools.

Social Significance

From the viewpoint of the social effects, ability and curriculum grouping are more alike than different. All variations share two characteristics:

1. Members of a group are similar to one another in some respects and segregated from other groups defined as different.
2. The criteria for grouping (ability, performance, future plans) are socially valued, thus ranking the groups in a status hierarchy.

The social aspect of grouping results in labeling effects, low motivation, nonconforming subcultures, and the high dropout rates typical of lower and low average groups. Indeed, students in vocational and general tracks are regularly treated with less respect by both faculty and peers.

Separating Myth from Fact

The dynamics of secondary schools are never the same, so differences found in the research studies on grouping may be due to actual differences between schools. But despite some exceptions, the research has identified a number of trends in the outcomes of grouping.

- *Achievement effects:* Findings for high-ability groups are mixed. Some studies show gains for the top group, while others indicate no difference. The gains appear unrelated to grouping per se, but to better or more advanced instruction. Middle and lower groups show consistent losses compared to heterogeneous groups. On balance, any gains by the top group seem to be at the expense of lower groups, with overall achievement for the school the same or generally lower.
- *Self-esteem:* Although the results are mixed, there is a tendency for gains in esteem for the top group to be offset by losses in lower groups.
- *I.Q. or aptitude:* Scores in top groups are likely to improve. Scores in lower groups are likely to decrease or to become more similar within a track.
- *Bias in selection:* Homogeneous groups are not always very homogeneous. Often the overlap is considerable between the bottom of one group and the top of the next. These placement "errors" almost always disadvantage low-income and minority youth and favor the more affluent.
- *Group transfer:* Extremely limited movement occurs between groups; most students remain fixed in a group. Those who move are much more likely to move down than up. Teachers and administrators consistently overestimate the degree of actual mobility.
- *Misperception of track:* Many students do not know in what curriculum track they are placed. Research shows a correlation of only .60 between actual and perceived track.
- *Effects of misperceived track:* A student's curriculum track is a major factor in future college or career plans. Students who believe they are in a college preparatory track, when they actually are not, can have their college plans frustrated when they fail to meet admissions requirements. Disadvantaged students seem to be disproportionately affected by this phenomenon.
- *Student choice in curriculum selection:* Curriculum grouping is predicated on career preference, yet many students (and parents) are not fully informed about career options. Nor are students always free

---

Stephen K. Miller is assistant professor, School of Education, University of Louisville, Ky.

Grouping Practices

to choose their preferred tracks. When choice is available, it may be influenced by such short-term perceptions as avoiding "tough" classes, influence of peers, etc.
- *Role of counselors:* Counselors play a key role in providing the information that students and parents have available for curriculum and course selection. Unfortunately, disadvantaged and working class students are less likely to seek out counselors. Many counselors tend to respond more to the academic students who seek them out more often. The result is unplanned bias.
- *Allocation of resources:* Grouping sometimes produces unequal distribution of resources within a school, especially in the assignment of teachers. Beginning and inexperienced teachers are more apt to be assigned lower groups than experienced teachers.
- *Feelings of failure:* Students experience the effects of grouping intensely and emotionally. Case studies reveal both student and teacher insensibility toward those in lower groups. Too often, lower-track students develop feelings of resentment, hostility, self-blame, hopelessness, and inadequacy.

Positive claims for homogeneous grouping are not substantiated by the research evidence. Instead, typical grouping is associated with social hierarchies, educational inequalities, and peer subcultures. Many negative outcomes are associated with (if not caused by) the rigid grouping systems that schools perpetuate.

What the Principal Can Do

Heterogeneous grouping across ability, race, and social class seems to produce the benefits sought by advocates of ability grouping without the negative consequences noted above. But high schools are often faced with vast differences in student achievement, attitude, and motivation that are fairly well-fixed by eighth grade. The recommendations that follow are an attempt to respond to this real diversity but to limit the effects of negative labeling.

1. *Provide inservice:* Inservice can create the awareness needed to counter unintended and unrecognized effects. Good diagnostic techniques are helpful. Diagnosing and accommodating individual student learning styles can contribute to student success in homogeneous or heterogeneous settings. (See Article 61.)

2. *Monitor track placement decisions:* Do all students have equal access to counselors and information? Are career options understood?

3. *Check allocation of resources:* Are competent, self-confident teachers assigned to students who need more individual attention? Are sufficient and appropriate resources provided for the less talented?

4. *Monitor racial and social class ratios* to avoid segregation by track. Very often, ability-grouped programs tend to resegregate a school.

5. *Increase the flexibility of grouping practices:*
- Monitor and inform staff of group transfer rates.
- Review student placement frequently.
- Consider achievement or readiness grouping instead of ability grouping. Ability grouping separates students into different tracks with all subjects taught in that track. Achievement or readiness grouping places students in each subject independently. (Students at one level for math may be placed at a different level for English.)

6. *Implement stratified heterogeneous grouping* (the Baltimore Plan): Assign students of high, average, and low achievement levels to each class. Example: 90 students are ranked on the basis of a standardized achievement test. Students in the 1–10 percentiles, 31–40 percentiles, and 61–70 percentiles are placed in one class. A second class receives 11–20, 41–50, and 71–80 percentiles. A third class receives 21–30, 51–60, and 81–99 percentiles. This approach reduces the diversity within a class but offers the benefits of heterogeneous placement. Other combinations are possible.

7. *Implement mastery learning* in heterogeneous classes with corrective instruction and enrichment: (See Article 31.) Institute cross-age tutoring, especially with older, low-achieving students helping younger students. The youngsters benefit and the older students improve in achievement, motivation, and responsibility.

8. *Utilize academic team games:* Organize small (4–6) heterogeneous teams of students to compete with other teams in academic contests. The inherent motivation improves attitudes toward learning. (See Article 32.)

The negative effects of grouping are more pronounced in some schools than others. More rigid homogeneous grouping seems to generate more negative outcomes and to increase delinquent subcultures. Heterogeneous grouping, generally, is preferable to any of the forms of homogeneous grouping.

Use of Time

Lorin W. Anderson

Schools are time-bound places: Elementary school days last from about 9:00 a.m. until 3:00 p.m.; high school classes run from about 7:30 a.m. until 2:30 p.m.; and college achievement is registered in terms of credit hours.

Much has been written and said about the importance of time spent to learning. Thirty-five states have increased or are planning to increase the amount of time devoted to instruction. Extending the school day, lengthening the school year, and reducing classroom interruptions have been suggested as ways to improve student achievement. Attention has turned to increasing the productive use of the available time; i.e., instructional time, time-on-task, and academic learning time.

- *Instructional time* is that portion of classroom time designated for teaching students the knowledge and skills of a particular subject area and age level. Instructional time does not include the time spent on discipline and routine procedural matters, such as the clerical tasks at the beginning of a lesson or class period or the time passing from classroom to classroom.
- *Time-on-task* is that portion of instructional time during which students are actively engaged in the process of learning or doing what teachers have assigned. Time-on-task does not include the time students spend daydreaming, socializing, or not giving full attention to the task at hand.
- *Academic learning time* is that portion of the time-on-task during which students learn. Evidence of learning includes answering questions correctly in class and completing assignments accurately.

Increasing Instructional Time

Effective instructional time use is largely a matter of planning and sustaining classroom routines.

- Intrusions into class time such as announcements on the P.A. system can be eliminated; announcements can be made orally or in writing during a "homeroom" period.
- Attendance can be taken while the teacher is monitoring student seatwork or unobtrusively by an aide or student assistant while the teacher proceeds with instruction.
- Materials needed for use in a class period can be readied and distributed before the class period or, at worst, at the beginning of the class.
- Supplemental activities can be available for students who complete their assignments before the end of the class period.
- Procedures for entering and leaving the room, sharpening pencils, and the like can be standardized so that students can act without having to seek permission or disrupting the flow of instruction.
- Changes from one classroom activity (e.g., lecture) to another (e.g., discussion groups) can be planned and carried out smoothly with minimal loss of time.

A decision to increase the actual amount of time allocated to specific instruction should be based on how time is used at present and how much time is needed. Teachers who devote an inordinate amount of time to noninstructional activities can regain useful time by careful self-monitoring. Even the best teachers may find a few minutes in each class period to use more effectively. By using three minutes a day more productively, nine hours of instructional time are regained each year.

Increasing Time-on-Task

Recent research proposes a set of teaching activities associated with high degrees of time-on-task. Teachers can do the following:

1. Clearly communicate the purpose or goal of the lesson. Students spend more time on task when they know what they are expected to learn.
2. Keep things moving and pace the lesson appropriately. Reduce the number of digressions, and move the class purposefully toward daily, weekly, and long-range goals.
3. Reinforce task-oriented behavior. Praise and encourage students for paying attention, hard work, and the like. If appropriate, provide incentives and rewards for such behavior. Be sure that students see the incentives and rewards as valuable to them, not just to the teachers.
4. Monitor the learning. Ask periodic questions during a presentation. Use short quizzes to check students' progress. Circulate during supervised study

---

Lorin W. Anderson is professor, College of Education, University of South Carolina, Columbia.

Use of Time

time to see if students are working on assigned tasks.

5. Help students correct errors and misunderstandings as they occur. If errors and misunderstandings accumulate, students become "lost" and time spent on task decreases dramatically. Also be sure that students possess the prerequisite background information before beginning a task.

Increasing Academic Learning Time

Increasing academic learning time ultimately means helping more students become more successful at academic learning. The learning objectives or content to be learned must be at an appropriate level of difficulty.

At least three approaches exist for managing the difficulty level of learning objectives and related content:

- Different objectives can be assigned to different students or groups of students according to an assessment of students' current learning strengths and weaknesses. The implementation of this approach requires some degree of individualization or in-class, instructional grouping. Research indicates that the interaction of teacher and students is more likely than unsupervised learning activities to increase academic learning time. One-to-one instruction yields the highest degree of academic learning time.
- Similar instructional objectives can be specified for all students, with different assignments given on these objectives to different groups of students. If the objective is to infer the main idea of a paragraph or longer passage, some students may be assigned paragraphs, some longer passages. Different groups may be assigned paragraphs with different levels of reading skill.
- The curriculum can be carefully sequenced, permitting students to move from one area of the course or curriculum to another when they have demonstrated sufficient knowledge or skill.

Time and Learning

While better use of time actually makes more time available for teaching and learning, schools still have too much to do. We must begin to assess how much students can learn in the available time. In some instances, no amount of time increase will matter given the tasks to accomplish. Examining the density of courses and curricula (how many objectives or how much content is included) and weeding out less important objectives and content may result in more productive use of time. Effective time use is also related to clear and comprehensive instruction, the ability to diagnose the skills students bring to a task, and knowledge of how to sequence instruction appropriately for individual students.

In a recent review of the time-on-task literature, Nancy Karweit (1983) of Johns Hopkins University found that effects of time on student achievement are small. Only 1 to 10 percent of the variance in student achievement could be attributed to the amount of engaged time. She concluded, "The view that time spent is equivalent to learning gained has become the newest myth to cloud our understanding of education."

Reasons exist to believe that time devoted to learning can raise student achievement, but the process may not be a straight line projection, as some would have us believe. Other variables impinge on the quality of time spent and should be considered before we apply quick solutions to complex educational problems.

Reference

Karweit, N. L. *Time on Task: A Research Review.* Center for Social Organization of Schools, Report No. 332. Baltimore, Md., 1983.

Use of Space

Carl L. Midjaas

The use of instructional space is perhaps the most neglected element in the effort to improve instructional effectiveness. Most of us tend to think of classrooms as interchangeable units and the space within them as usable in essentially the same way. Teacher evaluation, for example, largely ignores the impact of different instructional environments.

A growing body of research suggests that space is a very important component of the learning process. Consider some of the findings on which environmental characteristics enhance academic learning. (For more information, see Weil and Murphy, 1982.)

- Teachers who maintain an "academic focus" or task orientation achieve greater student involvement.
- Environments characterized as teacher-directed produce greater student achievement in basic skills tasks than those in which the students have greater freedom to act; environments characterized as open or learner-centered generate better attitudes toward school, improved attitudes toward teachers, and higher degrees of curiosity and independence than teacher-dominated environments. The impact of each environment on individual students varies depending on the characteristics of the student.
- Environments which are psychologically or emotionally negative inhibit learning.
- Supervised student seatwork is more effective in supporting achievement than unsupervised time; the amount and type of supervision needed varies with different students.
- Students working independently or in small groups without adult supervision spend significantly less time working on task than do supervised groups.

What implications can we draw from these research findings about the effective use of space? In the following sections, we will discuss various ways to improve the instructional environment. Some are directly under the control of the teacher; some require additional resources such as physical or visual barriers and acoustic controls; still others require administrative action to change schedules and revise procedures.

Academic Environment

Instructional space should convey serious intent, de-emphasizing nonacademic or noninstructional ma-

Carl L. Midjaas is director of personnel and management services, Independent School District No. 622, Maplewood, Minn.

terials. According to research, games, puzzles, decorative posters, and materials not directly related to the learning at hand are distracting to students and should be avoided. Bulletin board and other instructional displays should reinforce the content under study.

Supervisory Arrangements

Evidence suggests that too much emphasis on individualization and one-to-one teaching is not productive in a typical classroom setting. When students work independently without direct teacher supervision, they spend significantly less time working on materials. If the teacher concentrates on one or two students, class time-on-task inevitably suffers unless other help is available. Cooperative or team teaching, for example, can support varied activities simultaneously in the same instructional space.

Teachers also need to establish appropriate classroom procedures. Students need to know the rules by which the class operates, where to get supplies, how to signal for assistance, how to participate in small groups, large groups, etc. Signs, posters, storage cabinets, and well-organized work stations can lend appropriate structure to the environment.

When students are working independently, paired up, or in small groups, the teacher should move about answering questions, checking work, making certain all students know what to do and are doing it. The supervisory arrangements should encourage students to remain on task.

Non-Negative Affect

The evidence is inconclusive whether a psychologically warm, supportive, and comfortable physical environment has a positive influence on learning, but it is clear that instructional space should not be negative in affect. Students should not find instructional space so unattractive or undesirable that their willingness to work is affected. The environment should also accommodate individual preferences for formal or informal space. Some students concentrate and do their best in informal surroundings; others require a high degree of structure.

Privacy and Concentration

A serious learning environment demands reasonable focus on task and teacher control. Conventional

Use of Space

classrooms and laboratories present few control problems, but open-plan instructional spaces require special attention. Appropriate treatment of space in an open-plan school can effectively reduce the number of problems: acoustical treatment of older areas, careful scheduling of adjacent activities, elimination of cross traffic, reduction of outside interruptions, etc. Headsets can allow some students to use audiovisual equipment while respecting others' rights not to hear. Movable barriers can be used to separate individuals and groups as needed.

Different activity areas should be clearly evident. Students need to know what activities are appropriate in various areas of the instructional space, and this space should help to define student behavior.

Student Density and Level of Resource

Research shows a negative relationship between greater numbers of students in an instructional space and lower levels of available resources (materials, supplies, reference materials). Instructional space characterized as high density/low resource is associated with increased student/teacher conflict and poor student-to-student behavior. Instructional areas must have enough space, reasonable numbers of students, and adequate resources.

Guidelines for Effective Use of Instructional Space

Administrators will find the following questions helpful in evaluating teacher use of space:

1. Does the teacher use space to create a serious, academic atmosphere?
2. Does the design and use of the instructional environment promote student cooperation and sharing of resources?
3. Does the use of space allow for differential treatment of students according to their instructional needs?
4. Does the environment provide for sufficient structure and reduce the need for repetitive directions about learning tasks and activities?
5. Is the environment positive in affect and attractive without detracting from the focus on learning?
6. Do the bulletin boards and display areas support the content under study?
7. If the instructional space contains activity subareas, are they clearly defined in purpose and design?

If you can answer yes to all or most of these questions, teachers in your school are using space in ways that contribute to greater instructional effectiveness. The key is to control the use of space, not be controlled by it. The arrangement of instructional space should accommodate the purposes of instruction and provide for both reasonable structure and flexibility.

References

Peterson, Penelope L., and Walberg, Herbert J. *Research on Teaching: Concepts, Findings and Implications.* Berkeley, Calif.: McCutchan Publishing Corp., 1979.

Weil, Marsha L., and Murphy, Joseph. "Instructional Processes." In *Encyclopedia of Educational Research.* New York: Free Press, 1982.

Instructional Media/Materials

Gene L. Wilkinson

The materials of instruction and the devices to display these materials are almost limitless. They include: textbooks, workbooks, handouts, maps, charts, flat pictures, chalkboards, bulletin boards, flannel boards, exhibits, displays, models, slides, filmstrips, motion pictures, audiotapes, cassettes, television, videotapes, games, simulations, programmed instruction, microcomputers, and interactive videodiscs. The big question, however, is which devices to use and how to use them effectively.

Research on Media Effectiveness

Thousands of studies have attempted to determine which is the most effective form of media to use in instruction. The results have been mixed—no one medium is clearly superior to another (Wilkinson, 1980).

This conclusion should not be surprising. Richard Clark draws an analogy between media and a truck. The truck contributes no nutritional value to the food that it hauls to market. Similarly, the important factor in media use is the message and how it is used in the classroom, not the medium that delivers it. Clark's analogy can be taken a step further. The truck adds no nutritional value to the food, but the choice of an inappropriate vehicle can destroy existing value. Media choice is critical to the effective delivery of the instructional message.

In spite of conflicting results, research evidence supports the conclusion that:

- Educational media and materials, when they are carefully selected or produced and systematically integrated into the instructional program, have a significant impact on student achievement.
- Media are more effectively and efficiently used when teachers receive specific training in their use.
- Media are more effectively and efficiently used when the school has an integrated media center based on national guidelines (ALA/AECT, 1975).
- Media centers have a greater impact on media use in instruction (and on students) when they are staffed by trained, full-time media specialists.
- Media centers have a greater impact when materials and services are based on and integrated into the instructional program of the school.

Gene L. Wilkinson is associate professor of educational media, University of Georgia, Athens.

Patterns of Media Use

Leadership is necessary for effective media use. The most critical task of the principal in this context is to develop or locate a qualified, full-time staff member to organize media utilization for the school—a media specialist.

The three basic patterns of media utilization, each of which has different potential effects on program cost and effectiveness, are:

- *Additive Approach.* Materials are added to regular instruction as supplementary or enrichment activities and, as such, are not necessary for the achievement of basic instructional outcomes. Media use is dependent on the classroom teacher, does not have a significant impact on student achievement, and represents an added expense for the educational system. This approach is not cost-effective.
- *Integrated Approach.* Carefully selected or produced materials are integrated into regular instruction and become an essential element leading to the achievement of basic instructional outcomes. This approach represents an additional cost for the school/district and requires extensive teacher planning and preparation, but it has the potential of increasing student achievement.
- *Independent Approach.* Instruction is redesigned so that at least some basic instructional outcomes can be achieved through the interaction of students and instructional materials without the direct intervention of the classroom teacher. This approach represents a major initial cost to the school system, but it has the greatest potential for increasing the cost effectiveness of the instructional program.

Effective Media Integration

Whatever general pattern of media utilization is adopted, effective integration within the program is built on a number of general principles. One of the most basic of these is that media are not ends in themselves, but means to an end.

The design of media-based instruction begins, not with the selection of media, but with an instructional problem to be solved. Media should be selected only after the learners and content to be taught have been identified and analyzed, objectives determined, and the general instructional approach selected.

Instructional Media/Materials

The process of media selection should begin with no preconceived notions. All forms and combinations of media should be considered before any final selection is made. The array of alternatives can be reduced initially by determining what the media must be capable of doing—the mode of presentation.

Identification of the mode of presentation should be based on learner and content analysis and instructional design decisions. It should take into consideration the forms of information to be presented (still visual, motion, sound, print, etc.) and the tasks to be carried out (new skill learning, immediate reinforcement, independent practice, etc.).

When the viable alternatives have been identified, the choices can be further narrowed by considering the relative advantages and disadvantages of the media: physical characteristics; operational characteristics; and such administrative characteristics as cost, availability, etc. At this point, personal preferences can be considered.

Materials Evaluation

Once the media format has been selected, commercial or locally produced materials must be evaluated for use in the program. This evaluation should be based on the following criteria:

- Do the materials fit the objectives?
- Is the material the best available rather than the first located?
- Is the material geared to the appropriate maturity level of the students?
- Is the content accurate, up-to-date, and without bias?
- Is the technical quality good?
- Is the length appropriate and worth the time required to view, listen, etc.?

At times, parents or the public will object to instructional materials selected for use in a given program. Many schools/districts have developed a form based on the ALA/NCTE model complaint form to give protesters a formal hearing. (See Article 24.) Principals should be very familiar with this form.

Sources of Additional Information

The basic principles of effective media utilization are relatively stable, but the devices are constantly changing. Those who would use media effectively need both a broad knowledge of media currently available and a means of keeping up with the field.

A basic overview of the forms and uses of media can be found in such general textbooks as Brown, et al. (1977), and Heinich, et al. (1982). Factors involved in the selection of media format and materials are discussed by Anderson (1983) and Reiser and Gagné (1983). A comprehensive treatment of production principles and techniques for local use is provided by Kemp (1980). Detailed information on equipment operation and maintenance is available in Oates (1979), and Bullard and Mether (1984).

A number of periodicals, from association journals such as *Instructional Innovator* and *School Library Media Quarterly* to commercial publications such as *Educational Technology*, can help the administrator stay up-to-date with the field. A descriptive listing of more than 475 periodicals in the media field is contained in the annual *Educational Media Yearbook* (Libraries Unlimited, Littleton, Colo.).

References

ALA/AECT. *Media Programs: District and School.* Chicago: American Library Association, and Washington, D.C.: Association for Educational Communications and Technology, 1975.

Anderson, R. H. *Selecting and Developing Media for Instruction.* Englewood Cliffs, N.J.: Educational Technology Publications, 1983.

Brown, J. W.; Lewis, R. F.; and Harcleroad, F. *AV Instruction: Technology, Media, and Methods.* 5th ed. New York: McGraw-Hill, 1977

Bullard, J. R., and Mether, C. E. *Audiovisual Fundamentals.* 3rd ed. Dubuque, Iowa: William C. Brown, 1984.

Clark, R. E. "Reconsidering Research on Learning from Media." *Review of Educational Research*, Vol. 53, No. 4, Winter 1983, pp. 445–459.

Heinich, R.; Molenda, M.; and Russell, J. D. *Instructional Media and the New Technologies of Instruction.* New York: John Wiley & Sons, 1982.

Kemp, J. E. *Planning and Producing Audiovisual Materials.* 4th ed. New York: Harper & Row, 1980.

Oates, S. C. *Audiovisual Equipment Self-Instructional Manual.* 4th ed. Dubuque, Iowa: William C. Brown, 1979.

Reiser, R. A., and Gagné, R. M. *Selecting Media for Instruction.* Englewood Cliffs, N.J.: Educational Technology Publications, 1983.

Wilkinson, G. L. *Media in Instruction: 60 Years of Research.* Washington, D.C.: Association for Educational Communications and Technology, 1980.

Instructional Strategy

Jerry W. Valentine

Administrators have a responsibility to provide the teachers they supervise with meaningful feedback. Without accurate and appropriate feedback, teachers cannot be expected to improve instruction.

This article outlines a number of strategies that represent a common sense approach to classroom instruction that can be easily communicated to teachers, and that can be implemented within the typical school setting.

Basic Beliefs

Some basic premises are fundamental: First, all students without a major educational handicap can master basic skills. Second, the instructional process affects the level of student learning and mastery of skills. Third, the teacher must be willing to assume a personal responsibility for the education of each student. Fourth, the level of student achievement is directly related to the level of teacher expectation. Fifth, the principal must assume an active, supportive role in the instructional life of the school.

Understanding these basic beliefs is simple; internalizing and implementing them is complex. The end product is personalized and adaptive education.

Methodological Considerations

Personalized education does not mean that students in a given class operate at many different levels with the teacher serving as ringmaster. Personalization is an educational mindset that identifies and uses the best in instructional strategy. Currently, teachers should be attuned to the strong message in the effective teaching literature about the value of on task, teacher-led instruction, and the findings of cognitive/learning style research on the importance of diagnostic-prescriptive practices.

What specific teaching strategies can the principal emphasize to provide teachers with useful feedback? The literature of effective teaching, diagnostic-prescriptive education, and personal experience would suggest a focus on the following stages of the instructional process:

Jerry W. Valentine is associate professor of education, College of Education, University of Missouri-Columbia.

- *Establishing Set.* A smooth, efficient beginning to each class increases the potential for effective learning. Learners need to understand what is forthcoming—both what will be taught (content), and how it will be taught (process).

Establishing set means clarifying for the student what will be accomplished in class today, how that relates to what has been learned previously, and how all this relates to what will be learned tomorrow. Set enables the learner to see the larger picture of learning.

Set can vary in its affective component. An enthusiastic and creative teacher may excite students about the learning process and make them anxious to begin the experience. A less animated teacher may be more "matter of fact." But with whatever degree of enthusiasm, establishing set is good learning practice. If students understand what they are to learn and are motivated to learn, they will learn more.

- *Stating Objectives.* Stating objectives is an integral part of establishing set. A statement of desired outcomes increases the probability that teachers will teach the appropriate content. Identifying outcomes is appropriate to both traditional and personalized approaches to instruction; some districts/schools even require that teachers send home semester course outlines with goals and objectives specified.

- *Diagnosing Style.* Much of the research on teaching focuses on the behavior of the teacher, but teacher behavior is most effective when it builds on the diagnosed characteristics of students. The assumption that one method of teaching is appropriate for all students is rejected by cognitive/learning style research.

Dunn and Dunn (1978) have found, for example, that only 30 to 35 percent of all high school students learn new or difficult material auditorily. Yet, the dominant behavior in most secondary classrooms is "teacher talk." Tactual and kinesthetic students who make up 30 to 40 percent of the high school population have difficulty with highly verbal learning.

Letteri (1980) has identified seven control dimensions of cognitive style that predict success in academic subjects. Using a therapeutic approach in which diagnosed deficiencies in the seven dimensions are corrected, Letteri has realized more than three years of growth for some students in one year of training.

Instructional Strategy

The cognitive/learning style approach requires that teachers know students' information processing, motivational, and environmental preferences.

- *Modeling Behavior.* Modeling is simply showing students what you want them to do. If students see the teacher perform a skill that they are asked to achieve, they will learn that skill more quickly. Whatever the content—a math equation, a chemistry experiment, a poetry analysis, a critique of a political doctrine—the teacher can demonstrate skills and thought processes through modeling. And, if teachers enjoy the instruction, they can transmit their enthusiasm as well.

- *Checking Comprehension.* Student understanding should be assessed by formative and summative evaluation. Formative evaluation is ongoing monitoring during the actual teaching/learning process. Summative evaluation is determination of the mastery of content and skills. Both forms of evaluation are important.

   Through monitoring, the teacher assesses student progress and evaluates current instructional methods, making changes as appropriate. Monitoring may take the form of a paper and pencil test, a one-to-one conference between teacher and student, or verbal student reports to a small group of students. Summative evaluation determines the degree of learning and can result in decisions to reteach, review, and remediate.

- *Providing Practice.* Students need practice to develop skills and to internalize them. Guided and independent practice in school and at home are essential to skill learning, and should follow immediately after student exposure to new skills. Guided practice usually involves direct tutelage by the teacher. Formative testing is a form of practice. Homework can be used for independent practice assigned individually to students needing additional reinforcement.

- *Achieving Closure and Retention.* At the end of each lesson or learning sequence, key concepts and skills should be reviewed as preparation for the next segment of learning. Knowing the connection between current and future content endows students with a greater sense of meaning. Right brain students are especially helped by a global picture of what is to be learned.

Hunter (1979) suggests a number of practices to help students remember what they learn:

—*Meaning.* Students remember what has meaning for them. A structured curriculum and sequential objectives contribute to meaning. Students need to see the bigger picture of what they are learning, in the context of their own lives.

—*Degree of original learning.* Students retain what they learn well initially. Teachers need to assess the level of learning on important objectives and reteach if necessary.

—*Pleasant feeling tone.* Students remember and are motivated by success. Unpleasant feeling tone causes avoidance behavior.

—*Positive transfer.* Positive transfer exists when students' previous learning facilitates new learning and retention. Negative transfer is present when prior learning interferes with new learning. Experienced teachers teach to positive transfer (e.g., sentence writing skills building to paragraph writing skills).

—*Practice.* New knowledge and skills require frequent and closely spaced practice (massed practice); previous learning can be reinforced by more widely spaced practice (distributed practice).

Words of Caution

Teaching is not a definitive and scientific set of clearly sequential steps that can be done by the numbers. It is a complex process involving the interaction of teachers, students, and content. Fortunately, a body of research is growing that makes the challenge more achievable. The continuing dilemma of instructional strategy is avoiding the perspective that information on one aspect of teaching can be generalized to resolve all instructional problems.

References

Dunn, Rita, and Dunn, Kenneth. *Teaching Students Through Their Individual Learning Styles: A Practical Approach.* Reston, Va.: Reston Publishing Co., 1978.

Hunter, M. "Knowing, Teaching, and Supervising." In *Using What We Know About Teaching,* edited by P. L. Hosford. Alexandria, Va.: Association for Sueprvision and Curriculum Development, 1984.

———. *Retention Theory for Teachers.* El Segundo, Calif.: TIP Publications, 1979.

Letteri, Charles A. "Cognitive Profile: Basic Determinant of Academic Achievement." *The Journal of Educational Research,* March/April 1980.

Homework

Deborah B. Strother

What should principals do to respond to the demands of state and national commissions for "firm, explicit, and demanding requirements concerning homework" (ECS, 1983)? Two options are to review the research findings, and to develop a school policy.

Read What the Experts Say

Nicholas Beattie, in an article for the *London Times Educational Supplement* (1978), suggested four reasons for assigning homework: parents expect homework; homework extends the time available for formal learning; homework encourages youngsters to work on their own; and homework acknowledges the existence of learning styles (objectives).

- *Parents expect homework.* Homework provides a vital link between school and home. Work sent home gives parents insight into a school's philosophy, curriculum, and objectives. Parents give their youngsters the individualized help that is often neglected or missing in crowded classrooms.
- *Homework extends the time available for formal learning.* Every few decades the extended learning time debate resurfaces, influenced by changing views of leisure time and changing attitudes about learning and teaching methods.

During three decades of the twentieth century—1900–1910, 1930–1940, and 1970–1980—teachers and parents strongly questioned the impact of homework on students' mental health, their leisure activities, and their sleeping patterns. During each decade, homework assignments decreased. But when grades or test scores dropped (although no relationship was proven), the pressure to increase homework resurfaced.

Today, the amount of homework assigned in U.S. schools appears to be increasing again. Whenever basic education reformers attempt to improve the academic outcomes of American schooling, more homework seems to be one of the first steps. The justification for this approach probably has more to do with philosophy (students should work harder) and ease of implementation (more homework costs no extra money and requires no major program changes) than with research findings.

Does more time produce better student achievement? Until recently, research on the effects of homework yielded inconclusive results. Sometimes homework seemed to make a difference in achievement; sometimes it did not.

Several large research studies now provide useful data on the relationship of homework to school achievement. *High School and Beyond,* (National Center for Education Statistics, 1980), asked more than 58,000 high school sophomores and seniors how much time, on the average, they spent on homework each week. Keith (1982) used the NCES data to investigate the influence of homework on high school achievement as measured by grades. His findings suggest that individual ability influences grades the most, but the amount of time spent on homework also has a measurable impact.

Austin (1978) summarized the effects of homework on mathematics achievement through 1977. He concluded, for mathematics, that required homework may be preferable to voluntary homework; having no homework assigned in one grade can adversely affect performance in subsequent grades; and, having homework assigned in grades 4–10 seems preferable to not having homework. No studies relating homework to math performance could be located for other grade levels. Austin reported that routine drill-type homework was of limited value, and that teachers need to grade at least some assigned homework problems for learning effectiveness.

- *Homework encourages youngsters to work on their own.* Etzioni (1983) recently wrote that "the role of homework is pivotal. First, not because it provides more hours to pump information into pupils, but because it both encourages and measures the development of self-discipline and associated good working habits. Homework is typically done not under close supervision of teachers or parents, but by pupils on their own, to be evaluated later . . . hence, when systematically and fairly evaluated, (homework) fosters the crucial internalization of discipline, the foundation of self-discipline."

Etzioni concluded from his research that teachers in high-performing schools expect students to do more homework. He advises teachers to help students understand why they should complete their homework and to give them quick feedback on their efforts.

Deborah B. Strother is assistant editor, Phi Delta Kappa Center on Evaluation Development and Research, Bloomington, Ind.

Homework

- *Homework acknowledges the existence of different learning styles* (understood here as objectives). Lee and Pruitt (1979) developed a taxonomy of homework according to its purpose: practice, preparation, extension, or creativity. Assignments involving *practice* help students master specific skills. These practice assignments, according to Lee and Pruitt, should be limited to work in class. *Preparation* helps students gain the maximum benefit from future lessons. *Extension* assignments determine whether students can transfer specific skills or concepts to new situations. These assignments demand abstract thinking. Homework involving *creativity* requires students to integrate skills and concepts to produce original responses (e.g., book reports, research projects).

Develop a School Level Homework Policy

Antoinette Price, supervisor of guidance in the Caddo Parish School System (Shreveport, La.) suggests the following procedures for developing a school level homework policy:

1. *Select a policy development committee.* Gather input from the entire school community; include teacher, parent, and student representatives.

2. *Establish goals and objectives.* List the needs based on the input and then set goals. List objectives and decide on activities to meet them. Include activities that encourage self-direction, independence, and personal responsibility.

3. *Decide on time standards.* Keep in mind what the "experts" suggest:
   - Primary grades (1–3)—45 minutes maximum
   - Upper elementary (4–6)—60 minutes maximum
   - Junior high—90 minutes maximum
   - Senior high—120 minutes maximum

   Stay flexible. No single schedule will work for all schools or even for the same school over time.

4. *Emphasize the need for evaluation.* Demand that students' efforts be appraised and recognized. Homework should be graded or checked. Set up a system so that students can make their own comparative evaluations. Allow students to share with others what they have done.

5. *Make decisions about grading.* Predetermine appropriate rewards for homework and share the results with parents. Homework efforts should count toward a small portion of the overall grade. (If rewards are too high, problems can arise.)

6. *Communicate the policy.* Explain homework policy to parents in writing. Review the policy regularly with teachers, parents, and students.

Some Practical Tips

The Forum of Education Organization Leaders in Washington, D.C., recommends that schools assign one hour of homework per day to elementary students and two or more hours per day to high school students. The Forum adds the following cautions:

- Increasing the amount of homework will be useful only if students have appropriate places to study. (In this regard, schools may want to establish an after-school study hall supervised by an instructional aide or a volunteer.)
- Homework needs to be as carefully planned as classroom instruction; it can include such activities as creative writing, art, music, current events, and community involvement, in addition to reading textbooks.
- Teachers need smaller classes and adequate help to correct homework.

The Forum suggests that teachers individualize homework assignments (long-range as well as short-term projects), make relevant assignments, avoid busywork, and carefully evaluate or grade all homework.

References

Austin, J. D. "Homework Research in Mathematics." *School Science and Mathematics* 79 (1978): 115–122.

Beattie, N. "What's It All For?" *London Times Educational Supplement,* November 20, 1978.

Etzioni, A. "Self Discipline, Schools, and the Business Community." Final Report to the Chamber of Commerce Foundation, 1983.

Keith, T. Z. "Time Spent on Homework and High School Grades: A Large-Sample Path Analysis." *Journal of Educational Psychology,* April 1982.

Lee, J. F., and Pruitt, K. W. "Homework Assignments: Classroom Games or Teaching Tools." *Clearing House,* September 1979.

Task Force on Education for Economic Growth, Education Commission of the States. *Action for Excellence.* Denver, Colo.: ECS, 1983.

EVALUATION ELEMENTS

Assessing, Reporting Student Progress

James W. Keefe

Student grades can serve several purposes: an administrative function, to establish a permanent record of student achievement; a guidance function, to determine strengths, weaknesses, and needed goals and skills; a communication function, to provide information to students, teachers, parents, and others; a motivational function, as a reward or sanction. Well-conceived reporting systems exhibit five characteristics.

1. *Learning progress receives the primary emphasis*—reporting focuses on individual growth.

2. *Information is recorded on many objectives*—motivation, study skills, citizenship, mastery of subject matter skills, etc.

3. *Comparative achievement is reported*—for purposes of planning, promotion, GPA, class rank, etc.

4. *Parents and the public are able to understand the system*—parent-teacher conferences are incorporated for follow-up feedback.

5. *The system is cost-effective.*

Grading Models

Terwilliger (1971) cites four basic approaches to grading:

1. *Absolute or criterion model.* The standards of achievement are specifically defined and applicable to all students. Categories of achievement are criterion-referenced. In a mastery system, a single criterion level is chosen for mastery; e.g., 80 percent, or actual demonstration of a required skill. Sometimes, higher performance is assigned an "A" or "B" grade. This model encourages most students to achieve real competence, but it does present two problems: how to set appropriate standards of performance; and how to organize for individual differences in cognitive style, motivation, and academic ability.

2. *Relative or normative model.* The achievement of other students is the frame of reference. Assessment is based on some variation of the normal curve. The assumption that achievement in a regular class is normally distributed may be false, however, particularly if the class is highly selective (gifted, remedial, etc.).

James W. Keefe is director of research, NASSP, Reston, Va.

3. *Ability-achievement model.* Achievement is rated in relation to individual ability. Since greater ability generally makes for higher achievement, different standards of performance are set for different students. Equity may not be well-served in the long run, however, because students with lower ability may well receive good grades under this system yet not be able to achieve in the job market.

4. *Growth model.* The frame of reference is individual student growth. Achievement is assessed strictly in terms of individual progress. The motivational advantages of this model are obvious, but the premise poses some difficulty. On the one hand, growth occurs in students whose actual achievement is at a minimum; on the other hand, students who show little growth may actually be outstanding by any objective criterion.

Grade Reporting Systems

In practice, most grade reporting systems are eclectic, combining two or more of the above models. The following are the most widely used systems:

- *Percentages (100-point scale).* This system assumes a precision in evaluation that usually is lacking and tends to quantify the trivial; i.e., one percentage point separates grades. Percentages convey little information about learning progress and are difficult to interpret.

- *Alpha grading (5-point scale).* A, B, C, D, and F are given the value of 4, 3, 2, 1, and 0 grade points, respectively. There are few categories, but the dividing lines between the grading levels are arbitrary. Various distributions derived from the normal curve are used for grading. Generally speaking, alpha grades are poor indicators of individual progress. Their strength lies in simplicity and administrative convenience.

Visual Grading is a variation on alpha grading that starts with a frequency distribution of raw scores. The teacher decides how many grade categories to use; e.g., in a gifted class, only A, B, and C might be used. Grades are organized in a horizontal frequency distribution so that the "hills and valleys" of the rank order are apparent. The "natural breaks" become dividing lines for the grades. Visualization encourages assigning the same grade to close scores, but "natural" breaks are often hard to find. (See Figure 1)

Assessing, Reporting Student Progress

Figure 1. *Visual Grading Example*

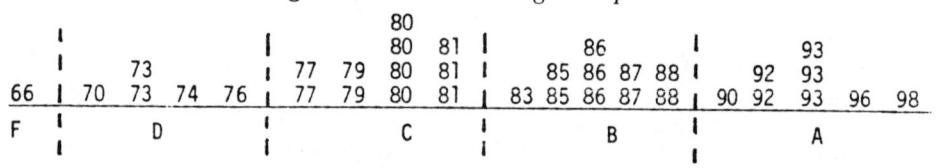

```
                            80
 |             |            80  81  |            86        |             93
 |       73    |     77  79 80  81  |     85  86 87  88    |      92     93
66 | 70  73  74 76 | 77 79 80  81  | 83 85 86 87  88   | 90 92   93  96  98
 F  |         D    |         C     |          B           |         A
 |             |                   |                      |
```

35 students: 8 As, 10 Bs, 12 Cs, 4 Ds, 1 F

Weighted grading is another variation on the alpha system, with differing grade points awarded to show course difficulty or student achievement. The simplest version awards 0.5 additional grade points for honors or gifted classes. More complex systems assign predetermined weights according to the achievement or challenge of the class. Weighted systems do tend to reward greater student motivation, but also higher academic ability.

- *Pass/Fail, Credit/No Credit, E/S/U.* Two or three level systems attempt to avoid the arbitrary features of percentage and alpha grading. The categories can be clearly defined, but little information is provided about student learning and any predictive value for college success is lost. Several studies also show that students opting for pass/fail show lower achievement than students graded by conventional alpha methods. Pass/fail and its variations are most often used in grading elective courses.

- *Performance or mastery grading.* A definite level of performance is assessed either by a test score or the mastery of a skill. A minimum level of acceptable performance is set as the criterion level. Two variations are in current use:

Contract grading, in which the teacher spells out the course and unit requirements, performance expectations, work requirements, learning tasks, etc. Students fill out a course or unit contract and work toward a specific grade. The contract approach uses alpha grades which students earn by reaching the predetermined performance level. Each student who completes the contract receives the contracted grade.

Criterion-referenced methods, such as competency lists and performance tests, in which a clear level of performance is established for each concept, skill, or attitude that the learner is expected to master. Alpha grades (without F) are used, as well as credit/no credit, checklists, and mastery criteria.

Performance approaches demand a systematic curriculum and outcome-based evaluation. They require more time to administer, but learning progress is clearer than in conventional systems. Parents may have difficulty understanding the progress reports.

- *Anecdotal or descriptive reports.* The teacher writes descriptive comments about student achievement, work habits, and citizenship. Descriptive reporting can provide a holistic picture and flexibility for assessing individual learning. Unfortunately, the process is time-consuming and tends to deteriorate into stereotypical statements of questionable value. Comparative ranking of students is virtually impossible.

The Principal's Challenge

Grading approaches that combine performance or mastery criteria with a modified alpha system and supplementary descriptive reports have been very successful. In many schools/districts, however, principals have little control over the actual form of grading. Nevertheless, responsibility for the supervision of grading practices almost always resides with building administrators. Supervising principals need to be alert to the following irresponsible practices:

- Grade inflation that pushes grades higher because of teacher unwillingness to discriminate among students' performance.
- Grade deflation that eliminates "A" grades when teachers structure courses or give tests that make top scores unattainable.
- Teachers not collecting enough data for valid judgment—giving few assignments or relying almost entirely on final examinations.
- Teachers changing grading criteria in the middle of the term.

Student growth should be the focus of the grading system; objectivity and consistency should be the basis for assessment and reporting.

Reference

Terwilliger, J. S. *Assigning Grades to Students.* Glenview, Ill.: Scott, Foresman and Co., 1971.

Teacher Performance Appraisal

Thomas L. McGreal

To improve the quality and reliability of teacher performance appraisal, schools and districts must meet the following conditions:

1. Administrators and teachers must be trained in effective classroom instructional practices, including observation and recording.
2. An evaluation system (procedures, processes, and instruments) must be adopted that encourages teacher input and focuses on classroom instructional improvement.

Successful Evaluation Systems

Evaluation systems perceived as effective by their participants share the following characteristics:

• *A realistic attitude exists toward the purpose of evaluation.* The purpose of the evaluation system, especially for tenured and/or experienced teachers, must be to provide assistance in improving instruction. Experience and available data suggest that systems built around the concept of improving instruction are almost always accompanied by acceptable levels of accountability.

• *The system includes complementary procedures, processes, and instruments.* The requirements placed on the participants must reflect the actual purpose of the system. Too often evaluation systems state that "the primary purpose of evaluation is the improvement of instruction," but saddle principals and teachers with procedures that require ratings on standardized criteria, produce high supervisor-low teacher involvement, and promote unfocused, superficial classroom visitation.

• *Supervisory behavior is separated from administrative behavior.* Administrators must strive to separate the evaluation of teachers from the evaluation of teaching. Minimum expectations for teachers that are primarily administrative and/or personal in nature (adherence to school policy, personal appearance, relationships with parents and community, etc.) can be monitored informally and unobtrusively. No special set of procedures or instruments is needed for these elements. As violations occur, they can be dealt with immediately and effectively. The principal and the teacher, then, can focus their time together on formative evaluation issues that foster a more collegial relationship.

• *Goal setting is the major focus of the system.* Goal setting is a logical alternative to the kinds of systems that contain rating scales and standardized criteria. In its most effective form, the goal-setting process is a cooperative activity between supervisor and teacher that results in a mutually agreeable focus. The goals become the core of the supervision/evaluation process.

• *A common set of terms about teaching is shared by all administrators and teachers.* Principals and teachers must have a common framework and a similar set of definitions about teaching from which they can operate.

Two very useful approaches come from the teaching effectiveness research (Rosenshine, 1983) and the work of Madeline Hunter (1984). Both approaches focus on teacher behaviors and common sense practices. Improving individual evaluation skills through inservice can be helpful, but without a system that encourages good practice, teacher evaluation will never be efficacious. Principals should adopt a realistic evaluation system and then seek training in the processes for themselves and staff members.

Developing a System

Teacher performance appraisal should focus on current teaching research as a framework for classroom observation. Current research emphasizes two dimensions that can significantly improve student learning.

1. *Classroom Climate.* The key words here are student involvement and opportunity for success. Teachers must create a classroom climate in which all students feel free to raise their hands, ask questions, take a chance, and get involved. Teachers must plan climate with as much diligence as they plan instruction. Principals will find the following questions helpful in describing and monitoring a teacher's attention to classroom climate.

- Who does the teacher call on?
- What is the percentage of direct questions (produce higher involvement) versus indirect questions?
- What is the approximate percentage of correct answers given?
- Does the teacher use praise and reinforcement to reward correct answers and successful experiences?

Thomas L. McGreal is associate professor, College of Education, University of Illinois at Urbana-Champaign.

Teacher Performance Appraisal

Figure 1. *Models of Instructional Strategy*

MODELS OF INSTRUCTIONAL STRATEGY

Theory into Practice (Hunter)

1. Anticipatory set
2. Statement of objectives

Direct Instruction (Rosenshine)

1. Review of previous day's work

- These are teacher preparatory moves designed to tie lessons together and to inform students of the purpose and direction of the day's lesson.

3. Instructional input
4. Modeling

2. Explanation
3. Demonstration

- This developmental stage of teaching focuses on clear, logical presentation of new learning material, with teacher modeling, demonstration, examples, etc.

5. Checking for understanding

4. Initial practice
5. Feedback and correctives

- Monitoring of student learning must be visible and continuous. If students are not operating at about a 70 percent correct answer rate, the teacher stops and reteaches.

6. Guided practice
7. Independent practice

6. Controlled, prompted practice
7. Independent practice

- Students must practice new learning under the direct supervision of the teacher. Only after the students have demonstrated understanding or minimal skills (low error rate) is independent practice or homework appropriate.

- Does the teacher deal appropriately with incorrect responses?
- Are instructional experiences available that give all students a chance to be successful?
- Does the teacher attempt to personalize instruction according to the student need?

2. *Classroom Planning.* One of the most useful classroom observation techniques looks at the sequence of events that characterize teacher planning for classroom presentation. Hunter (1984) and Rosenshine (1983) have developed models of effective instruction that can be used as frameworks for this process. (Fig. 1)

Current research and practice clearly indicate that teacher performance appraisal can be both reliable and helpful. Teacher evaluation and instructional leadership are virtually inseparable. For many principals, the visits and conferences mandated by the evaluation system are their major instructional contacts with teachers. Principals committed to instructional leadership, then, should hold teacher performance appraisal among their highest priorities.

References

Hunter, M. "Knowing, Teaching, and Supervising." In *Using What We Know About Teaching,* edited by P. L. Hosford. Alexandria, Va.: Association for Supervision and Curriculum Development, 1984.

Rosenshine, B. "Teaching Functions." *Elementary School Journal* 83 (1983): 35–351.

Program Evaluation

Warren B. Newman

Honesty is essential to program evaluation. You must know and admit to yourself why you are conducting the evaluation because it is intrinsically worthwhile to do so; because you have a predetermined prejudice about a program (good or bad) and you want documentation to substantiate your belief; because the superintendent or board wants the evaluation. Honesty is essential because the process of designing, implementing, and reporting on evaluation requires compromises. These include:

- The scope of the evaluation (breadth and depth)
- The available resources, including the time you devote, the personnel you assign, and the money you spend
- The kinds and quality of instruments you use to gather information
- The rigor with which you will analyze data
- The comprehensiveness of the reporting process
- The openness of the final report.

When so many points require compromise you need to know where and why you are making them.

The Statement of Purpose

It is necessary to state the purpose of your evaluation. If you do not set your course clearly in the beginning, you probably will not find what you are looking for. Consider the following sample statement:

> The purpose of this evaluation is to determine if students in grades 9, 10, and 11 read better as measured by performance on nationally-standardized norm-referenced tests of reading comprehension and vocabulary. Test scores will be compared with those of the three previous years to measure any changes in the mean percentile rankings of classes as well as the Q3 (third quartile—top 25%) and Q1 (first quartile—bottom 25%) scores. Individual student scores will be plotted to determine the changes during the past three years. Test information will be analyzed for any correlation between the scores and grades earned in the academic subjects of English, history, and science. Finally, students will be given an attitudinal survey to assess whether they think they are better (or worse) readers than in the two previous years. Those who believe they have changed will be asked to cite examples of performance in support of their belief and reasons why they think that they have changed.

The sample statement is complete enough to develop an entire evaluation design. It describes exactly who the target group is, what measures will be used, what other information may be important (e.g., correlates of grades), and, perhaps best of all, whether the target group has evidence of and reasons for any change.

What is most helpful about the example is that it includes descriptive, correlative, and causative factors and attempts to gather such information directly and indirectly.

Most testing is indirect. To measure vocabulary strength, for example, students match selected words with meanings. Indirect measures may indicate vocabulary power, but they tell us nothing about its relating (correlation) function or what causes it to be what it is.

To know that factor A correlates in a high positive or negative way with factors B, C, and D does not describe factor A better, but it does give us some idea of its relationship to the other factors. This kind of information may be critically important. Educators frequently would like to know why something happens and whether it happens consistently enough to allow us to predict outcomes.

What Data Should We Collect?

Many kinds of data are useful to program evaluation. Most schools/districts collect all or part of the following information:

- *Standardized Test Scores.* The ranking of students on national norms in various subject matter content.
- *Criterion-Referenced Tests.* Locally normed tests keyed to local subject matter goals and competencies.
- *Survey Data.* Written and oral feedback from students, teachers, parents, and community surveys.
- *Graduate Follow-Up.* Mail or interview data from graduates on the efficacy of the curriculum in preparing them for college or the job.
- *External Evaluation.* Accreditation team visits by regional accrediting agencies and/or independent evaluations by local subject matter experts (district personnel, university consultants, etc.).
- *Self-Study.* Specialized self-evaluations by depart-

Warren B. Newman is assistant superintendent, South Pasadena Unified School District, South Pasadena, Calif.

Program Evaluation

ments or teachers, usually for new programs or special objectives.

Can We Do It?

Good program evaluation is complex and time-consuming (the reason that it is costly), but it is also possible, desirable, and necessary. Evaluation is *possible* because we already collect enormous amounts of data. The data have to be sorted out; not everything is relevant. But once the data are identified and recorded, technicians can analyze them. Statistical methodology has a language for specialists, but let those who are familiar with research and statistics give you the reports. Then, look at the data from an *educational* point of view.

Evaluation is not only possible, it is *desirable*. A profession is partly defined by the control its members have over related behaviors and outcomes. Program evaluation can give you conscious control of many aspects of schooling. Your instructional decisions will be based on valid, reliable, and timely information, enhancing the probability that your decisions will be good ones.

And, finally, program evaluation is *necessary*. Education—public, parochial, and private—is the largest industry in America; more people are involved and more money is spent on training and education than any other economic sector, including the military. But precious little information exists on the efficacy of what is done or how much it really costs in terms of student outcomes.

What if we could achieve the same level of performance in skills, concepts, or behaviors at half the cost if we did x instead of y? To know how much those vocabulary basic skills are costing, we need both vocabulary scores and the cost of the resources to bring achievement to a certain level. Evaluation can provide the answers.

How To Get Started

Several useful program evaluation models exist, but the CIPP Model developed by Daniel Stufflebeam at Ohio State University is both comprehensive and flexible. CIPP (*c*ontext, *i*nput, *p*rocess, *p*roduct) deals with four kinds of decisions and the related evaluation issues. The decision types are: planning decisions about objectives; structuring decisions about strategies and procedural designs; implementing decisions about carrying out the design; and recycling decisions about whether to continue, modify, or terminate the design. These decision types are served by four kinds of related evaluation:

- *Context evaluation* provides information about needs, problems, and opportunities as a basis for identifying objectives. It records the objectives and the reasons for their choice.
- *Input evaluation* provides information about the strengths and weaknesses of alternative strategies for achieving the chosen objectives. It records the strategies and the reasons for choosing them.
- *Process evaluation* provides information about the strengths and weaknesses of a strategy during implementation. It records the actual implementation process as it occurs. If a particular strategy is unsuccessful, it assesses whether the design was inadequate or simply never implemented.
- *Product evaluation* provides information about objectives achieved and whether the strategies chosen for implementation should be continued, modified, or terminated. It develops a record of outcomes and modifications based on them.

Basically, the CIPP model suggests that we ask and record the answers to four questions:

1. What objectives should be accomplished (context)?
2. What procedures should be followed (input)?
3. Are the procedures working properly (process)?
4. Are the objectives being achieved (product)?

Some aspects of program evaluation are technical in nature, particularly the statistics, but specialists can help you with them. Try your district office, a local university, the nearest research laboratory, or intermediate unit. All kinds of reference books, how-to kits, and resource people are available to help you. In the final analysis, however, you alone know what the key evaluation questions are and how important the findings can be.

Take up the challenge: evaluate because you can and because you must.

Community Feedback

Thomas L. Fish

Community feedback is an important and often overlooked element of program evaluation. Such opinion is important because schools depend directly on community support to function. Prior to setting goals, schools/districts regularly attempt to assess the community's needs and seek support for instructional improvement. Community involvement in program evaluation, however, is often weak.

If principals believe, as evaluation expert Daniel Stufflebeam notes, that "the purpose of evaluation is not to prove, but to improve," they should seek community feedback as part of the total evaluation process. In the average community, only 26 percent of the families have children in school, but the other 74 percent have a stake even though they have no direct connection with the schools. The survey is a key tool for reaching out to the total community to assess judgments, opinions, and feelings about the school.

Developing the Survey

A community survey should be developed very systematically. Several questions should be asked before the survey is developed.

- What questions do we want to ask? Are these questions clear and concise?
- What is the best way to obtain the answers to these questions? A community survey may or may not be the best way to secure the information.
- How will this information be tied to the data collected from teacher, student, and program evaluations?
- Who will do the survey?
- How much will it cost?
- When should the survey be done for greatest effect?
- How many people must be sampled to achieve valid results?
- Which method—mailed questionnaire, the dropped-off/picked-up questionnaire, telephone interview, or personal interview—is best?
- How will the data be analyzed?

The more time that goes into planning a survey, the more effective and useful it will be. (Generally the dropped-off/picked-up questionnaire and the telephone interview achieve the highest response rate. A random sample with high response provides the greatest validity.)

If a random sample is taken, large numbers are not necessary for accuracy. (Note the success of pollsters in projecting political winners on the basis of a small sample of voters.) If the survey is to be used internally for projecting trends in an average district, as few as 100 randomly sampled individuals would be sufficient. If the survey will be the basis for decision-making, about 400 randomly selected families would be enough for results within a predictable plus or minus 5 percent rate of error, regardless of the size of the community.

The key is to draw a truly random sample. Most computers (even micros) can generate random numbers for sampling purposes.

Survey Construction

In constructing a survey, keep a few guidelines in mind.

1. Make the questions simple and brief.
2. Avoid leading questions.
3. Avoid emotionally loaded words.
4. Avoid ambiguous and threatening statements.
5. For each item ask, "Is this question really necessary?"
6. Place the questions in a logical sequence.
7. Place open-ended questions last.
8. Pretest the survey. This is the most important guideline. Pretesting the survey on a small group similar to the sample can anticipate and eliminate many problems.

One other item is worth mentioning. Be sure to develop a cover letter (for mailed or dropped-off/picked-up surveys) or a set of directions (for interviews). The content of the cover letter/directions should include: who is doing the survey, the purpose, instructions on how to complete it, how the community will be informed of the results, and a word of thanks for taking time to participate.

Other Methods of Sampling Opinion

A well-done survey will pay dividends to the principal who is willing to take the time to develop it. But the

---

Thomas L. Fish is director, Community Education Center, College of St. Thomas, St. Paul, Minn.

Community Feedback

survey is not the only way to find out what the community thinks. Many less formal approaches provide very useful feedback to school administrators.

- *Key Communicators*—Key people located throughout the attendance area who talk to other people regularly (barbers, beauticians, service station attendants, and so on), and on whom the principal can call to share or to seek information. These people also may contact the principal when important issues arise relating to the school.
- *Advisory Council*—A group of individuals who are representative of the entire attendance area, not just parents. The council meets regularly, usually monthly, with the principal.
- *Question/Idea Card*—Cards placed where people wait (doctors' offices, dentists' offices, grocery stores, pharmacies, and so on) inviting the community to submit questions or ideas to the school.
- *Telephone Calls by Staff*—School staff members make random calls to community members to inform them about the school and to seek reaction and comment.
- *Hotline Phone*—A phone with a 24-hour answering machine for community members to voice their concerns, comments, or questions to the school.

Obtaining community feedback is not difficult, but the information must be used for ongoing planning and program revision.